KEY THEMES IN
QUALITATIVE RESEARCH

KEY THEMES IN QUALITATIVE RESEARCH

Continuities and Changes

PAUL ATKINSON
AMANDA COFFEY
SARA DELAMONT

ALTAMIRA
PRESS

A Division of Rowman & Littlefield Publishers, Inc.
Walnut Creek • Lanham • New York • Oxford

Library
University of Texas
at San Antonio

ALTAMIRA PRESS
A Division of Rowman & Littlefield Publishers, Inc.
1630 North Main Street, #367
Walnut Creek, California 94596
www.altamirapress.com

Rowman & Littlefield Publishers, Inc.
A Member of the Rowman & Littlefield Publishing Group
4501 Forbes Boulevard, Suite 200
Lanham, Maryland 20706

PO Box 317
Oxford
OX2 9RU, UK

British Library Cataloguing in Publication Information Available

Library of Congress Cataloging-in-Publication Data
Atkinson, Paul, 1947–
    Key themes in qualitative research : continuities and changes / Paul
Atkinson, Amanda Coffey, and Sara Delamont.
        p. cm.
Includes bibliographical references and index.
    ISBN 0-7591-0126-4 (hardcover : alk. paper)—ISBN 0-7591-0127-2
(pbk. : alk. paper)
1. Social sciences—Research. 2. Qualitative research. I. Coffey,
Amanda, 1967– II. Delamont, Sara, 1947– III. Title.

H62 .A78 2003
305.8'007'2—dc21

                                                    2002152409

Printed in the United States of America

♾™ The paper used in this publication meets the minimum requirements of
American National Standard for Information Sciences—Permanence of Paper for
Printed Library Materials, ANSI/NISO Z39.48-1992.

CONTENTS

ACKNOWLEDGMENTS

We would like to thank Mitch Allen for his support of this project. We would also like to take the opportunity to thank all of the authors who contributed to *The Handbook of Ethnography*, along with members of the editorial boards of both the *Handbook* and the journal *Qualitative Research*. Their contributions and comments have been valuable in informing and shaping our own ideas about the pasts, presents, and futures of qualitative research. The anonymous referee made very useful suggestions, and in preparing the final version of this book, we adopted nearly all of them with alacrity. We dedicate this book to Virginia Olesen, who is always a staunch friend, patient and generous in her support for younger colleagues, and who balances skepticism with enthusiasm for work at the fuzzy borders.

PREFACE

This book is our manifesto for a mature approach to ethnography: a brave or foolhardy task we have imposed on ourselves. In this preface we set out clearly what the book does, and, equally importantly, does not do. We hope that you will enjoy the book whether you are a seasoned veteran ethnographer or a relative beginner, whatever discipline(s) you come from and are going towards, whatever empirical area(s) you conduct research in, and wherever you live. The book outlines a number of key issues that we think contemporary researchers—whether they be novices or experts—need to keep in mind when thinking about ethnographic, qualitative methods.

WHAT THE BOOK DOES

There is an enormous literature on qualitative methods in general and ethnography in particular, and a substantial portion of that literature talks enthusiastically, or in horrified outrage, about crises, turmoil, rapid change, and zesty disarray. Such proliferation, and its emphasis on change, leaves the basics, the strong deep roots, and the continuities of ethnography invisible to novices, and in danger of extinction. Our aim is to restate and reiterate those basic continuities via an exploration of key themes. We believe that the current state of qualitative methodological writing and research practice is muddled. We also think that, in some respects at least, it is overheated. There is need for a cooler appraisal of research and its possibilities. We believe that the proliferation and promotion of qualitative research in recent years has, on the whole, been beneficial to the social sciences. Good research will not proceed without a collective appreciation of good research strategies and a sound appraisal of their outcomes. We are heartily gratified by the fact that research methods have changed and developed. We thoroughly approve of debate and experimentation. Indeed, we endorse and encourage dispute and contention about methodology. Our purpose is certainly not to close down change and exchange. We do, however, believe that in the process of change things have been lost as well as gained, and the time is right for some judicious review of key issues and ideas.

Amid the disputes about the past, future, and present of ethnography we have consistently tried to steer a course between the wilder excesses of novelty and a stolid reactionary conservatism (Atkinson, Coffey, and Delamont 1999; Delamont, Coffey, and Atkinson 2000; Delamont, et al. 2001). Moreover, we have asserted the importance of continuity as well as recognized the value of change. As this book will reveal, we have engaged with the debates at the fuzzy borders of ethnographic research (Atkinson 1990 and 1992; Coffey 1999), but have done so with a healthy skepticism and a degree of caution.

In the rush to advocate "new" ethnography—with emphases on auto-ethnography, cultural studies, narratives and voices, messy or layered texts, appeals to postmodernist theories, and other innovations—some of the basics are in danger of being forgotten. The innovators of the past, the intellectual pioneers who wrote major ethnographic monographs, also mapped out the methodological terrain. Their empirical works have endured and should continue to inspire the work of younger generations. They laid down the traditions that have nurtured many of today's researchers and teachers. In doing so, they raised many key methodological questions, including those we have chosen to revisit in the course of this book. These pioneering researchers and mentors include Everett Hughes, Anselm Strauss, Leonard Schatzman, Blanche Geer, Hortense Powdermaker, John and Lyn Lofland, and Virginia Olesen. Taken together, they and their publications have helped to define the traditions of qualitative research. Several of the key authors to whom we refer continue to make distinguished contributions to the field. They had some important things in common throughout their research careers: They believed that the work of the ethnographer is to study and understand a social setting, a social group, or a social problem (a "social world" as some of them might have put it). They believed in documenting *and analyzing* those phenomena for an audience of fellow scholars and students. Their work was firmly grounded in their respective disciplinary traditions, and their observations of life in their chosen research sites were inextricably linked with their theoretical commitments. While they were self-conscious about their own research—how could they not be when they pioneered methods texts and training?—they were not self-obsessed. We believe that too much contemporary work advocates and celebrates self-referential work, with little relevance to our understanding of actual social worlds. Moreover, we fear that too much ethnographic and other qualitative work has broken from its moorings in the disciplinary traditions of social science, only to float free. Qualitative research, we strongly believe, does not constitute a quasi-discipline or quasi-paradigm in its own right. Without the hard graft of working with theoretical ideas, research traditions, and bodies of literature, any research strategies—qualitative or quantitative, positivist or hermeneutic—are likely to prove futile. If we collect narratives and life histories, we should be doing so in order to analyze their production, construction, and cultural significance, not merely to reproduce them. If we conduct ethnographic fieldwork, then the prime purpose should be to document social worlds, not to provide opportunities for self-absorbed reflections on the researcher. If we experiment with our styles of scholarly writing, our purpose should be to improve the reconstruction and extend our representation of the social world, and not to transform all social phenomena into the products of creative writing classes.

The developments of the past twenty-five years are exciting, and it is easy for people to get swept up in that excitement. There is no need to reject all new developments out of hand. However, their experienced exponents can build upon the more solid foundations of the enduring ethnographic monographs and the classic methodological debates. When they experiment, innovate, cross boundaries, and blur genres, they can do so from a solid disciplinary background. The danger is, however, that with all the talk and publication that claims and endorses novelty, contemporary students do not have access to the same foundations. We believe that many of the classic studies and the classic themes retain their relevance for today's research community.

Much of the more fevered writing about intellectual crises and methodological novelty fails to recognize that the central issues concerning good qualitative research have long been recognized and debated. Our argument parallels those of Maines (2001) and Atkinson and Housley (2003), in their respective discussions of the fate of symbolic interactionism, who assert that many of the central concerns of so-called postmodernism recapitulate ideas that were, long before, associated with interactionist sociology. Both of those books invoke the notion of *sociological amnesia* to capture how, in their search for novel ideas, contemporary sociologists ignore the past and periodically reinvent the wheel. Ideas of the past get reformulated in new vocabularies, while their original inspirations are too easily overlooked.

While methodological and epistemological novelty is celebrated in the research community (or at least among methodologists) and past ideas are paid insufficient attention, in practice, the classic ethnographies of previous generations are what endure. While fashions proliferate, scholars and students alike return to classic ethnographies for inspiration. The classic urban ethnographies such as *Street Corner Society*, *Tally's Corner*, *Soulside*, or *Slim's Table* continue to nourish the sociological and methodological imagination of successive generations. Heyl's life history of a madam (1979), or Strong's ethnography of pediatric clinics (1979/2001), or Olesen and Whittaker's account of socialization into nursing (1968) continue to demonstrate the value of fieldwork conducted in accordance with careful attention to the representation and reconstruction of social worlds and social actors. Myerhoff's account of the lives of older Jewish people; Kondo's ethnography of family, work, and identity in Japan; or Krieger's account of a radio station, although they have newer features in their approaches to research and writing, are all grounded in the same virtues—of careful attention to concrete detail, of equal attentiveness to the social actors and their accounts, of clear writing and disciplinary relevance. They, too, continue to inform and inspire. There are many others; these are but examples. The enduring quality of the best ethnographic work rests on a relatively simple set of foundations, resulting in original work that demonstrably engages simultaneously with the particularity of social lives and social worlds and the generality of sociological or anthropological interpretation.

WHO SHOULD NOT START FROM HERE

This book is not designed as a primer in qualitative research methods for absolute beginners. Novices should read some classic ethnography, some introductory methods texts, and engage with fieldwork of their own before tackling this book. Between us we have written a very basic introduction (Delamont 2002), a classic bestselling and more advanced introduction (Hammersley and Atkinson 1995), a text on how to organize, analyze, and theorize about qualitative data (Coffey and Atkinson 1996), and a reflection on the "ethnographic self" (Coffey 1999). We have also edited a large volume of papers on many aspects and applications of ethnography (Atkinson et al. 2001). If you are new to all this, please read some of the more introductory material first, and come back when you have absorbed a basic book and done some fieldwork yourself. Then you may find this book illuminating and informative. In Gary Alan Fine's (1985) study of working-class

Americans learning to be chefs, their lecturer explains that their future customers like foods which the apprentices themselves have probably never tasted, and will not like to begin with, such as olives, paté, and brie; when they are skilled chefs in good kitchens they will like these foods, because their palates will develop as they are socialized as chefs. This book is our plate of paté and brie: we want you to enjoy it when you are a skilled chef, not be put off by it because you are not ready.

In contrast, anyone who has read a basic text on ethnography already, has taken a course on it, has done a small project, is ready for this book. Discipline, nationality, and theoretical stance do not matter.

WHAT YOU MIGHT WANT TO KNOW ABOUT US

Given the confessional tone, and the celebration of the personal, found in much qualitative writing published over the past decade, we have offered brief sketches of ourselves to conclude this introduction.

Paul and Sara are white British people who grew up in England, did their Ph.D. degrees in Scotland, and have lived in Wales for thirty years. Within the United Kingdom, therefore, they do not feel any nationalist identity within any one territory. They both studied anthropology as students, but chose to move into sociology at doctoral level, pioneering symbolic interactionist, "Chicago" fieldwork in Britain. Paul has regularly done research in medical settings, and is currently holding grants to study the social implications of the new genetics. He has also conducted an ethnographic study of an opera company. Sara has mainly done educational research, and is also particularly interested in Mediterranean anthropology. In the 1990s, Sara and Paul collaborated with Odette Parry in a study of United Kingdom doctoral studies in social and natural sciences, including social anthropologists (Delamont, Atkinson, and Parry 2000); they therefore write about anthropology from two sources—one data driven and the other autobiographical. Paul worked briefly but inspirationally with Virginia Olesen and Anselm Strauss, and has taught with Lyn and John Lofland in Davis, California.

Amanda is also white and British, but has Irish heritage, too. She moved to Wales to do her Ph.D. and take her first post. Her research has been on gender, occupations, work and education, and on the frontiers of hypermedia ethnography. She is currently part of a team exploring the potential of ethnography in the digital age. She also has a particular interest in the relationships between ethnography, representation, and the self.

All three of us have taught in Scandinavia, especially in Finland, which provides a good intellectual distance from British and American preoccupations. Together we have built up a distinct ethnographic approach in Cardiff (Delamont et al. 2001). We have published and edited as a trio, and in all the possible pairs, for a decade. We do not always agree: indeed, we know we differ and the arguments are often fierce. This book was prepared by each of us doing a draft of a pair of chapters, and then each of us working through the whole manuscript to improve it—Paul the first time, then Amanda, and finally Sara. We are still on speaking terms.

Introduction

THE OLD GUARD
AND THE AVANT GARDE

There are probably already too many books devoted to qualitative research methods. Within the relatively short space of twenty years, the literature on ethnographic and related research strategies has grown exponentially. The state of the literature, and indeed the state of the market in textbooks, has gone from bust to boom. Why, then, should we want to make yet another contribution to that literature? Any such undertaking surely needs a strong justification.

Our rationale for this book derives directly from the remarkable increase in recent writing. On the one hand, we welcome the degree of informed interest in the strategies of qualitative research— its methods, proper conduct, and ethical considerations. On the other hand, we think that with this growth of interest, there is a good deal of muddle and confusion. In particular, as we outline in this introduction and exemplify in greater detail in the chapters that follow, we believe that amidst the contemporary enthusiasm, some have lost sight of the basic issues in the tradition of qualitative research. In this introduction, we outline some of these issues and some of the intellectual context for the chapters that follow. More detailed discussions of the literature appear in the relevant chapters.

The book is structured around what we call key themes—big issues that were discussed fifty years ago and are still being discussed today. We have chosen a classic text on each theme, a journal article or book chapter, in which a major figure in the history of ethnography addressed that issue. All these texts should still be read today, because their authors conducted exemplary fieldwork and wrote benchmark reports on it. Some of these pioneers are dead; others are still productive scholars. Ethnography today exists because of their efforts. We have chosen to organize the book around classic papers, just as many women organize a wardrobe around a little black dress, a classic Chanel suit, or an Yves St. Laurent blazer. The papers are classics the way a Leica camera or a Thunderbird is a classic: we would all love to own one and be able to live up to it.

In each chapter, we outline the argument of the classic paper, review how its premises can be supported, (re)designed, or made problematic today, and then state our position on that theme. The papers we have chosen are those we regard as important. Where we criticize them it is because ethnography itself has changed.

We have written primarily about ethnography in sociology and anthropology in Britain and North America (the United States and Canada). Ethnography is used in many applied fields, such as education, nursing, and social work, and in interdisciplinary fields such as urban studies, cultural studies, and women's studies. The disciplinary roots are, however, clear. Ethnography began in the 1890s in anthropology and sociology, and the innovations have come predominantly from scholars based in these two disciplines.

In this introduction, we draw a rhetorical contrast between the Old Guard and the Avant Garde. It must be emphasized that we do not discuss the members of the earlier generation in this way in order to treat them in a derogatory manner. Our contrasts are certainly not designed to suggest that our intellectual forebears were in error or have been consigned to the dustbin of history. On the contrary, we remain indebted to their pioneering work. Moreover, we do not wish to imply that the methodological commentators of the 1960s or 1970s are relegated to the past. They all continued to produce work of great distinction after the publication of the work we discuss. Indeed, several are still doing so. They themselves moved on and developed new ideas and made further original contributions to research. Our aim in reexamining their pioneering work rests on the strong belief that it deserves continuing respect and close attention—not least because we think that contemporary developments have not always been well founded.

In recent years, scholarly reflection on research methods (both qualitative and quantitative) has been enlivened by a number of fresh and controversial perspectives. These have included the postmodernist turn in the social sciences; the crisis of representation; and feminist and other critical standpoints. In various ways, these perspectives have led to both renewal and critique in the social sciences generally, and in the conduct of qualitative research in particular. We ourselves have contributed to some of the ensuing debates, and have endorsed many of the positive effects of renewed research activity and methodological reflection. We believe, however, that some confusion has entered the literature in the wake of these recent innovations and reevaluations. Ours is not a wholesale critique of recent developments, such as the collective appeal to postmodernism, nor is it a comprehensive manifesto for qualitative research in general. Our approach follows a specific strategy, which we outline here. The introduction is not packed with citations, because the ideas are used in the following seven chapters and the explanations and citations are there. Our purpose here is to provide a general overview of how our arguments will develop as the book unfolds.

Some elementary aspects of our characterization of the field can be summarized in terms of the following, exaggerated thumbnail sketches. Our book is structured by means of a series of comparisons and discussions predicated on a distinction between the methodological pioneers of the 1950s and 1960s and the contemporary writers on qualitative methods, roughly since 1985.

> *Methodological pioneers* ("The Old Guard"). We need to reflect upon and provide written guidelines for field research, using participant observation and/or interviewing, in order to establish criteria; the individualized and oral tradition of field research needs to be translated into explicit, written methodological advice.
>
> *Adherents of new ethnography* ("The Avant Garde"). We are in a postmodern world, and ethnography is the best-placed method to embody that world, breaking with positivist knowledge claims, drawing inspiration from feminism, postcolonialism, queer theory, and celebrating a diversity of methodological criteria.
>
> *The central tenets of our book.* Differences between the past and the revolutionary present are more apparent than real; methodological questions raised in the 1950–1980 era are pertinent today. Focusing on them provides clarity; revisiting them is an illuminating way to think about methods for the future. Comparing and contrasting them with current debates remains worthwhile.

In addition to these methodological positions, there is yet another, which we can refer to as the "diehard traditionalists."

> *Diehard traditionalists.* Qualitative research can, and should, continue to provide reliable and valid knowledge about the social world in accordance with clear criteria; trends since 1985 have undermined this with relativism, French theory, feminism, queer theory, and postmodernism.

We need to emphasize at the outset that we do not align ourselves with this last position. In revisiting the methodological questions posed by the pioneering generation, we are not trying to turn the clock back. Equally, unlike several recent methodological commentaries, we are not contrasting past and present in order to denigrate the past and celebrate novelty. Our series of discussions of key themes and questions is intended to be more subtle than that. We believe that it remains worthwhile to engage with the key methodological issues of the past that helped in large measure to establish the character of qualitative, ethnographic field research.

Before we go on to characterize the Old Guard and the Avant Garde in more detail, we also want to establish that this book discusses literature from sociology (and cultural studies) and anthropology, drawn from the United Kingdom and from North America. We do not attempt to cover all the possible literature from other national traditions, such as continental European nations or Australasia. This is not because there is no significant work being done in other national settings; we recognize that qualitative research is now conducted globally. Rather, it reflects the need to impose some limits on an otherwise very diffuse field of relevant literature. It is important to recognize that there are disciplinary and national differences; there is no single "ethnographic" tradition—let alone one single broader category of "qualitative research." There are some differences between the United Kingdom and the United States, between anthropology and sociology, and between "pure" and "applied" research, which we outline briefly below. We are confident, however, that the core issues addressed in this book are pertinent in all those intellectual contexts.

Anthropology

In the United Kingdom social anthropology is a high status but relatively small discipline, concentrated in the top universities. "Applied" anthropology barely exists, has not enjoyed much recognition, and is concentrated largely in medical anthropology. British anthropologists today do undertake fieldwork "at home" in the United Kingdom, have been influenced by the so-called "crisis of representation," but have not become substantially involved in autoethnography. Fieldwork overseas continues to enjoy high esteem. There are very few links with sociology at either institutional or intellectual levels. Monographs and journal articles remain conventional in style. In the United States and Canada, cultural anthropology is strong in the elite universities, but also exists more widely across higher education. Applied anthropology is strong, with its own organizations and journals; it also figures strongly within mainstream programs, organizations, and conferences. Boundaries between anthropology and other disciplines such as sociology are weaker than in the United Kingdom, with some scholars working in both disciplinary domains. North American anthropologists have always worked "at home," especially on indigenous and immigrant ethnic communities. Overseas fieldwork has high status, but research at home is perfectly fine. The crisis of representation was expressed most vigorously by American anthropologists and is widely understood there. Despite that, most monographs and journal articles remain conventional in form and style. Autoethnography is still relatively rare, but more visible than in the United Kingdom.

Sociology

Sociology and cultural studies in the United Kingdom are strongest where other social sciences are also strong, which include some of the relatively new universities, outside the Oxford/Cambridge/London "golden triangle." Qualitative and ethnographic work is strongest in education, medicine, and criminology, but interactionist sociology is relatively underdeveloped, although the work of American interactionists had a major influence on the development of qualitative research traditions as well as the initial methodological work on ethnography and qualitative research. Qualitative research is especially strong in cultural sociology and in cultural studies: the disciplinary boundary between those two domains is increasingly blurred. Work on consumption and popular culture is especially strong. Most monographs and journal articles remain conventional in style, and the crisis of representation has not resulted in a large number of experimental publications. Autoethnography remains relatively rare. The cultural turn has added new empirical domains of research but has not resulted in wholesale transformations in the style of work. Feminism and postmodernism have had significant impact on methodological and empirical work.

   In North America, the interactionist tradition was strong, and continues to provide the background to much innovative work in empirical research and methodological commentary. Many contemporary avant garde figures have come from that strong tradition. Contemporary interests are also informed by cultural interests and communication studies. While conventional styles of writing are numerically predominant in monographs and journal articles, there is a highly visible style of work that celebrates experimental and postmodern modes of work, with prominent exemplars among the published monographs, edited collections, methodological works, and journal articles. Varieties of feminist, postcolonialist, and critical race theory exert noticeable influence.

There are, then, differences within and between national and disciplinary bodies of work. Innovation is experienced and performed in different intellectual contexts. It is important to bear in mind these differences when considering the current picture of qualitative research more generally. The distinctions become even more difficult to trace when one realizes that patterns of explicit influence and citation also differ. The patterns of explicit influence are not symmetrical across the national and disciplinary boundaries. For instance, anthropologists tend not to cite the work of non-anthropologists, and North American authors tend to refer primarily to American work. Likewise, British anthropologists were, for a long time, relatively impervious to American cultural anthropology. British sociologists working in empirical fields have long acknowledged the relevance of American literatures, but the cultural turn in sociology has weakened those direct influences, as attention has been turned more towards European social theory.

THE OLD GUARD

We have used the label "Old Guard" to cover sociologists and anthropologists who did ethnographic research and published it in the 1950s and 1960s, before the ruptures of 1968. We are contrasting them with those writing since the 1980s, when reflexivity about methods and texts has proliferated. Some scholars, such as Howard Becker and John Lofland, have careers that span the two eras. Many practitioners of the avant garde studied with the old guard and revere them. Many members of the old guard welcome the avant garde. They are not mutually antagonistic camps within the academy. More recent generations have built on the foundations laid by the older generations of scholars. In the intervening years, however, the key methodological themes and problems have been transformed. In that process, too, the contributions of our predecessors can become distorted or overlooked. We believe it is time to revisit them.

The literature on qualitative research methods had a major flowering in the 1960s, when sociologists in the United States began to reflect upon their own experiences, and to codify the methodological principles of qualitative research. Those authors were by no means the first researchers to use field methods (as they might well have been called at the time). On the contrary, ethnographic field research had been a trademark of social and cultural anthropology for decades, but anthropologists took for granted methods of data collection through ethnographic fieldwork. Mastering them was treated as a matter of personal apprenticeship rather than a topic for explicit instruction. The same was partly true of earlier sociological fieldwork as well. The classic early years of the Chicago School of Sociology (Abbott 1999; Deegan 2001) did not give rise to a large volume of methodological work, although it was methodologically influential. Likewise, the exponents of earlier community studies (Brunt 2001) did not devote a great deal of time to methodological reflection. In many ways, the relative lack of methodological literature reflected a positive commitment on the part of the social scientists themselves; they devoted their time and energies to the conduct of practical field research and to publishing the results rather than writing extensively about their research methods.

To a considerable degree, social and cultural anthropologists have continued to relegate research methods to the periphery of their collective vision. They have written more and reflected more on matters of method over the past twenty years or so, but it is not an extensive literature. In many quarters, anthropological fieldwork is still seen as the extension of personal qualities—to be grounded in implicit principles rather than the application of explicit methodological precepts. Anthropologists are fond of citing the unpredictability of practical fieldwork as a reason to adopt an essentially pragmatic approach, and they regard the conduct of fieldwork itself as an emergent and contingent phenomenon. The major growth and distribution of research methods books was initially associated with the work of members of the so-called Second Chicago School of Sociology. In addition to the conduct and publication of major works of empirical sociological research, leading authors such as Howard Becker, Anselm Strauss, Blanche Geer, and Leonard Schatzman published major contributions to methodological debate and advice.

A set of methodological issues was established through the codification of qualitative methods in what we might call this "classic" period. The authors we have referred to, and others, started to publish textbooks and methodological reflections on their work. Through the influence of scholars, including Herbert Blumer, people like John and Lyn Lofland also promoted the Chicago-style fieldwork. The publication of anthologies of influential papers also promoted canon formation. These collections of papers themselves helped to define the overall shape and content of methodological work. They helped to disseminate and institutionalize the methodological literature of the day. It would be unfair to imply that all of this classic work was from the same mold. There were, however, significant themes that colored the literature and its reception.

As we have said, the postwar Chicago School was a major influence (Fine 1995). The group around Everett Hughes carried forward his view of sociology through their empirical research studies and the resulting papers and monographs. They also brought the inspiration of Chicago field research—in urban settings, in places of work, and in organizations of different sorts—to a wider audience through their methodological publications. While field research escaped complete codification, there were a number of methodological approaches that became established as orthodox, even if they were never part of a completely dominant paradigm. Ideas like "grounded theory," that Barney Glaser and Anselm Strauss established in their jointly-authored book became especially influential, not least because they seemed to furnish methodological justification for the kind of approach that people were taking anyway. In a similar fashion, key papers in the methods anthologies helped to set the agenda and to guide research strategy for subsequent generations of researchers and graduate students.

To a considerable extent, the Chicago influence added a strongly interactionist flavor to the methodological literature. It is usually wrong to assume or to attribute a simple correspondence between schools of social theory and methodological strategies or inspirations. Nevertheless, the broad continuities between symbolic interactionism and ethnographic field methods—both deriving from Chicago and its products—were significant in the development of methodological literature. Subsequent contributors to the methodological literature carried that influence forward. Insofar as there was ever a dominant set of perspectives, strategies, and methodological precepts, therefore, they derived from that strong set of influences, and owed much to those classic methodological publications to which we have already referred.

In the intervening years, the "qualitative" methodological literature of sociology and its related disciplines has continued to expand. Where once it was almost exclusively North American, it now derives also from the United Kingdom and continental Europe, as well as Australasia. It is now much more diverse in terms of its disciplinary bases and derives from a much wider array of research domains than those of the Second Chicago School. There are now many more alignments and traditions that have contributed to the stream of methods texts. Disciplinary research traditions have, in turn, generated their own distinctive contributions. There are now specialist literatures—including specialist journals—on qualitative research in (for example) educational, medical, and healthcare settings. The growth in sociological and anthropological research on cultural production and reception has also generated a distinctive literature of its own (see Denzin 1991, 1992, and 1995). Feminist scholarship has developed a particular affinity with qualitative research and has developed a methodological literature that reflects that particular stance. The more traditional kinds of field research have been added to and combined with other, more innovative strategies. They include varieties of visual ethnography, biographical and narrative methods, online and cyber-research techniques, and other research strategies that are either new or have been given renewed impetus in recent years.

As we have already acknowledged, social and cultural anthropologists have now come to the party. They have devoted some of their collective attention to the pragmatics of ethnographic data collection, but the practicalities of ethnographic fieldwork still have not captured their collective imagination as firmly as other issues such as representation and authority. The anthropologists have introduced a deeply skeptical and potentially dangerous turn to the discussion of qualitative research, transforming it from a confident and empirically grounded approach to understanding a social world, to a troubled and hesitant undertaking—only to reconstitute it again in the reflexive moment of textual experimentation and autoethnography. Sociologists and cultural analysts, too, have sought to develop and exploit novel forms of research and expression. In the process, qualitative research methods have been disseminated yet more widely, and have simultaneously become more complex and more problematic.

Arguably, then, recent generations of social scientists have experienced a radical shift in the intellectual foundations and the realizations of qualitative research. The range of methods themselves has been extended, while the very nature of research has become increasingly problematic. In the 1960s, the sociologists who inspired and guided so many students and others were able to enunciate relatively straightforward justifications and perspectives on their research enterprise. Even when the research had to be justified and defended against hostile criticism—notably of course from critics, in the United States especially, who believed in crude versions of science and measurement—the objectives and outcomes of ethnographic or life-history research seemed relatively unproblematic to their practitioners and advocates. In recent years, however, these objectives and outcomes have seemed thoroughly troubled and troubling even to many of those scholars who profess them. This apparent paradox has not been confined to the adherents of qualitative research in the social sciences. It is apparent across the cultural and literary disciplines. Critical theory has, for instance, steadily transformed and questioned the objects of scrutiny—and indeed the subjects that undertake the analysis—so that the categories of literature, theory, and analysis have seemed increasingly unstable. The same can be said of critical and aesthetic theory as applied to the graphic and performing arts. The categories of analysis and the appropriate ways in which to approach the task of scrutiny have become increasingly problematic.

There has been, it would seem, a passage from relative certainty to radical skepticism, from relatively stable categories to highly volatile ones, and from an emerging orthodoxy to a state of permanent revolution. This book is poised somewhere between that starting point and that end point. We have deliberately structured it so. Each chapter starts from one of the classic formulations of qualitative research that informed the emerging consensus of the 1960s. We have drawn upon a number of highly influential papers, by some of the key authors in the field. We use each of these papers as a starting point in tracing some of the changes that have taken place in recent years. But we do so with a particular purpose. We do not employ this organizational device to criticize the earlier contributions. We are not lining up distinguished and influential professional colleagues like Howard Becker in order to take cheap shots at them. To criticize them now for views they—very cogently and successfully—expressed in the 1960s would be gratuitously impolite. We use the papers as jumping-off points precisely because they were good examples of their kind. There would be absolutely no point in selecting weak arguments for our purposes. On the contrary, we have selected them because as well as being classic statements, they are eminently sensible statements of significant issues. Far from dismissing them, therefore, we use them in order to demonstrate how our collective thought has been transformed by subsequent interventions.

Equally, we do not undertake this process in order to celebrate all of the newer accounts. We believe that some of the more recent innovations have been excessive. There has indeed been far too great an emphasis on novelty for its own sake. There have, we maintain, been too many attempts to write intellectual histories of research methods that stress radical discontinuities and that overemphasize the claims of the new. There is a danger of celebrating the radical chic of postmodernism or postcolonialism by writing off past achievements, and—worse—by distorting the history of ethnographic and other qualitative research.

It is, therefore, our intention to provide a balanced view of change here. We are not neoconservatives, trying to recapture a more certain and more comfortable world of methodological certainty. We have jointly and severally contributed to some of the recent developments in the field, and we have no desire simply to put the clock back. Equally, however, we are not uncritical adherents of the latest versions of "post" theoretical or epistemological innovation. Our reasoning will become clear in the course of the detailed discussions in the chapters that follow. Before moving on to those specific discussions, however, we outline some of the main lines of cleavage and continuity, paying particular attention to the current state of innovative thinking. In particular, we examine claims that have been made on behalf of "postmodernism" in the general context of methodological renewal. These are part of a more general avant garde of research approaches, which we shall address throughout this book.

THE AVANT GARDE

It is virtually impossible to summarize the contemporary field of writing about qualitative research, except to note its extreme diversity. In contrast to the early classics of methodological writing, through which methodological canons for qualitative work were formulated and disseminated, the contemporary scene is not conducive to the promotion of orthodoxy. Indeed, one is tempted to suggest that heterodox positions are the new orthodoxy. Without preempting the main arguments of the book, here we outline in brief how this highly variegated array of methods and justifications is shaped.

The main characteristic of today's diversity derives from a pervasive anti-foundationalism. This is justified by various appeals to postmodern social theory and epistemology. This in turn has led commentators to brand earlier attempts to justify and to conduct qualitative research as unduly grounded in scientistic and positivist intellectual frameworks. Contemporary approaches are sometimes described as post-paradigmatic, suggesting once more that they have escaped or transcended what are seen as unnecessarily restricted or inappropriate canons of rigor and the boundaries of disciplinary knowledge. This implies a rejection or a reevaluation of long-established, conventional criteria for the adequacy of research.

It is quite wrong to assume that ethnographers and other qualitative researchers of previous generations unequivocally saw themselves and their work in "positivist" terms. That is to overlook the long traditions of interpretative social science that informed much ethnographic and cultural research. It does not do justice to the influence of interactionism or phenomenology in sociology, and it distorts the recurrent inspirations of social and cultural anthropology. However, advocates of postmodernism have, perhaps appropriately, called into question the conventional criteria for research. They reject the kinds of criteria for the validity of research that were the benchmarks of earlier generations of researchers and methodologists. Rather than searching for universalistic criteria for the validity or adequacy of research, therefore, adherents of the avant garde stress that notions of validity are themselves culturally and socially specific: that validity is always constructed within specific interpretative traditions, ideological positions, and in accordance with sectional interests. They question the possibility of universally valid and disinterested knowledge. This is not tied to the conduct of any one particular research strategy, but it is applied with special vigor by those who seek simultaneously to question and to renew the possibilities of ethnographic inquiry. Insofar as they exist in these terms at all, postmodernist notions of adequacy for research are thus rendered in explicitly relativist terms. The general position reflects a thoroughgoing skepticism concerning the authority and legitimacy of more conventional notions of methodology, epistemology, and research practice.

In that sense, therefore, members of the contemporary avant garde represent the research act as an inherently political one. This goes well beyond controversies about the proper *ends* of the research process. From this perspective, the *means* of research are themselves shot through with ethical and political import. The personal and political relationships between the researcher and the researched, for instance, are subject to critical scrutiny and reflection. The fieldwork encounter itself is politicized. This reflects various influences that have rendered the "fields" of "field research" contested domains. These include the reappraisal of anthropology as a discipline, and the parallel influence of feminist critiques.

Anthropology has been especially sensitive to and—in some quarters— responsive to criticisms of its historical relationships with the social actors and the cultures that it takes as the topics of inquiry. These include accusations of *orientalism* (Said 1978) and similar inappropriate constructions of the "others" on whom and with whom they work. Social and cultural anthropologists have become increasingly sensitive to the charge that their traditional subject matter, and their distinctive treatment of it, has led them to represent "others" as exotic and alien in inappropriate ways. The stark contrasts drawn in the past between, say, indigenous and Western styles of thought, between cosmopolitan science and local belief systems, or between different modes of rationality have been called into question. In a world of global communications and influence, it is not clear that such contrasts remain valid. The "othering" of the anthropologists' hosts has been questioned. The ready equation of anthropological fieldwork as encounters with geographically and/or culturally distant peoples has been further undermined by the increasing propensity of anthropologists to work with groups and organizations within their "own" culture. This has thrown into relief not just the problematic nature of the "other," but also what counts as one's "own" culture.

Anthropology has also been the site for a parallel set of debates that have called into question the authority of the ethnographer and the authority of the author (Clifford 1988; Marcus and Fischer 1986). From this perspective, the ethnographer is engaged in two kinds of practical activities, neither of which is neutral, neither of which results in an unmediated representation of an independently truthful representation of the social world. First, the conduct of fieldwork is dependent on a protracted series of transactions and negotiations with one's hosts or informants. Through that practical work, a version or series of versions of the world is jointly produced. Rather than seeing the fieldwork encounter in terms of the ethnographer's disengaged gaze, or in terms of an interrogation of informants, the craft of ethnography is seen in dialogic terms. The product of those encounters—the written ethnographic monograph or paper—is equally crafted. It is made through the textual work of the ethnographer, who draws on a variety of literary conventions in order to construct a written reconstruction of the social world (Coles 2000). These conventions are also far from neutral, and inescapably mediate the textual representation of the social world (Denuvo 1992; Sparkes 1995). Textual forms inscribe aesthetic conventions of representation, and they equally inscribe representations of the researcher/author.

The so-called crisis of representation among anthropologists has taken a somewhat different turn among sociologists. Responses have been decidedly mixed. For instance, the *Journal of Contemporary Ethnography* (August 2002) carried a review symposium on the "crisis in representation" with papers by Flaherty (2002a and 2002b), Denzin (2002), Manning (2002) and Snow (2002). Flaherty (2002a) sets out a brief history of the debates within the United States; Denzin (2002) sees the *nouvelle vague* as a wholly positive move. Snow (2002) argues that there is no crisis because classic, traditional ethnographies are still published and from that will come the new classics that will be re-read and cited in the future, not the experimental works. Flaherty (2002b) concurs, in his overview of the three papers. All these authors write as if the issues— whatever conclusions might be drawn—are entirely confined to American literature. Writing from the United Kingdom, we find this casual, unthinking ethnocentrism odd: for a decade, we have been actively engaged in aspects of the debates (Atkinson 1990, 1992, and 1996; Coffey and Atkinson 1996; Coffey 1999).

Whereas anthropology tended to perceive things in terms of a crisis of authority, sociologists, over the same period, have tended to respond in more positive terms. They have traced the rhetorical and literary conventions of ethnographic texts, but they have tended to see these issues in terms of the *possibilities* they present, rather than as a shaking of the foundations. Consequently, the avant garde of qualitative research in sociology have embraced the opportunities of textual experimentation. "Alternative" literary forms have been deployed in a variety of modes. Examples and works of advocacy are to be found among an influential network of established and younger scholars (e.g. Angrosino 1998; Banks and Banks 1998; Ellis and Bochner 1996; Goodall 2000; Jones 1998).

Explicit attention to literary form has led a number of contemporary researchers and commentators to acknowledge the role of writing as a mode of ethnographic analysis in its own right (Richardson 1994). Writing up the results of field research is not seen as a technical matter, to be completed as a neutral exercise after the data collection and analysis are complete. Rather, the process of inquiry is itself an exercise in authorship. Textual work is integral to the creation of "data," from the construction of fieldnotes to the transcription of interviews or other spoken interactions. Equally, the creation of interpretative analyses is an exercise in authorship. As a consequence, authors working in a self-consciously experimental vein have treated authorship as a *personal* matter. Rather than writing themselves out of the account, therefore, authors write in much more explicitly autobiographical modes.

The exploration of the ethnographer's own self is an increasingly visible aspect of contemporary writing. Indeed, this has been combined with newer modes of scholarly writing to the effect that there is a blurred line between the ethnography of "others" and the ethnography of the self. Autoethnography and autobiographical reflection have become a distinctive genre within contemporary ethnographic writing. Likewise, ethnographers are increasingly willing, even eager, to explore their personal and emotional responses to research in the field. Of course, sociologists and others have written autobiographical accounts and personal reflections on their fieldwork experience for many years. What is intended to be distinctive about the more recent style is the extent to which authors foreground their own reflections and responses. These are not removed to confessional accounts that are separate from the major publications. Rather, they are integral to the work of analysis and representation. In autoethnographic work, indeed, they form the central focus of attention.

QUALITATIVE RESEARCH—NOVELTY AND DIVERSITY

Contemporary qualitative research is, therefore, a highly variegated domain. The range of actual methods deployed is diverse. The methods that are routinely discussed include not just participant observation and interviewing, but also the collection and analysis of life histories, biographies and autobiographies, the recording and analysis of spoken discourse, a variety of visual methods, as well as "virtual" methods for the investigation of online interactions. The subject matter of qualitative research has also grown. Such research strategies have become firmly entrenched in major substantive areas, and newer methods are in turn suggesting newer fields of application.

The literature on ethnographic and other qualitative research is burgeoning. It is easy to see how a degree of confusion can result, not least from the explosion of methodological innovation and innovative writing about methods. Arguably, the methodological literature has moved beyond much of the actual practice of social scientists. Purely methodological interventions can readily give the impression that entire disciplines are in epistemological and methodological ferment—that all the products of field research appear as "messy texts" or other kinds of literary invention, that "we are all postmodernist now," and that earlier methodological formulations are redundant. We do not believe either of those to be the case. There is a great deal of work that is conducted and reported according to conventional criteria and in traditional formats. Moreover, the issues raised by earlier scholars remain pertinent; we do not believe that they have been swept away by a tide of innovation and experimentation. In many ways, the purpose of this book is to provide a balanced view that partly redresses excesses of recent commentary and advocacy.

Equally, we believe that the novelty of recent contributions may have been exaggerated. The structure of this book is based on a contrast between methodological perspectives of earlier generations of distinguished methodologists and contemporary views. We do not do so in order to imply that there is a linear developmental progression from one to another. Closer inspection of the relevant literature suggests that the novelties of recent years are not all that new. It is not the case that all the work done before the most recent "new wave" was modernist, positivist, or lacking in self-conscious aesthetic influence. We expand on these observations later in the book, when we discuss specific research issues. We want to emphasize at the outset, however, that we are definitely not trying to turn the clock back. We do not adopt the approach in this book in order to dismiss current approaches; on the contrary, we have contributed in various ways to recent thinking. We do not discuss earlier publications in order to suggest that they are out of date, or in order to contrast them with superior and more sophisticated recent arguments. Rather, we want to suggest that questions raised in "classic" methodological papers and studies remain important ones. At the same time, we do not think that all of the most recent interventions provide "solutions" to those issues, much less render the questions themselves obsolete.

CLASSIC THEMES

We address the issues we have outlined above through a series of specific questions. These have been among the defining issues of qualitative research methods. They represent some of the most abiding, recurrent questions that researchers have to address. There have been, as we shall see, various responses to these issues, and the nature of those responses accounts for much of the newer thinking in the field. We argue that these "classic" themes continue to have significance for contemporary research. Although responses to those questions have changed over the years, these transformations have not removed their importance for methodological thinking, nor has their urgency been diminished.

We begin in chapter 1 with a discussion of the related themes of familiarity and strangeness. We do so by addressing Blanche Geer's classic paper on first days in the field. Geer's discussion of the ethnographer's first encounters with "the field" has undoubtedly become a *locus classicus*, through which researchers have encapsulated the dynamics of strangeness. The ethnographic researcher has been characterized repeatedly in terms of a tension between the extremes of outsider and insider. Equally classic formulations have included the anthropologist Hortense Powdermaker's evocative phrase of "stranger and friend," or the sociologist Michael Agar's telling emblem of the "professional stranger" (Agar 1980), or indeed the formulation of the "marginal native" (Freilich 1970). The Chicago sociologists traced a homology between the urban ethnographer and the social type of the "marginal" social actor. The sociologists Lyn and John Loflands' allusive notion of the "socially acceptable incompetent" also captures dimensions of the tension (Lofland and Lofland 1984). Although the phenomenological movement was not always used to the same ends, the image of the ethnographer encountering a new social world has been supplemented by Schutz's invocation of "the stranger." The stranger is at once a social type, as described by Georg Simmel, and a metaphor for the social phenomenologist, who finds that his or her taken-for-granted stock of knowledge will not serve for practical purposes in a newly encountered social environment.

Geer herself does not deal with just the obvious issue of a "strange" research site. She also raises the equally fundamental analytic problems that "familiar" settings can create. Famously—and in a way that must have rung true for countless teachers and dissertation supervisors—she writes about the problems of understanding that present themselves when the research setting is, broadly speaking, a familiar one in one's own culture. If Schutz's archetypal stranger finds too little that fits with common-sense understandings, then the ethnographer of her or his own culture may find too much that chimes with preconceived understandings. Strangeness provides too much novelty, familiarity too little. The intellectual trick for the ethnographer, in whatever setting, has conventionally been portrayed as the attempt to make the familiar strange, and the strange familiar. Since Geer's account, and other classic formulations of the problem, the issues have not been resolved. Indeed, they have become more complex. We have come to recognize that "strange" and "familiar" are not easy terms to apply, any more than are terms such as "distant" and "at home" for anthropologists. The cultures of "our" society have become—or at least have been understood to be—more fragile and more complex than such dichotomies would readily permit, while the "strangeness" of our research settings has become less self-evident. Ironic contrasts between "mainstream" or "conventional" society and local subcultures lose their analytic simplicity and instead throw into doubt the construction of conventionality itself. Equally, contrasts between "our" culture and "other" cultures have been regarded as thoroughly troublesome.

The ambiguities of familiarity and strangeness carry through into the social processes and relationships that underpin the conduct of field research. Chapter 2 takes as its starting point Hortense Powdermaker's classic discussion that locates the anthropologist in the space "between stranger and friend." Such formulations of the issue suggested that the personal position of the ethnographer paralleled the intellectual posture of the marginal native. The researcher was portrayed as poised between intimacy and distance. There was the ever-present danger of "going native" (both practically and intellectually), and so losing the analytic cutting edge of marginality. Socially, this was paralleled by the perceived dangers of "over-rapport" in the field. The problem—enunciated by Powdermaker—was simultaneously practical and methodological. The danger was that the ethnographer would become too closely identified with the social actors who were the focus of the research, or with a particular segment of those actors. The ethnographer should, it was argued, seek to avoid unduly close social relations with individuals or groups in the field. The rationale for such a standpoint includes the practical requirement to maintain some degree of interpersonal mobility within the field setting; unduly close identification with particular individuals or groups may place limits on social engagement with others. More profoundly, perhaps, over-identification would blunt the ethnographer's analytic capacities. It would lead her or him to exchange one taken-for-granted stock of knowledge for another. The field researcher who was guilty of over-rapport would be in danger of reproducing or advocating the culture or subculture in question. The ideal was to maintain the ethnographer's liminal position—socially and intellectually—in order to retain the capacity for critical reflection on social action and cultural categories, and to be able to translate between the researcher's own academic subculture and that of the chosen field setting. The classic formulation of social relations in the field was, therefore, the advocacy of a "cool" approach. The ethnographer in the field should maintain a degree of self-possession, reserve, and social distance.

In more recent years, however, the conduct of ethnography has come to be a less cool medium of exploration and expression. Anthropologists and sociologists have come to explore and even to celebrate relations of intimacy in the field, and equally to treat intimate relations (such as their own family members) as legitimate topics for scholarly research. Likewise, more researchers have singled out and explored the sources of personal transformation in the field—religious conversions, sexual liaisons, personal dangers, extraordinary experiences—that severely undermine any pretense to cool detachment. In the process, the ethnographer has come to be portrayed as a more complex actor than might otherwise be the case. Distinctions between the "self" of the ethnographer and the "others" in the field have become problematic. Selves are constructed and reconstructed in kaleidoscopic ways, and the patterns of social relationships are densely woven. Simple dichotomies will not suffice to capture them. Contemporary methodological reflection celebrates more than the one-dimensional field worker of older formulations. In that sense, the "field" has become a more richly layered site of social relations through which the anthropologist or sociologist explores a variety of inter- and intrapersonal perspectives.

A similar shift can be detected in the politics and ethics of field research. We explore some of the key issues in chapter 3, where we begin from Howard Becker's oft-quoted paper in which he asked rhetorically "Whose side are we on?" It would be a gross oversimplification in itself to suggest that Becker's formulation—and his answers to his own question—were naive. But they do display a perspective characteristic of its time. We find, once again, that the categories within which the argument is framed are relatively straightforward. The ethical issues are predicated on relatively simple and stable social differences. Becker writes—persuasively and with great clarity—about the hierarchies of credibility within which and against which the social analyst must work. In essence, Becker argued for a kind of moral and epistemological symmetry, through which normal social categories and values are suspended, and the values of the marginal, the discredited, and the "underdog" are treated seriously. From a contemporary perspective, however, one can see that Becker's original formulation begged a number of questions. We now would recognize that invocations of "we" are problematic. Who "we" are is far from self-evident. We certainly cannot assume a stable and homogeneous community of research scholars, sharing common identities, goals, and values. Moreover, the research community cannot necessarily be assumed to share the authority to speak for others. Indeed, if it is no longer clear who "we" are, it is also no longer clear who are the "others" about whom and for whom the researcher might speak. In that sense, then, Becker's invocation of "sides" seems difficult to sustain, and seems redolent of a more settled moral universe than many contemporary researchers find possible. Lastly, Becker and his contemporaries did not seem to find any intrinsic ethical or political difficulties in the use of field research methods. The ethical issues were not indigenous to the research process itself, but in its applications and interpretations. Some contemporary positions imbue the research process itself with greater ethical moment.

Research methods themselves, and the proper relationships between them, are returned to in the chapters that follow. Moving from their more overtly ethical dimensions to problems of interpretation, we consider two recurrent problems concerning qualitative research. First, in chapter 4, we look at the proper relationships between participant observation and interviewing. This again was one of the key questions formulated during our "classic" period. Our chosen paper, by two distinguished authors—Blanche Geer and Howard Becker—reflected on the relationship between these two methods of data collection. Our own discussion traces out the original formulation of the question, and then looks at the development of the issue subsequently. What is again striking is that while Becker and Geer ponder interview and observational data, they again treat the methods and the data they generate as relatively unproblematic. Their paper derives from a period when methodological commentary was directed at the choice of appropriate methods, the best ways of combining research methods, and their respective strengths and weaknesses. The methods themselves are treated relatively unproblematically. In the intervening years, the status of data and the methods used for their generation have received more critical scrutiny. In particular, the nature of interview data and the proper treatment of accounts derived from interviews have become more controversial. We therefore discuss the relationship between observational and interview data from the vantage point of the intervening debates. We suggest that while the comparatively simple formulations of the 1960s may no longer hold, radical claims for or against interview-derived accounts and narratives are not necessarily valid either.

In chapter 5, we focus on Dean and Whyte's reflections on one of the key issues of qualitative research, especially in its formative years: "How do you know if your informant is telling the truth?" This is something that has occupied many commentators, and has sometimes been portrayed as a weakness of all social research, especially that based on interviewing. It can be extended from informants' truth telling to the assumption that participant observation must inescapably alter social actors' behavior—so that any interpretation of the social setting is rendered inauthentic. We discuss some of the issues that underlie this longstanding research question. Again, we suggest that it is possible to derive a sufficiently sophisticated approach to the issues involved without resorting to the most extreme or radical versions.

The chapters have, to some extent, followed the logic of a research project, with focuses upon initial encounters, field relations, data collection, ethics and social responsibility, and the reliability and validity of data. In chapter 6, we move on to analysis, focusing on another classic paper by Howard Becker about "problems of inference and proof" in field research. The relationships between methods and the interpretation of data form the basis of our chapter. This was one of several influential statements through which field researchers reflected upon their proper modes of analysis and reasoning. We suggest that Becker's approach is part of a more general one that encouraged a convergent model of analysis, and was part of the movement whereby field methods became codified. The convergence towards a single orthodoxy included the widespread endorsement of the principles, triangulation of methods and sources, and of the methods of grounded theory. We argue, in passing, that these principles sometimes became oversimplified and vulgarized in that process of codification. In contrast, the contemporary picture is characterized by divergence, in that a multiplicity of strategies and justifications flourish.

In our discussion of classic methodological questions, we finally consider the issues of representation and writing. This forms the subject matter of chapter 7. In one sense, we are cheating a little here. The classic papers we have used to launch our discussions paid little attention to matters of writing and representation. In the "classic" period, this was not a major preoccupation of methodologists. It would be wrong to imply—as we point out—that there had never been any interest in matters of form and representation on the part of field workers, but they were rare experiments and were not part of the core repertoire of methodological or epistemological issues. We have identified one very good paper by John Lofland as our starting point, for his was one of the very few papers of methodological advice that explicitly took writing and form as a set of issues. It is entirely characteristic of the time that those matters are raised primarily as practical and stylistic, rather than reflecting more profound and destabilizing tendencies in the social sciences. In the intervening period, the representation of ethnographic work and the textual forms of ethnographic writing have been placed at the very heart of methodological debate. Here, then, we reflect on the implications of this textual turn in qualitative research and some of its implications.

In each of these chapters, therefore, we follow the same underlying pattern. We trace the arc of change from a period when there were concerted and highly successful moves to codify qualitative research to the contemporary scene where methodological perspectives are far more diverse—where methods, representations, and ethics are all contested. As we have emphasized already, we do not do so in order to trace a simple developmental or evolutionary movement. We have discussed this at greater length elsewhere, but we are not convinced that the kind of intellectual history repeatedly sketched by Denzin and Lincoln is wholly adequate. We do not believe that one can really identify a kind of Comtean progression from modernism or even from positivism towards a triumphant poststructuralism/postmodernism. Rather, we think that qualitative research is a more variegated domain of activity than that model would allow. We also do not think that the kinds of transformations to which we have just alluded, and which will be explored in the chapters to follow, are necessarily "progress." The newer ideas have certainly not been implemented and adopted as universally as the avant garde methodologists might wish to imply. Indeed, as we have suggested elsewhere, innovative ideas seem to be clustered in particular enclaves within the discipline—a series of *rives gauches* within disciplines and areas of specialization.

This volume, then, is not a textbook on how to conduct qualitative research. There are more than enough such texts already. Rather, it is a series of reflections on key themes and classic questions. We have written them as more-or-less self-contained essays. There is of necessity a good deal of cross-reference between the themes, and we have allowed ourselves a modicum of overlap between the chapters. These themes are of such pervasive significance that they all cross-refer anyway, and we have not sought to impose unduly rigid boundaries between them. We would like each of the essays in this volume to be read alone, as well as part of the broader argument.

There is also a wider framework that unites the chapters and that constitutes our collective view on these matters. In brief, we believe that the *answers* to our classic questions have changed and become more complex in the years since they were first posed (or at least were posed in this form) but the *questions* retain their significance for today's researchers. We have ourselves contributed to some of the developments in qualitative research, and we are not seeking to repudiate all of the innovations that have been introduced. On the contrary, we believe that the degree of interest and debate surrounding qualitative research in the social sciences is one of the most exciting aspects of social research in recent years. If the disciplinary boundaries could be shifted accordingly, we would have the opportunity for a remarkable program of social research that spans the current divisions of social and cultural anthropology, sociology, discursive psychology, human geography, health and educational research, criminology, and other closely related fields of inquiry. The boundaries between these exercises in interpretative social science and the humanities are also becoming increasingly blurred. The anthropological, cultural, and historical influences on the "new historicism" in literary studies are an example of such convergence; the increasing awareness of literary forms by social scientists implies convergence from the opposite direction.

CONCLUSION

We have set out the underlying contrasts on which our reflections are based. We have introduced and juxtaposed some of the foundational methodological questions for qualitative research. We do not do so in order to condemn the past, nor to celebrate the present. The earlier generations did not have everything right. The current generation does not either. There is an element of radical chic to be found in contemporary methodological pronouncements. Excessive methodological positions have been granted considerable prominence through high-profile publications and through the work of prolific authors. This brings with it a danger; it can sometimes seem as if the Avant Garde approach is the only game in town, and that less heady and innovative perspectives have been abandoned altogether. In the chapters that follow, we have therefore set out to redress the balance somewhat—pointing out not only the rich and productive diversity (and potential) of current methodological understandings but also some of the confusions, difficulties, and excesses that are detected in the current research environment. In essence, we argue that contemporary authors can exaggerate the differences between their own perspectives and those of earlier generations. We think that the claims for "postmodernism" and similar positions can lead researchers and methodologists to overlook key issues that retain their significance. We believe, therefore, that it is important to understand the continuities in methodological thinking and writing as well as the changes and discontinuities.

1

STRANGENESS AND FAMILIARITY

FIRST DAYS IN THE FIELD

We begin this chapter by revisiting the classic paper by Blanche Geer (1964), "First Days in the Field." Like the other formulations of recurrent methodological issues we examine, this has become a *locus classicus* in the methodological literature of ethnography. It addressed a problem that was—with subtly different nuances—shared by sociologists and anthropologists. As anthropologists have increasingly undertaken research close to "home" their interests have increasingly converged with those of sociologists. Equally, as other disciplines have adopted field-based ethnographic research, their practitioners too have needed to think about these issues. Like the other methodological topics we address, it derives from a period in which major authors, thoroughly engaged in empirical ethnographic research, combined their own experiences of field research with general methodological precepts. Geer reflected on the significance of the early period of field research—a potentially crucial time when the ethnographer encounters her or his research setting for the first time. She examined, from the point of view of the sociological field researcher, the practical phenomenology of estrangement and the processes of familiarization. In doing so Geer captured recurrent issues that confront all researchers "in the field." She explored the problem of "making strange" the familiarity of social worlds from within one's own culture, together with the field researcher's accommodation to the unfamiliarity of the research setting in terms of its local particulars. When Geer was writing, the majority of anthropologists did their research in foreign countries or on ethnic minorities different from their own at home, such as Inuit and other Native American peoples, and their debates were about culture shock rather than the need to create strangeness. The passage in which Chagnon (1968) described his first encounter with the Yanomamo was more colorful in style than most, but not essentially different in meaning. There were undeniably exceptions, such as Victor Turner's (1978: ix) celebration of Srinivas's proposal that anthropologists should be "thrice-born": first, born into their own culture, then undergoing a second birth into the culture of the field site, then a third birth back home when one's natal culture should now be "strange." We return to anthropology after our discussion of Blanche Geer.

Writing about her experience of research on student cultures at the University of Kansas—published as *Making the Grade* (Becker, Geer, and Hughes 1968)—Geer (1964: 379) wrote:

> Throughout the time the undergraduate study was being planned I was bored by the thought of studying undergraduates. They looked painfully young to me. I could not imagine becoming interested in their daily affairs—in classes, study, dating, and bull sessions. I had memories of my own college days in which I appeared as a child: overemotional, limited in understanding, with an incomprehensible taste for milkshakes and convertibles.

Geer's "problem," then, was to overcome her own "knowledge" about undergraduate students in order to find new sources of sociological interest and new topics for research. She and her colleagues did so. Once immersed in the fieldwork, Geer found that the social world of the students was fascinating. Her classic paper is, in part, an essay that reflects on that process.

Among other things, she comments on the deadening effect of general knowledge or acquaintance with cultural settings. While the novice observer may have no direct or sustained personal knowledge of a setting, she or he may nonetheless find its surface appearance unhelpfully familiar. There can therefore arise a sort of observational *ennui* (the term is ours, not Geer's). Geer herself suggests that an untrained novice can, for instance, spend time observing in a setting like a hospital, and come back from the field with a virtually empty notebook and little or nothing to report: "Untrained observers, for instance, can spend a day in a hospital and come back with one page of notes, and no hypotheses. It was a hospital, they say; everyone knows what hospitals are like" (Geer 1964: 384). The problem is that for the naive observer, there is nothing special to see. "Everyone knows" what to expect in many a setting, and so the inexperienced can find nothing newsworthy to report if what they see conforms to what they would normally expect on the basis of general cultural knowledge. The lessons that have to be learned, therefore, include an intellectual process of defamiliarization. The would-be field researcher also has to learn that "nothing never happens" and that even the most apparently mundane of occasions have to be accomplished by their participants. The seasoned fieldworker, unlike the novice referred to above, must find ways of rendering the field observable, in such a way as to derive fruitful working hypotheses. Geer herself continues:

> My comments in the fieldnotes suggest that working hypotheses are a product of the field data itself and of whatever ideas the field worker can summon. The initial stimulus may come from repetition or anomalies in the data which catch the observer's attention so that he [*sic*] searches his mind for explanations, or he may start from the opposite end—what is in his head—and search the data for evidence of stereotypes from the general culture or notions derived from discussions with colleagues, previous research, and reading. (384)

In other words, the first days in the field are described in terms of a somewhat anxious set of practical and intellectual engagements. Geer's ideal of the typical field researcher has to engage with the field, apparently in a somewhat anxious search for fruitful ideas in an ambiguous context of strangeness and familiarity.

Becker (1971:10) also paralleled the general argument in a much-reproduced footnote. Also writing about research in educational settings, Becker suggested:

> We may have understated a little the difficulty of observing contemporary classrooms. It is not just the survey method of educational testing or any of those things that keeps people from seeing what is going on. I think, instead, that it is first and foremost a matter of it all being so familiar that it becomes impossible to single out events that occur in the classroom as things that have occurred, even when they happen right in front of you. I have not had the experience of observing in elementary and high school classrooms myself, but I have in college classrooms and it takes a tremendous effort of will and imagination to stop seeing only the things that are conventionally "there" to be seen. I have talked to a couple of teams of research people who have sat around in classrooms trying to observe and it is like pulling teeth to get them to see or write anything beyond what "everyone" knows.

Becker thus reaffirms the apparent problem of working on aspects of one's own society. Just like Geer's hypothetical hospital or Becker and Geer's real undergraduate students, Becker's school classroom is a site of phenomenological problems. We can appreciate its general character by virtue of its relative familiarity as a constituent element in our own culture, yet that familiarity is itself a potential handicap. Familiarity, while possibly a desirable end of research is not, from this point of view, a desirable starting point. Geer and Becker are undoubtedly right in a practical sense. "Observing" in social settings is not a straightforward matter. One cannot just walk into a setting and "see" sociologically or anthropologically: Davies (1999) makes this point forcibly. We need to look a little further beneath their formulations, however, in order to examine the underlying assumptions and tensions before going on to reflect on how those issues may have been recast in the subsequent years.

STRANGENESS AND FAMILIARITY

In general, we wish to argue that the differences among ethnographers between what is "strange" and what is "familiar," and our attitudes towards those categories, have undergone subtle shifts. We can no longer assume, for instance, that the familiar is quite so familiar, nor can we take for granted what will count as strange. Anthropologists no longer concentrate on alien and exotic cultures; the geographical and cultural distance between "home" and "elsewhere" has decreased. In parallel, many sociologists have dissolved the social and intellectual difference between the "observer" and the "observed." In the 1960s, the classic methodological literature on qualitative research stressed the dangers of "over-rapport" between the researcher and the researched. In chapter 2, we explore in more detail the move from a fear of over-identification ("over-rapport" and "going native") to a celebration of intimacy. Here, therefore, we parallel those concerns with personal relationships with the equivalent interest in conceptual or cultural difference and distance. While sociologists and anthropologists have become more sensitive to the nuances of "difference" as a research topic, simple assumptions of strangeness and difference have become less sustainable.

The classic formulations of the Second Chicago School authors like Becker and Geer reflected an ethnographic tradition that repeatedly drew on the trope of the stranger and the marginal man. The descriptions of the modern metropolis—of which Chicago was both locus and archetype in American sociology—were inspired by the urban sociologists' explorations of the city as a site of dislocation, juxtaposed natural areas, and a new frontier. The urban setting thus became a contact zone between social worlds in transition. Large-scale migration meant that the Old World of Europe met the New World of North America; the American South met the North. If America had had a frontier that moved progressively West across the interior of the continent, it now had a new frontier, located in the heart of the metropolis, at the intersection of those urban zones where new immigrants first settled. The progressive wave of newcomers arriving at this frontier and the human traffic across the cultural frontier were among the driving forces for the "natural" development of the city as an organic whole.

Within this seething flux, the marginal person was not merely a social type, but a metaphor for the wider social condition. Marginality captured the cultural dislocation of the metropolitan dweller. It also captured the social and intellectual stance of the sociologist explorer of the same metropolitan setting. The sociologist thus engaged with a social world that was already populated by "strangers" to one another, and entered it as yet another form of stranger. European and American social observers and theorists were in agreement as to the social nature of the modern metropolis—Berlin, Paris, or Chicago. It was a physical and social setting in which city dwellers were brought into close proximity with large numbers of anonymous strangers, whose paths crossed in fleeting encounters and temporary relationships. The imagery and methodological thrust of the social type of the stranger was closely related to Simmel's interest in the same topic (Simmel 1971). Robert Park was a direct conduit between Simmel's work and the emerging Chicago school, and Simmel was one of the major theoretical influences on the American agenda (Park and Burgess 1925). The "stranger" was a key type in German social thought, of which Simmel was but one prominent example. Again, the stranger represented both a social archetype and an allegory for the social explorer. The city of Chicago was paralleled in the exploration of Berlin's cityscapes by Simmel himself, and by other authors such as Kracauer and Benjamin; see Frisby (1985) for a summary of these authors' general contributions to the observation of urban modernity.

The stranger-observer was captured in the person of the urban *flâneur*—the leisurely observer of the passing scene. There was, however, a major difference between the urban ethnographer who emerged out of the earliest years of Chicago urban sociology and *flâneurs*. The latter remained a detached onlooker, whereas direct participation in the social life about them characterised the urban sociologists in America. The famous "Arcades" project that was the unfinished legacy of Walter Benjamin (1986, 2000) illustrates the point. The shopping arcades of Paris (and other cities) provided Benjamin with the opportunity to exercise a kaleidoscopic imagination, ranging over a bewildering variety of goods, displays, associations, and connotations. In the arcades, Benjamin excavated the archaeological record of bourgeois capitalist consumption. But he was not a participant observer in even the broadest sense. He remained detached from the various social worlds that might intersect in the streets, shops, and other sites of consumption. His remained an optical exercise, reproducing the *flâneur's* scopophilia (the act of getting pleasure from something observed). In contrast, the commitment that came to define the ethnographic imagination reflected a different kind of "stranger." Estrangement might be thought of as a social barrier to be overcome—if only to a limited degree—as well as being marked by an intellectual difference that was to be explored and exploited. The *flâneur* enjoys her or his disengagement, and maintains it as the source of optical imagination. He or she remains *dégagé*. In contrast, the classic ethnographer as described by Geer and Becker sought to transcend the gulf of difference, or at least to work within that social and conceptual space. Moreover, with the development of sociological research, researchers—as we have seen—found themselves not so much "marginal" persons, but thoroughly socialized and competent members of their own society, attempting to make sociological sense of settings that were over-familiar. If the *flâneur* retained an ironic detachment from a passing social scene, the ethnographic fieldworker needed to work within a more ambiguous conceptual space. The detachment or estrangement needed to be preserved to some degree, in that the difference between researcher and hosts was held to provide a key analytic resource. Equally, the disengagement of the *flâneur* could not satisfy the imperative of *participant* observation. The ethnographer of urban social sites or organization settings needed to gain *access* not only to the actors and organized settings, but also to the personal and social worlds of her or his informants and hosts.

Classic formulations of ethnographic fieldwork therefore stress the tension between familiarity and strangeness in these terms. Paralleling the social relationships of distance and intimacy we discuss in chapter 2, the intellectual stance of the classic ethnographer straddled estrangement and familiarity. Estrangement could be expressed in terms of the role of the "outsider" and her or his marginal social position. Trice (1970), for instance, in a paper reproduced in one of the classic methodological anthologies, commented on his own experiences of field research among Alcoholics Anonymous members. In addition to the management of social relationships, Trice identified an analytic advantage:

> The utilization of the "outsider" role allows for a maintenance of objectivity that would become weakened if roles other than this one were at-

tempted. It is a maxim of rapport development that the researcher makes certain he [*sic*] is not allowing himself to be labelled as a representative of any group or interest, i.e., that he remain impersonal. It seems that when the outsider role is given a neutral flavor, it can be a most effective vehicle for securing this objectivity. It is difficult for the researcher to become emotionally involved in the viewpoint of any particular group if he continues to view himself as someone apart from the organization in which his research is taking place. (Trice 1970: 81)

Here the social role of "outsider" is closely linked to the intellectual stance of the field researcher. Social neutrality and lack of partisanship in the field is equated with the analytic virtue of *objectivity*. There is a homology between the nature of social relationships and the nature of the analytic perspectives that are enabled. By implication, therefore, social engagement would lead to a loss of objectivity, with the consequent dangers of bias.

This is perfectly apparent in the various accounts of "over-rapport" and the dangers of "going native." Miller's (1952) much-quoted paper on the dangers of over-rapport in the field is another standard point of reference. Again, the social and the analytic are brought into close proximity. Over-rapport implies the researcher over-identifying with particular individuals, cliques, or interest groups. This implies a degree of social intimacy and comfort, but also an alignment of the researcher's developing interpretative understandings with the perspectives of those with whom he or she identifies most closely. From this point of view, therefore, researchers may be accused of losing their capacity to explore the multiplicity of perspectives or to grasp a social world holistically if they become too closely allied with just one, partial interpretation. The researcher should, on the contrary, maintain the social freedom that marginal status confers, and which in turn engenders a certain intellectual freedom. The ethnographic gaze, so conceived, is productive within this conceptual space that opens up between the familiar and the strange, between the social positions of "insider" and "outsider."

Philosophically, ethnographic difference was sometimes fleshed out in terms of phenomenological "strangeness." The work of Alfred Schutz, among others, provided a philosophical account of the intellectual consequences of strangeness and estrangement (Schutz 1967; Berger and Luckmann 1967). In particular, the essay on "the stranger" continued the work of authors like Simmel, translated into social phenomenology (Schutz 1964). The social position of the stranger or newcomer is treated as a vantage point for the investigation of mundane reality. The stranger who encounters a new social situation for the

first time, Schutz argues, will discover that his or her taken-for-granted assumptions concerning everyday life do not work in the new circumstances.
This refers not only to the most florid of social differences, but also operates at
the most basic level of practical knowledge and action; the stranger's stock of
everyday knowledge, especially those preconscious background assumptions
that constitute what Schutz and the other phenomenologists refer to as the
"natural attitude." This refers to the bedrock of unexamined assumptions that
constitute the common sense of practical social actors. The "stranger" for
Schutz is not merely a specific topic for an investigation into social psychology.
The stranger is also a microcosm for phenomenological inquiry in general.
The crucial difference between the philosopher—and hence also the social
scientist—and the everyday social actor in a strange situation resides in the phenomenological work that the analyst has to perform. For the ordinary stranger,
the initial encounter with social novelty produces the sense of estrangement
"naturally" as it were. For the phenomenologist, on the other hand, the philosophical point at issue is to *make* strange the familiar features of one's own cultural milieu. This is the essential point of the phenomenological move of
"bracketing" one's own background knowledge in order to address afresh the
phenomena of everyday experience.

The phenomenological spirit was also incorporated into some of the
earliest ethnomethodological work in the famous "breaching" exercises undertaken by Garfinkel and his students (Garfinkel 1967; Heritage 1984). By
deliberately breaking the conventions of everyday conduct in one's imme-
diate mundane surroundings, one could render them visible. Normally they
would pass unnoticed in the flow of mundane talk and action. Infraction
renders them available for inspection. Furthermore, members' attempts to
make sense of the disrupted flow of everyday social action render visible
their sense-making practices, which would again pass unnoticed in the
smooth progress of practical social life. (These illustrative exercises were
sometimes mistakenly taken to be the main thrust of ethnomethodological
work.) The practical and intellectual exercises involved in ethnomethodological work were often referred to as making everyday life "anthropologically strange." This was but one example of the invocation of anthropological understanding to develop the analytic significance of strangeness in the
social sciences.

A standard reference point in the construction of the intellectual space
between the familiar and the strange was the model of social anthropology,
a discipline in which the dynamics of distance and difference have been a
central motif. Classic formulations of the anthropological enterprise stressed
the cultural difference between the researcher and the researched. Social and

cultural anthropology were grounded in the relationship between the two worlds of the anthropologist and his or her "people." While the cultural and analytic distance that confers "strangeness" in anthropological work has been a recurrent exemplar for many generations of researchers and methodologists, it no longer remains uncontested or unquestioned. Indeed, contemporary anthropology has transformed the underlying assumptions. For example, the conceptualization of "the other" has been radically questioned. Likewise, easy assumptions about cultural difference have been rendered problematic.

This reflects several tendencies in contemporary anthropological thought. They include the growing trend for the discipline to incorporate "anthropology at home" (Messerschmidt 1981; Jackson 1987) and the critique of "othering" the subjects of research. These are accompanied by parallel arguments concerning the appropriateness of "insider" research in anthropology, privileging not the distance of strangeness, but the capacity to understand cultural phenomena from an internal perspective. These issues are rendered not merely in technical analytic terms, but are also intimately related to the politics of anthropological legitimacy and authority. They are thus closely implicated in the "crises" of authority and representation that we return to in chapter 6. They thus illustrate the important point that those so-called crises are not to be thought of in negative terms only. While they may challenge certain foundational assumptions of the discipline, they also have productive and positive consequences, in opening up new understandings of the ethnographic enterprise.

An interest in "anthropology at home" betokens a shift in perspective of greater moment than just the location of anthropological fieldwork. It transforms the conceptual relations between "near" and "distant," "familiar" and "strange," or "insider and outsider." The picture is rendered in far greater complexity than in earlier formulations of the "self" and "other," of field researcher and the actors with whom they worked. These in turn reflect current preoccupations with the politics of cultural difference, reflecting concerns with postcolonialism and orientalism. Anthropology at home refers to a tendency for anthropology to abandon any implicit assumptions that anthropological fieldwork should be conducted in distant and exotic social settings. In practice, the great majority of anthropologists still contrive to sustain that image: most research still explores and most monographs still report field research on geographically and/or culturally distant settings. Research students in the United Kingdom, for instance, still feel in key departments that overseas field research counts for more than research in settings near to hand (Delamont, Atkinson, and Parry 2000). Nevertheless, there have been changes in normative terms. Research "at home," in one's own culture, is at least thinkable in a way that it might not have been to earlier generations. Anthropology in one's own culture removes the easy assumption of difference as the intellectual and imaginative motor of anthropological understanding. It changes the perceived relationship between the anthropologist and her or his chosen research site (see Strathern 1987). Anthropology at home has meant that anthropologists have, collectively, come to reconsider the nature of their own status as "outsiders" and to rethink the nature of their own conditional marginality. Indeed, the new anthropologist cannot base her or his research on the tacit value of cultural strangeness. It renders much more complex the claim to strangeness itself. Moreover, it has led anthropologists to re-evaluate the traditional and conventional appeals to cultural difference. The anthropologist working in his or her own culture is more likely to be confronted by the problem articulated by sociologists like Blanche Geer—rather than experiencing "anthropological strangeness" as a given, she or he is more likely to try to render the more familiar social world analytically strange.

In the United States and Canada, there has been a strong tradition of applied anthropology. These scholars frequently conducted their fieldwork at home, geographically at least. Some did foreign fieldwork, but many studied ethnic minorities, social problems, and institutions in North America. There is a flourishing Society for Applied Anthropology, with its journal, *Human Organization*; and in education a fifty-year tradition of research (Spindler and Spindler 2000) showcased in *Anthropology and Education Quarterly*. These anthropologists are often active in the American Anthropological Association alongside the "pure" anthropologists. We have written about the anthropology of education elsewhere (Atkinson and Delamont 1980; Delamont and Atkinson 1995). Classic examples of this genre are Gibson (1982) on schooling in St Croix, Virgin Islands, and Levinson (1998) on secondary schooling in Mexico. British anthropology has no equivalent. Over the past fifty years there have been attempts to establish and popularize applied anthropology in the United Kingdom, but with little success.

One example of the changes in North American anthropology is apparent from the research on the education of Navajo adolescents, especially at Rough Rock, an innovative school. The early research on Rough Rock was done by Anglos (Erikson 1970) and criticized by other Anglos (Wax 1970), while debates were also reported by Anglos (Collier 1988). In the past twenty years, the research has been conducted by Navajo scholars such as McCarty (McCarty et al. 1991) and Deyhle and Margonis (1995). These Navajo scholars do not themselves herd sheep in a harsh landscape, of course. However, they are studying the education of their own people, even their own clan siblings. LeCompte (2002) explores these changes.

Despite the strong tradition of anthropology at home, North American anthropologists also gain status from exotic and dangerous fieldwork sites. Harriet Rosenberg (1988: xi) did her research in an isolated French alpine village:

> I loved living in France and was amused when my anthropologist colleagues who worked in more exotic locales asked about my time in the bush. I would bravely attempt to match their stories of hardship by pointing out that "my village" was more than twenty-four hours away from the nearest three-star restaurant.

In practice, anthropologists have rarely undertaken research "at home," in that even within their own cultures they have still tended to seek out the more distant cultural settings. Anthropological research at home has concentrated on small-scale communities, disadvantaged groups, and ethnic minorities within European and other Western societies. Indeed, the anthropological research on contemporary Europe is barely distinguishable from the work of earlier generations that focused on small-scale rural "communities" on the margins of advanced societies (Bell and Newby 1971); Delamont (1995) contains a thorough review of this literature. There is research evidence to suggest that the individual researchers treat their local fields as if they were distant, by divorcing themselves from their academic departments and mentors while "in the field," and placing themselves in a kind of internal exile. They thus mimic the social and geographical distance conferred by research "elsewhere" (Delamont, Atkinson, and Parry 2000). However, the increasing prevalence of anthropological research that is at least close to home has helped to transform the disciplinary self-identify of its practitioners, and to throw into doubt some of its historical assumptions. Furthermore, feminist sociologists and anthropologists have been particularly active in making problematic the concepts of "home." Olesen (2000) explores these, including work by, for example Kondo (1990).

AMBIGUITIES OF STRANGENESS

The tendency to incorporate research "at home" has also been accompanied by the increasing practice of so-called insider research. This has reversed the classic formulation of the anthropological enterprise. What one might think of as the classic view celebrates the difference between the anthropologist and the people being studied. A growing number of commentators and practitioners have reversed the polarity, arguing that anthropological research should be conducted by scholars who are indigenous members of the culture in question. Insider or indigenous research, rather than celebrating difference, transforms and questions the implicit values that valorize such difference in the first place.

The topic of *orientalism* has led anthropologists to reconsider their relationship with their field sites. The term derives from Edward Said's work, specifically on the Near and Middle East in the Western imagination (Said 1978), and has subsequently been extended to cover a more general phenomenon—that is the problematic and increasingly contested constructions of "others" in the Western gaze of anthropology and other disciplinary knowledge (J. Marcus 2001). The orientalist gaze, Said suggests, constructed "Levant" in various and particular ways; it projected, for instance, characteristic kinds of motifs. Sexual imagery was, for instance, used to code the otherness of the Turk or the Arab. The harem provided a key reference point, an imaginary site of lascivious excess, effeminate luxury, and cruelty that exercised a recurrent fascination for Western observers.

The "Orient" was thus appropriated in imagination and in material terms by the West. Said's treatment of the theme highlighted one historical example of the discursive and pictorial representation of the exotic and the alien. The orientalizing gaze rendered "the other" in terms of cultural codes that stressed difference and exoticism. While it is wrong to extrapolate from orientalizing literature, art, travel writing, and so on to all of anthropology, critiques of orientalism were among the several intellectual currents that contributed to successive crises of legitimation among social and cultural anthropologists. Certainly a general re-evaluation of the object of anthropological scrutiny was given increased urgency by the general currency of orientalist critiques (J. Marcus 1992 and 2001).

Critical understanding was not confined to debates surrounding orientalist representations alone. More generalized anxieties concerning the representation of other cultures have been pervasive in anthropology, and have reflected wider preoccupations concerning the appropriation of the other. (See Lutz and Collins 1993, on *National Geographic*, for example.) These include the growing body of practical and reflective work on the collection and display of ethnographic materials in national museum collections. The spectacle of exotic cultures within the confines of conventional museum practice has in many ways paralleled the anthropological anxieties concerning the proper relations—social, political, and analytic—between Western intellectuals and the people with whom they have worked. Likewise, the appropriate stance toward the artistic representations of other cultures has been the context for considerable debate and controversy over our appropriation and appreciation of "otherness." The impact of so-called primitive art on the development of twentieth-century European and North American art is but one well-known moment in a changing climate of reception of images and artifacts from other cultures. The connotations of that otherness have been increasingly contested, and rendered a topic for explicit critical commentary in recent years.

There is a further layer in the story of familiarity and strangeness in the accounts of anthropology in one's own culture: the problem of academic estrangement between disciplines. In the introduction to his edited anthology, Jackson (1987), for instance, includes a baffling bit of boundary maintenance between anthropology and sociology. Clearly any discussion of anthropology in one's own culture invites comparison with the discipline of sociology. One is allowed to wonder at the difference between sociological ethnography and anthropological ethnography. The answer, at least from Jackson, was based on a risible distinction, which is worth quoting in full if only to document its absurdity. Commenting on the potential relationship between sociology and anthropology, Jackson (1987: 7–8) wrote:

> There is certainly very little relationship today. Anthropologists have abandoned the idea of a universal theory about the evolution of human societies, but sociologists fear to do so, since it would undermine the whole rationale of their existence. Sociologists are wedded to the notion that all societies can be explained in terms of some universal law of human development. Sociology is premised [*sic*] on its claimed ability to predict the course of social change—if it had not done so then it would be no different from history. This claim, however, has never been sustained and disillusionment has set in.

It is clear that Jackson's exploration of his own culture did not extend to any serious acquaintance with decades of empirical sociological research. The absurd statement does, however, reflect a broader tendency within anthropology: the desire to reaffirm the discipline's distinctive identity even when it serves no intellectual purpose, the desperate desire to establish difference from others, and to cling to an image of anthropology as occupying a unique position. When we were studying doctoral research students and established academics in British social anthropology, using ethnographic interviews, our informants frequently told us that we sociologists only used questionnaires, worked with quantitative methods and stressed that fieldwork was unique to anthropology (Delamont, Atkinson, and Parry 2000). Likewise, the papers edited by Gellner and Hirsch (2001) are framed by an introduction stating that the noun "ethnography" to describe a monograph "is confined to anthropological circles" (1), and that other disciplines "are beginning to be dissatisfied with the jejune results of positivist paradigms" (2). The individual chapters in that collection then resolutely fail to cite any ethnographic work on their particular subject matter by sociologists. Simpson (2001), for example, studied divorce mediation, but does not even cite Riessman (1990).

In practice, the justifications and critiques of anthropology at home seem to recapitulate the kinds of issues that have been explored by sociologists and others. Indeed, the more fruitful approach would seem to be a common set of understandings that reflect the shared interests of sociology, anthropology, cultural studies, and other disciplines committed to social exploration and interpretation.

Aguilar (1981) essayed a major review of the debates concerning insider research as they were at the time. In essence, the debate as he summarizes it is directly parallel to the sociological accounts with which we began this chapter. Aguilar begins to outline the issues in terms of familiarity and strangeness that are already familiar to us:

> In their zeal for intercultural investigation some anthropologists assert that Western social science is too culture bound because its research is too close to home. This, they say, results in a number of epistemological restrictions. For one, the conduct of research at home often inhibits the perception of structures and patterns of social and cultural life. Paradoxically too much is too familiar to be noticed or to arouse the curiosity essential to research. Intercultural or outsider research, on the other hand, involves a comparative orientation in which contrast promotes both perception and curiosity. The researcher undergoes a kind of heuristic culture shock that operates through curiosity as an impetus to understanding. (Aguilar 1981: 16)

Aguilar added that outsider research might be less biased and "more conducive to disinterested scientific behavior" (16). He also recognized the counterclaims that had been entered. They include the suggestion that culture shock could be a barrier to comprehension, leading the ethnographer to recoil from, rather than explore, the social world in question. Indeed, it is suggested that the imagery of culture shock is itself inappropriate, in that the anthropologist's personal experience more often feels like long-term disorientation rather than sudden dislocation. Moreover, as Aguilar conceded, culture shock and novelty-driven curiosity may not lead the observer to focus on scientifically significant phenomena. Advocates of insider research,

Aguilar added, argue that insiders are less likely to disrupt social settings, and may find members less likely to conceal things from them. They also advocate insider research on the basis that the insider has already acquired an enormous amount of cultural knowledge that the "outside researcher will have to learn either before entering the field or as an early part of the field experience. Insider research is therefore seen as more economical and efficacious."

The examples and debates outlined by Messerschmidt in his introductory essay to the same volume (Messerschmidt 1981), and by Aguilar, traverse unremarkable terrain—shuttling between familiarity and strangeness, culture shock and acculturation, insider competence and outsider curiosity. The essays anthologized under Messerschmidt's editorship, in fact, display a diverse range of positions of inside and out. More importantly, they also show that there are different social criteria used to attribute or to claim to be "at home." The editorial gloss is revealing. For instance, Messerschmidt (8) says that four of the authors are "closely identified" with the subjects of their research: Gwaltney working with "his own folk" (urban black Americans); Aamodt, a Norwegian-American woman working with her own kin in Wisconsin; Light and Kleiber "as women studying a Canadian feminist health collective." On the other hand, there are those with similar social backgrounds to their subjects, but "who are nonetheless unable to breach professional, philosophical, or subtle class boundaries to identify closely with their subjects." Messerschmidt cites here the chapters by Molgaard and Byerly, who worked with a New Age subcultural group, and Serber, who studied state insurance agencies.

What is clear is that within the broad definition of anthropology in one's "own" society, the definitions of identity that are invoked can differ markedly. Indeed, it appears to be the case that the social situations that anthropologists might describe as anthropology at home include encounters that sociologists have been equally likely to invoke as examples of "strangeness." We shall return later to this issue; it appears to be the case that a calculus of different degrees of "strangeness" or "familiarity" is inappropriate. What is certainly problematic is the easy assumption that one can treat either cultures or social identities in an essentialist manner. Before developing this argument, however, we turn to discuss two other strands in this literature. They are the advocacy and practice of indigenous and standpoint ethnography. (The terminologies vary, but they capture two constellations of ideas—themselves closely related.)

It has become increasingly common in anthropological contexts to recognize and to advocate the work of indigenous ethnography. That is the study of societies and cultures by scholars who are themselves members. This reverses the historical process of investigation and interpretation for anthropology, although it very much parallels—at least in purely personal terms—the stance of the majority of sociologists working on some segment of their own society. Strathern's intervention provides one of the classic statements of the ambiguities of anthropology at home (Strathern 1987). She outlines two assumptions that she suggests are commonly made concerning anthropology at home. First is the proposition that anthropologists working on familiar territory will achieve greater understanding because they do not have to overcome cultural and linguistic barriers. Secondly, there is the proposition that anthropology at home will render transparent the "contrivance" of anthropology in general—showing it up for reproducing and mystifying commonplace knowledge, producing only "unnecessary mystifications" (Strathern 1987: 17). Both propositions concern the nature of familiarity. Strathern suggests that they are in apparent contradiction. The first implies greater and deeper understanding, and the second implies the achievement of trivial understanding. At root, however, the arguments are the same. The cultural congruence between the anthropologist and the host culture raises the problem of familiarity in two guises. Familiarity holds out the appearance of ready understanding, while exposing the potential danger that the outcomes of the ethnography will appear too familiar to one's audiences—fellow academics in the same culture or the hosts themselves.

On behalf of anthropologists, therefore, Strathern rediscovers the tensions between familiarity and strangeness that the sociologists had explored a generation before. She disposes of the simple argument concerning congruence and understanding. She illustrates the argument with reference to the study of Elmdon—an Essex village studied by a series of Cambridge anthropology students (including Paul Atkinson) and subsequently drawn together into a monograph (Strathern 1981):

> The Elmdon project might have begun in a milieu in which it could be assumed that the villagers broadly participated in the worldview also held by the anthropologist. Yet what started as continuity ended as disjunction. The ethnographic text was hardly continuous with indigenous narrative form; one was not rendering back to the residents of the village an account immediately contiguous with those they had given, as social history or as biography might be regarded. It is clear that simply being a "member" of the overarching culture or society in question does not mean that the anthropologist will adopt appropriate local cultural genres. On the contrary he/she may well produce

something quite unrecognisable. Common-sense descriptions are set aside. (Strathern 1987: 18)

Strathern points out that the indigenous understandings are treated as anthropological *data*, rather than being merely reproduced in the anthropologist's account. In other words, difference is to be found in the work of the anthropologist that reformulates everyday life in terms that are neither inherently familiar nor strange to the indigenous social actors. In these terms, therefore, Strathern asserts the analytic distinction between anthropologists' and members' accounts. The work of the anthropologist is grounded in the systematic knowledge of the discipline: "For the ethnography is always to be compared and brought into relationship with a body of shared knowledge, and the contrivances of method and theory" (Strathern 1987: 26).

What Strathern highlights is the extent to which ethnographic understanding is produced through the work of reconstruction, not least through *writing* that constitutes the means of anthropological interpretation. Strathern argues that debates about autoethnography (see her chapter 3) and anthropology at home need to be very careful about what is assumed about culture. She suggests that it is dangerous to assume that all societies "have" culture in the same sense. While it may be true that all societies have techniques for ordering experience and for understanding their social world, one may not assume that those techniques of self-understanding or theorizing are identical.

DIFFERENCE AND IDENTITY

Debates about anthropologists at home and recent contributions from sociologists and others highlight the problem of arguing from identity. The argument from identity would suggest that cultural understanding is facilitated by a close relationship of identity between the researcher and the host culture. There is, however, the danger of oversimplified assumptions concerning cultural identity. Indeed, it would be ironic were social scientists— whose task it is to explore the nuances of enacted identities within concrete social settings—to account for their own work in terms of crude social and cultural categories. The complexities of insider and outsider roles and their embeddedness within the multiplicities of social identities are illustrated very aptly by Motzafi-Haller (1997), who reflects on fieldwork in Israel and in Botswana. Motzafi-Haller was born and brought up in Israel, in a family of immigrants from Iraq, as an oriental Jew, or Mizrahi. She attended a boarding school in Israel for Mizrahim who were judged clever enough to benefit from an Ashkenazi elite education away from their disadvantaged homes. There, and subsequently at university, she learned to stigmatize her own Arab heritage. As an American-based graduate student she did field-work in Botswana, where she was considered white among the poor vil-lagers but black as far as apartheid-segregated white South Africa was con-cerned. Reflecting on all her experiences she writes of her struggles to "fit into the dominant male-Ashkenazi-positivist discourse of Israeli scholar-ship" (218). Commenting on her work in producing a text on Mizrahi identity, she renders problematic any simplistic notions that ethnic origin guarantees authenticity in the rendering of cultural accounts. She dismisses "reductive essentializing" versions of ethnic or other identities, and the claim for privileged standpoints on the basis of such ascribed characteristics (214–15). Such perspectives, she maintains, over-determine the categories of here and there, center and periphery, self and other.

The argument from experience seems equally troubling. This strand of argument suggests that researchers' or authors' own experiences render them more able to achieve authentic understandings. This argument derives from the assumption that shared experience confers the capacity to secure more authentic insider interpretations. Like arguments concerning indige-nous anthropology, such a perspective closes the conceptual division be-tween the researcher and the hosts, seeking similarity and familiarity rather than distance and difference. Claims from identity are most clearly seen in the celebration of testimony by indigenous members of particular cultures or groups. This finds clearest expression in the genre of *testimonio*, in which members are the authors of their own cultural and political experiences or manifestos. The creators of such testimony are often represented as spokespersons for their own people, normally marginalized or oppressed minorities, translated into bearers of national aspiration and indigenous au-thenticity (see Warren 1997).

The more traditional treatments of difference and distance have, as we have seen, been confronted by a variety of perspectives that challenge its foundations. These have reflected a fundamental shift in critical thought surrounding ethnography, difference, and strangeness. They have challenged the dualisms between observer and observed, between subject and object, between near and far, insider and outsider, familiar and strange. Insofar as they reflect broader tendencies in postmodern thought, these contemporary currents demonstrate the proliferation of perspectives, and a de-centering of knowledge.

Approaches enshrined in the more conventional literature have been predicated on relatively fixed positions and bodies of knowledge. The social researcher, whether sociologist or anthropologist, has approached a particular group or culture from a fixed point of origin, and has progressed toward a particular mode of understanding. Current practice reveals a multiplicity of modes of understanding. The fixed positions of insider and outsider have been transformed into a kaleidoscopic array of practices. Rather than knowing "the other," the work of the ethnographer has been seen as a series of interactional and interpretative actions that simultaneously construct and question the processes of othering. There is, therefore, a shift from viewing the sociologist or the anthropologist as a knowing subject to the advocacy of de-centered and polymorphous ways of knowing. There has been a collective move away from an image of the ethnographer as the romantic subject who is the heroic center of a struggle to bridge a cultural divide. The quest for knowledge is transformed into a more problematic kind of journey, which has no determinate end any more than it has a fixed origin.

We would argue, however, that such perspectives, while abolishing facile characterizations of strangeness and familiarity, could also lead to unhelpful methodological practices and precepts. The appeal to shared identity or shared experience, while undermining the self-image of the anthropologist as heroic outsider, is itself grounded in a romantic myth of the subject. It too easily leads to a celebration of an internal world of subjectivities, biographies, and autobiographies. Likewise—as in Strathern's contrast—it reduces the ethnographer (sociologist or anthropologist) to someone who reproduces local knowledge, members' experiences, and the indigenous genres of knowledge. Behar (1993), in reflecting on her work with a Mexican woman that resonated with her own Cuban ancestry, expressed its difference from her earlier (to our mind exemplary) monograph on Northern Spain (Behar 1986). That former work had, she writes, "no link" to "her life" (331). It was, however, an evocative study of social change in Spain, including heartrending accounts of poverty and hunger. Her realist monograph is an important investigation of social change in rural Spain as it underwent transitions from being a village of peasants on the breadline under a fascist dictatorship and a repressive church to a condition of relative affluence in a democracy within the European Union and with choice in religious affairs. These are, we suggest, rather more important issues for social science in the long term than Behar's personal identity.

We have started from accounts that deal with relatively taken-for-granted categories and boundaries. The categories of insider and outsider, or the stances of familiarity and strangeness, were originally constructed in rather unproblematic ways. The anthropologists' contrasts of home and away were originally posed in similarly simple terms. While different kinds of justifications and values were attributed to the different poles of those dichotomies, the contrasts were sharply drawn. Anthropologists were relatively untroubled by the contrast between "inside" and "outside," even while they were debating the advantages and disadvantages of the different positions. Indeed, we note that in several of the earlier formulations, those positions are treated as relatively fixed, and the dimensions of congruence or difference rendered in simple terms. Often, indeed, the dimensions of membership or strangeness are represented in terms of ascribed social characteristics—ethnicity, citizenship, or gender. Moreover, those categories themselves are sometimes treated somewhat simply. Ethnic self-identity, say, is no guarantee of productive discovery any more than the status of outside observer.

What is clear from our discussion so far is that the distinctions between inside and out, home and away are not straightforward. Likewise, the categories of familiarity and strangeness are not pre-given. It is not productive—indeed it is not really possible—to *assume* that particular phenomena will fit one or other category of understanding in principle. Moreover, what strikes the stranger ethnographer on the basis of novelty during first days in the field will not automatically prove to be the most analytically significant issues. Indeed, the sociologist or anthropologist who stresses what is most immediately striking will be in danger of treating the culture in question in unnecessarily exotic terms. This is apparent to social scientists who are themselves members of an organization or culture that is the topic of some ethnographic account.

We can illustrate this phenomenon with reference to an anthropological account of the national setting with which we have some familiarity—contemporary Wales. Wales and the Welsh have provided settings for various ethnographic accounts—most notably, in the past, a number of classic community studies. We want, however, to highlight one particular "outsider" anthropological monograph (Trossett 1993) in which a North American anthropologist describes "Welsh" culture in terms that are entirely familiar to United Kingdom readers, whether or not they actually live in the country. The account focuses on the most distinctively "different" and culturally distinct aspects of life in Wales. She focuses, for instance, on the most obviously exotic and "ritualized" aspects. She stresses, for example, the tradition of the *Eisteddfodd*. This refers to a type of cultural festival, conducted through the medium of the Welsh language, which features competitive cultural performances—including poetic composition on set topics in strict metres, and individual and ensemble singing. There are local festivals, including those specifically for young people, and there is an annual national *Eisteddfodd*, where ceremonies like the crowning or chairing of winning bards are major highlights. The festivals are part of an invented tradition, based on nineteenth-century ethnology and philology, and based in part on an invented Druid tradition. Likewise Trossett stresses the place of rugby union in Welsh cultural life. Undoubtedly the national sport, and a major focus for national pride, rugby is one of the most distinctive features of a "Welsh" national self-identity. Success by the national side on the rugby field (rare in recent years) certainly colors local pride and satisfaction. Yet the social organization and culture of contemporary Wales is rendered in almost caricature form. The anthropological account focuses disproportionately on those aspects that are most likely to strike the stranger as most exotic, colorful, and alien.

It is, however, no accident that in this anthropological account Wales is rendered in these exotic terms. These are precisely among the cultural categories *used* by individual and collective Welsh actors to render the distinctiveness and specialness of Wales—for purposes of tourism or nationalist aspiration, for instance. Likewise, they are among the repertoire of representations that can be deployed by people from outside Wales to generate Wales as a distinct and different social or cultural milieu. We need, therefore, to treat such enactments in sensitive analytic ways. We should not confuse the ceremonial performances that individuals and collectives use—sometimes quite rarely but at specific junctures—to affirm a particular identity with the everyday realities of the relevant social worlds. Some of the people of Wales may deploy symbolically marked enactments in order to affirm their distinctive national identity. But they do not spend much of their ordinary time engaged in such practices.

What is arresting to the outside observer, especially the sociologist or anthropologist who is looking for what is "strange," may thus lead the observer to exaggerate the exotic or the unusual. The occasional ceremonial observance or collective performance may seem more significant than the ordinary realities of mundane social activity. The deviant may prove more striking than the routine and conformist. On the other hand, the insider or indigenous ethnographer may prove equally blind to the ordinary and the taken-for-granted. The observer who is already deeply immersed in the everyday world of the setting in question may find it hard to gain analytic purchase on phenomena that are so thoroughly habituated as to prove immune to research-oriented scrutiny.

In recent years, anthropologists and others have confronted a rather different set of issues concerning their relationships with the "others" with whom they work and whose worlds they seek to document. Far from feeling the danger of over-identification, and far from needing to maintain social or intellectual distance from the "others," some researchers have overtly explored the processes of research with groups or institutions for which they feel repugnance. This has been given special force by ethnographers engaged in explicitly critical social science. They see the end of ethnography in terms of a value-laden orientation towards major social institutions. They retain the long-standing ethnographic commitment to explorations of local organization and culture, but insist on locating the local within global contexts. They may, therefore, engage with others from whom they explicitly wish to maintain their distance, and whom they wish to criticize. Moreover, some cultural critics find themselves attempting to document dispersed and disembodied practices of power, so that personal relations of difference and distance are even more problematic to capture. As Springwood and King (2001: 410) summarize the problems:

> The difficult question is, How do researchers, writers, feminists, activists or critics *ethnographically engage* those folks who are implicated in the (re)production of those *very* sites and practices they seek to excavate, deconstruct or reconstruct, and perhaps challenge and eliminate? Wherein is rapport? Mutual collaboration? At a time when critical ethnographers have largely embraced the notion of collaboration in lieu of rapport . . . how does one collaborate with a signifying practice? Or a sociocultural landscape? Or a racist? A capitalist? A misogynist?

G. E. Marcus (1998 and 2001) has been a prominent author in this vein, commending multi-site ethnography that is justified by cultural critique. Marcus suggests that this critical vein has not been motivated primarily by systematic social theory—such as Marxism—but by the radical reappraisal of ethnographic fieldwork that has been pervasive in anthropology, sociology, and the cultural disciplines. These reformulations and re-evaluations have led ethnographers toward a reappraisal of the more traditional views of proper relationships between themselves and others.

CONCLUSIONS

Contemporary research in the social sciences has led to a multiplicity of stances, from those that stress distance between researcher and researched, to those that emphasize close, even intimate, relations. Moreover, the social and intellectual distance between researcher and researched has sometimes become so thoroughly collapsed as to result in an identity of researcher and researched through the move towards autoethnography. These intellectual and personal moves form the subject matter of the next chapter.

In exploring some of these topics, we have emphasized the degree to which notions of "strangeness" and "familiarity" have become increasingly problematic and complex. The relationships between the "observer" and the "other" certainly cannot be treated as self-evident. On the other hand, it is important not to lose sight of the original inspirations for ethnographic exploration. While we do not make facile assumptions about the difference between ourselves and those we research, and while we may also make of ourselves an object of reflective inquiry, we should not forget the underlying message of the methodological classics. It remains of fundamental importance to *make* phenomena strange or familiar, near or distant, rather than basing our analyses on easy assumptions about our own identity or our stance towards other cultures. "Othering"—in the sense of treating cultures and social groups as inherently exotic and alien—is no longer acceptable, intellectually and morally. On the other hand, we still need to recognize that the purpose of ethnographic field research is to make sense of social settings we are not familiar with, and to make strange social contexts that we assume we understand by virtue of our taken-for-granted cultural competence.

2

FROM OVER-RAPPORT
TO INTIMACY
AND AUTOETHNOGRAPHY

STRANGERS AND FRIENDS

In *Stranger and Friend*, Hortense Powdermaker (1966) provides an autobiographical account of anthropological fieldwork. Through rich descriptions of her own fieldwork experiences, Powdermaker locates her own anthropological career and makes explicit the relationships between personal feelings and intellectual perceptions.

Powdermaker's work in this vein was pioneering: Hier and Kemp (2002) provide a contemporary review of her scholarly contribution and of the enduring relevance of *Stranger and Friend*. Powdermaker takes the reader backstage into the life world of the fieldworker, illuminating the personal and emotional dimensions of participant observation. She describes her book as "an attempt to stand outside and observe one anthropologist— myself, the only one I can really know—stepping *in* to societies and *out* of them" (Powdermaker 1966: 15). Her objective is to provide more than mere glimpses of the fieldworker, rather to situate the personal characteristics and relationships of the fieldworker within and without the research experience. At the same time, however, Powdermaker is keen to stress the limits to her personal involvement in the field. In her descriptions of fieldwork in Lesu, a village on an island in the Southwest Pacific, she cautions against over involvement and the possibility of "going native" [*sic*].

> Although I had enjoyed those brief moments of feeling at one with the women dancers at the initiation rites and although I was fairly involved in this Stone-Age society, I never fooled myself that I had "gone native." I participated rather freely but remained an anthropologist. (Powdermaker 1966: 115)

Powdermaker presents a role of partial member (or marginal native) for the anthropologist. One who joins in but remains apart; has personal experiences and feelings of the field, but does not become part of that field; is there but not there; engaged but distant. Laura Bohannan's fictionalized account of her fieldwork in West Africa, written under her *nom de plume* Elenore Smith Bowen (Bowen 1964), represents an earlier attempt to navigate this same journey between engagement and distance. Her account, like that of Powdermaker, (re)presents an autobiographical and emotional version of qualitative fieldwork. Prolonged participant observation is described in personalized, emotive, and evocative ways, involving "a sea change in oneself that comes from immersion in another and savage [*sic*] culture" (Bowen 1964, *author's note*). However, immersion does not imply conversion here. Nor does it suggest over-familiarity with people, place, or culture. The self that Bowen (re)presents is still that of a stranger in an alien (and indeed "savage") culture. While she lived in the field, got to know and become known by the people, Bowen's account continually positions herself as a distant or marginal native (Freilich 1970). The personal impacts and emotions of fieldwork experiences are recognized, while at the same time the researcher remains poised on an interface between familiarity and strangeness.

Powdermaker's observations were derived from her experiences of anthropological fieldwork. Sociologists had their equivalent concerns, articulated in one of the earliest of the "classic" papers, frequently cited and anthologized in the codification of methods texts. Miller (1952), basing his remarks on his experience of field research with local labor union leadership, commented on the dangers of "over-rapport" in the field. Miller summed up the kind of problems he had experienced:

> Once I had developed a close relationship to the union leaders I was committed to continuing it, and some penetrating lines of inquiry had to be dropped. They had given me very significant and delicate information about the internal operation of the local [union branch]: to question closely their basic attitudes would open up severe conflict areas. To continue close rapport and to pursue avenues of investigation which appeared antagonistic to the union leaders was impossible. To shift to a lower level of rapport would be difficult because such a change would induce considerable distance and distrust. (Miller 1952: 98)

The very fact that Miller had established close rapport with the union leaders—potentially productive in research terms—in turn became a limiting factor. Indeed, Miller also suggests that the union officials might have fostered close, personal relations with him as a strategy to manage (or limit) his data collection opportunities. Moreover, the establishment of close rapport with the union leaders was more of a limiting factor when it came to Miller's field relations with rank-and-file union members. Miller's paper has been widely cited in order to emphasize the delicate balance that field researchers need to strike. On the one hand was the need to establish relations of trust and familiarity adequate to the practical needs of data collection in the field; to establish a manageable social role, of marginal membership, socially tolerated and free to come and go. This might well entail the aid of a sponsor to help establish social relationships, and to stand guarantor for them. On the other hand there was the desire to avoid undue close identification with particular social actors or categories of actor, recognizing that over-rapport in one direction, or with one subgroup, can lead to undesirable social distance in other directions or from other groups. Moreover, the establishment of close relationships can shut off lines of inquiry just as surely as it might open up others. The implication of Miller's advice is clear: the successful researcher should strive to maintain a degree of social flexibility, freedom to move between different individuals and groups, while balancing the interests of investigation against the niceties of trust and friendship. The problem of over-rapport thus encapsulates the orthodox ideal of the marginal person. The objectives of research access and the daily negotiations of field relations mostly preclude intimacy and close identification.

Sociologists readily adopted the vocabulary of anthropologists, in warning themselves, their colleagues, and their students against "going native." The vocabulary of going native or remaining a marginal native is no longer acceptable to some writers; others (e.g., Delamont 2002) use it deliberately to jolt readers into facing up to the issues. The connotation of "native" does not sit happily with an intelligentsia sensitized to the realities of colonial and postcolonial relations. It smacks too much of anthropology's imperial legacy. We are also less likely to hear the issues posed in such terms because sociologists and anthropologists are, collectively, less committed to maintaining social and intellectual distance. Empirical literature and methodological commentary both contain accounts of much more personalized approaches to research, in which varieties of intimacy are promoted and celebrated.

The personal approach is certainly not a new direction for ethnography (see Reed-Danahay 2001), although personal narratives of fieldwork have, at best, been seen as parallel texts to the more formal ethnographic monograph. At worst these personalized accounts have been viewed as bordering on dangerous self-indulgence. While it has become increasingly acceptable to chronicle the personal journeys of and in fieldwork experiences, the ethnographer's tale and self still remain as adjuncts to the main story or event. Clifford (1983) has even suggested that personal accounts of field-work became less necessary as anthropology established itself as a discipline. Ethnographic research no longer required explicit demonstrations of validity through descriptions of fieldwork experiences. However, the imagery of the fieldworker as a marginal participant—recognizing the personal contexts of fieldwork while simultaneously maintaining a professional distance—has long been propagated in texts on the conduct and epistemology of ethnographic research. Straightforward readings of standard qualitative methodological texts, for example, have usually implied a starting position of ethnographer as relative stranger, progressing toward a measure of familiarity and enlightenment, while simultaneously achieving a professional and personal distance. These readings are usually located within more general articulations of "appropriate" locations of the self and others within the research endeavour.

BIOGRAPHIES AND INTIMATE RELATIONS

Relationships between researcher and researched have long been the subject of debate and scrutiny in qualitative research. Qualitative methods texts, for example, have always, as a matter of course, offered comment and advice on personal field roles and the managing of relationships in the field. Often this advice has focused on issues such as guarding against over-familiarity and the effects of context on the relationships that are formed in the field. The general emphasis has been on the negotiation and crafting of personal and social "research" relationships in order to facilitate the expedient collection of data. Methodological and political critiques of ethnographic research have, in recent years however, called into question this marginal status—on both practical and ethical grounds. Taken-for-granted dichotomies of observer and observed, the stranger and member, innocence and experience, have been challenged and troubled. While there are long established justifications of the methodological and epistemological value of personal estrangement in the field (Geer 1964)—whereby strangeness provides an analytical cutting edge—increasingly attention has been drawn to the difficulties (or indeed impossibilities) of sustaining an engaged, yet distant self. If we follow this through, then the earlier personalized accounts of fieldwork experiences (such as those of Powdermaker and Bowen) walk the wire between personal involvement and over-familiarity, and in doing so represent only partial explorations of the myriad of relations between the self and the field. While they present vivid and emotive accounts of field-work experiences, they also give sanitized versions, recognizing the personal and the emotional in partial rather than holistic ways. That is, (auto)biographical involvement remains tempered by concerns of over-familiarity, over-rapport, and perhaps worst of all, conversion or "going native." Recent articulations of the ethnographic endeavour have sought to reexamine these partial positionings, and the extent to which they are, or ever were, realistic, tenable, or desirable.

Increasingly, attention has been paid to the range of experiences and emotions inherent in prolonged fieldwork, and they ways in which these should be harnessed, recognized, even celebrated. Hence the researcher-self has become a source for reflection, reexamination, and (re)presentation. In more general terms, the personal narrative (of *both* researched and researcher) has developed as a significant preoccupation for many of those who espouse qualitative research strategies (Atkinson and Silverman 1997). There is a widespread assumption that personal narratives offer uniquely privileged data of the social world; data that are grounded in both social contexts and biographical experiences. The personal narratives of the *researcher* have formed part of this movement. The researcher's tale has increasingly been told and celebrated in the research and writing processes. These build upon earlier (auto)biographical accounts of fieldwork, such as those of Bowen and Powdermaker (see also Berreman 1962)—in recognizing the personal dimensions of fieldwork. However, some go further, embracing the centrality of the researcher to both the processes and outcomes of fieldwork. Hence the (auto)biographical *work* of undertaking qualitative research strategies has been revealed.

It has, of course, long been recognized that ethnographic fieldwork has a biographical dimension. Ethnographers are, after all, concerned with observing, (re)constructing and writing about *other* people's lives and experiences, such as Adler's (1985/93) or Bourgeois's (1995) ethnographies of drug dealing, or Lofland's (1973/1985) ethnography of urban interaction orders, or Duneier's (1992) study of African-American men in Chicago. In observing, writing, and representing the social world, ethnographers are primarily in the business of analyzing and reproducing lives (Stanley 1993). In this context the researcher can serve as a biographer of *others*. And we now have more recognition that the ethnographer is simultaneously involved in autobiographical work of his or her own. Moreover these autobiographical positions are not simply apparent and played out as a means to an end (the collection of data). We now have a much better appreciation that experiences in the field cannot help but be personal and emotional. That is not to say that fieldwork experiences will always (or even often) be life enhancing or autobiographically momentous. Nor can they be denied as irrelevant or marginal to the understandings and articulations of the self.

The perceived "dangers" of over-familiarity and over-identification do little to make sense of the practices and process of fieldwork. Presenting the ethnographer as navigating a middle way between engagement and distance is to set up a false dichotomy, masking the lived experiences and realities of fieldwork. Simplified and unqualified versions of strangeness, immersion, and familiarity fail to engage adequately or completely with the positionality of the self in the context of fieldwork. Conversion and/or over immersion have conventionally been perceived as negative, undesirable, analytically weak, as well as (in research and personal terms) deviant and dangerous in the extreme. In many methodological texts we still find warnings and morality tales about the stereotype of "going native." We recognize here that contemporary sensibilities about linguistic practice lead us to question the appropriateness of this term, while at the same time an increasing tendency to conduct fieldwork "at home" renders the term meaningless. Nevertheless there continues to be a methodological assumption that the researcher should resist total absorption or immersion.

We are not supposed to undergo transformations in the course of fieldwork. And while we should appreciate and look forward to a growing sense of familiarity and knowing, a distance is still to be observed. Yet the "choices" between involvement and immersion or over-engagement and distance are often too starkly drawn to be realistic or desirable. The issue is not necessarily one of conversion or over-immersion, but rather recognition that ethnographic work is the outcome of complex negotiations and relations, where the self has a central, rather than peripheral, role. The balance between engagement and distance, often stressed in pragmatic terms, is not an easily accomplished state, especially during prolonged fieldwork. As Kondo—herself a Japanese-American—has written in her account of fieldwork in Japan (Kondo 1990), the process of immersion and the formation of field relations involved a process of identity fragmentation. Her own multiple field roles and "fragmentation of self" were the result of complex collaborations between her self (or selves) and her hosts.

This chapter is not the place for detailed and lengthy descriptions of the myriad ways in which the self is intimately embedded in the ethnographic endeavor. At its simplest, we recognize the reliance on the researcher–self in the collection and representation of ethnographic data about social worlds, and that this reliance assumes and dictates the formation of personal attachments and relationships. Roles are created, managed, and maintained over the course of prolonged fieldwork. Fieldwork is not a passive activity. We actively engage in identity (re)construction, and this is not simply an instrumental process. The actual lived experience of conducting fieldwork confronts, disrupts, and troubles the self. This argument takes us beyond simple understandings of appropriate or fruitful field roles to a much more sophisticated and realistic appreciation of the intimate relations of the field. Thus fieldwork can reconstruct, restore, or rewrite identity and sense of self; fragment or challenge the self; and provide new and different ways of understanding the self. Prolonged fieldwork has emotional connectedness. It can be lonely or rewarding, but certainly provides space and place for self-reflection.

We know that there are many long-lasting relationships that have been struck during fieldwork, and that these can be enduring in both real and symbolic ways. Some field relationships are inevitably short or medium term, lasting no longer than the period of fieldwork itself. This does not necessarily absolve them from being mutual and meaningful, nor prevent their ending from signifying a loss. Indeed the ending of fieldwork is a distinctive phase of the ethnographic endeavor. It acknowledges a temporal and physical boundary between the field and the self, while at the same time recognizing the potential to trouble that same boundary. Leaving the field means leaving people and places that have become familiar to us, and often represents a transition in our own life and career. The ending of fieldwork is thus a signifier of lives changing. Accounts of the difficulties (or relief) of leaving the field symbolizes that we were physically and emotionally *there* (see for example, Cannon 1992; Blackwood 1995; Fowler 1994). Some fieldwork relationships last well beyond the research proper. Long-term friendships are often made during prolonged research, and these will draw on the usual conventions of trust, rapport, mutual respect, commitment, and emotional attachment. Equally some individual field relations can be testing and difficult to endure, yet no less difficult to walk away from in the context of the research. Indeed, genuineness and reciprocity are vexed questions for the ethnographer. Imbalances in the degree of trust or commitment or personal involvement can lead to potentially exploitative or difficult relations, for either or both parties (not so different from conventional friendships). Yet fieldwork relies on a high quality of personal relationship. This reliance can bring to the ethnographer great joy and fulfilment, but also exposes us to the risk of vulnerability, exploitation, hurt, and rejection. There are accounts of enduring and rewarding personal relationships being forged during (and some times beyond) fieldwork. Key informants can become best friends (see for example El-Or 1997; Crick 1992; Hendry 1992; Wolf 1992). These can be rewarding, but also bring with them difficulties.

Hendry, for example notes the difficulties of combining fieldwork and friendship, and the ways in which the coinciding of the two can be challenging (though epistemologically productive). Yet the difficulties she describes—of knowing when to "speak" are not so different from the general dilemmas of friendship:

> In general, during fieldwork, it might be better to avoid expressing negative opinions about matters close to the hearts of informants. In other words, one can really only pretend to be a friend. Nevertheless . . . I sometimes grew tired of the role I was playing, and made the mistake of revealing this to my host as friend, rather than informant . . . however, my mistake actually led to a deeper understanding of the people I was investigating. (Hendry 1992: 172)

There are also accounts of pseudo-familial relationships formed during fieldwork. Indeed fictitious kin are a relatively common feature, certainly of anthropological fieldwork. These relationships encompass friendship and familial ties. Briggs (1986) and Kondo (1990), for example, have described the process of becoming an honorary daughter during fieldwork. Macintyre (1993) entered into adoptive motherhood, which lasted long after fieldwork had formally ended, and Fowler (1994) describes her key informants as Grandma and Grandpa. Prolonged fieldwork can also lead to lovers (Blackwood 1995; Dubisch 1995), sexual liaisons (Bolton 1995), and marriage (Gearing 1995). These represent instances of the weaving of intimacy into fieldwork endeavors and roles. These friendships and other relationships denote the inherent contradictions and ambiguities of fieldwork. They are not quirky exceptions or failed research projects. Rather they expose ethnography for what it is—relational, emotional, and personal. Field relations are rewarding and problematic, not least because they do trouble the accepted or "conventional" boundary between fieldwork and self. These relationships should absolutely not be viewed as failed fieldwork endeavors. Rather they provide concrete examples of more general processes at work, revealing the self as intimately part of, rather than adjunct to, fieldwork. Fieldwork is *also* (auto)biographical or "life work." They are not even joined at the hip—they share the same spaces. This is vividly illustrated in Moreno's (1995) account of sexual intimidation and rape that occurred during her fieldwork. This could not be brushed under the ethnographic carpet, nor used to invalidate the fieldwork:

> In the field the false division of time and space between the "professional and the private" that underpins the supposedly gender-neutral identity

of the anthropologist collapse[s] completely. In the field it is not possible
to maintain the fiction of a genderless self. In the field, one is marked.
(Moreno 1995: 246–47)

Of course the puritanical might argue that close friendships and sexual relations during fieldwork are undesirable, wrong, and unethical. They
are certainly and undeniably part of a more general ethical problem of
power and exploitation in research. Although as Dubisch (1995: 31) has argued, a sexual relationship may not "be any more intimate, committing, or
exploitative than our normal relations with the 'natives' (and indeed may be
less so in some contexts)." We would certainly not wish to argue for the
explicit utilization of fieldwork settings for romantic moments or intimate
encounters. However the very fact that friendship, familiar ties, sexual relations, and romantic interludes occur is indicative of the very essence of
ethnographic fieldwork as a personal and emotional process and as a series
of relationships. Gearing argues for an emotionally aware ethnography. This
recognizes the personal commitment and processes of identity construction
present in fieldwork.

> I do not think that effective ethnographic research can be done without
> emotional engagement, and the pursuit of a methodology that ignores
> what we learn from our emotions is undermining the validity of the re-
> sulting information . . . in fieldwork as in all of life, sensation, emotion,
> and intellect operate simultaneously to structure and interpret our expe-
> rience of the world. Our emotional reactions and those to which we in-
> teract, guide our analysis of life "at home" as well as "in the field." (Gear-
> ing 1995: 209)

It would be easy to deduce from our discussion thus far that rather than
guarding against over-rapport and conversion, full immersion and identification are always possible and desirable, and furthermore fieldwork is only meaningful when we are completely engaged (and even challenged). This is not
what we are arguing at all. Rather it is necessary and desirable to recognize that
we are part of what we study, and are shaped and affected by our fieldwork experiences. To deny the self an active and situated place in the field is only fool-
ing ourselves. However, we are not suggesting here that the self should become
the sole focus of fieldwork. Indeed, to do so would render many ethnographic
archives meaningless. We should not lose sight of the ethnographic imperative
that we are seeking to understand and make sense of complex social worlds, of
which we are only part (but a part nevertheless). It is methodologically naïve
to presume that we fundamentally change the lives of our informants or the

settings we encounter. But we should not deny our place within their social world, and their place within ours. How we choose to represent these shared spaces is the subject of the next section.

REVEALING THE ETHNOGRAPHER

There has been a marked shift in the ways in which ethnographers reflect upon their fieldwork experiences. In particular, attention has increasingly been paid to the intertextuality of (auto)biography and ethnography. As we have already noted in this chapter there have been recurrent attempts to integrate ethnographic data and personal experiences. These are exemplified in the texts by Powdermaker and Bowen, although personal discussions of the conduct of fieldwork goes even further back, to anthropologists like Malinowski (1922), Mead (1928), and Evans-Pritchard (1940). However while these "revealings" demonstrated the personal undertaking and conduct of prolonged fieldwork, they did so within tightly defined understandings of over-familiarity and the dangers of immersion. Of course it has always been the case that ethnography has provided opportunities for self-reflection. Fieldnotes and research journals have long been used to record the feelings, emotions, and personal identity work that can come with prolonged research engagement (see Sanjek 1990).

In recent articulations of the presents and futures of qualitative inquiry, it is easy to assume that the self in the text is a relatively recent phenomenon. And to some extent this assumption has merit. Denzin and Lincoln's periodization of qualitative research substantiates this view. In classifying the development of qualitative inquiry in terms of key "moments," the self is most clearly revealed from the mid-1980s—Denzin and Lincoln's fourth moment—and the crises of legitimation and representation. Here the received canons of truth and method were challenged, not least through the critical examination of textual practices. This moment was signalled by the publication of *Writing Culture* (Clifford and Marcus 1986), and placed in hazard both the textual products of qualitative work, and the authority of the researcher. One of the main consequences of the fourth moment was what has been variously termed the linguistic turn, or the interpretative turn, or the rhetorical turn, and signalled an enhanced awareness of ethnographic writing (Atkinson 1990). Hence the fourth moment encouraged a revisiting of qualitative accounts and analyses, in order to grapple with issues of legitimacy, authority, and the conventionality of texts. This heralded the movement of qualitative research into new directions and representational territories. This moment was consolidated into a fifth moment—"the postmodern period of experimental ethnographic writing" (Denzin and Lincoln 2000: 17). This characterizes contemporary ethnography through diversity and a continuing series of tensions, as a mechanism for making sense of crises of legitimization, representation, and praxis, and responding to postmodernism and the interpretative turn. In their earlier-developed account of this moment, Lincoln and Denzin (1994: 576) observed that

> Qualitative research embraces two tensions at the same time. On the one hand, it is drawn to a broad, interpretative, postmodern, feminist, and critical sensibility. On the other hand, it can also be drawn to a more narrowly defined positivist, postpositivist, humanistic and naturalistic conception of human experience and its analysis.

Denzin and Lincoln identified a sixth "messy" moment (see Denzin 1997), capturing the discourses of the late 1990s. This noted the emergence of "a cacophony of voices speaking with various agendas" (Lincoln and Denzin 1994: 409) and was characterized by reflexive, experimental texts, multiple stories, styles, and futures (Atkinson, Coffey, and Delamont 1999). Subsequently, a "seventh moment" was constructed (Lincoln and Denzin 2000). Our own critique of the idea of moments and of the ways in which Lincoln and Denzin have written their history of the field has been elaborated on elsewhere (Atkinson, Coffey, and Delamont 1999; Delamont, Coffey, and Atkinson 2000; Atkinson, Coffey, and Delamont 2001).

As part of the development of ethnographic/qualitative texts, authorship, authenticity, and voice have all been repositioned. Part of this process has been the adoption of innovative textual mechanisms for writing the self into the text. But it is worth acknowledging that there are a range of examples of those engaged in ethnographic or qualitative research reflecting upon and rewriting the self into research texts and representations. Moreover, these are historically situated, and are certainly not all new, or necessarily innovative. They have included fieldnotes and research diaries as well as personal narratives of the research process. Personal accounts of fieldwork have been published as confessional tales (cf. Van Maanen 1988) or fables of rapport (Clifford 1983), and have been used as mechanisms for establishing authenticity and authority. More recent ethnographies have moved beyond these parallel projects of ethnography proper and confessional account, to more holistic or joined up tales of the self—texts that treat the self as a unit of analysis and/or subject of representation. All of these recognize, though to differing degrees, the authorship of research texts as well as the positionality of the self within both the research and representational processes.

Fieldnotes and journals are an obvious and longstanding form of embracing the self in the products of qualitative research, though they are often overlooked as such. These are the building blocks of qualitative research, a place for the accumulation of data and reflections (Emerson, Fretz, and Strauss 1995; Jackson 1990; Sanjek 1990). Field journals, personified in the diaries of the social anthropologist Malinowski (Malinowski 1967), serve as classic examples of these autobiographical, textual products. Field journals and diaries provide textual (though essentially private) space for the recording of research experiences, feelings, and emotions. Often these texts are kept separate from field data, that is notes on the research setting, people, places, and events. While personal, autobiographical narratives may form part of fieldnote writing, this does not necessarily imply any kind of public reflection or reclaiming of the self, although it does acknowledge that ethnographic accounts are mediated by autobiographical experiences. Fieldnotes are, though, relatively private texts and are rarely shared in their raw (emotional) form. Quoted fieldnote extracts are usually tidied up or edited, and relatively few researchers choose to share their personal "sacred" diaries of the field (Lederman 1990). Yet, while there is now a greater tolerance or expectation of a revealing of the self in the ethnographic text, the personal has never been subordinate in the private world of fieldnotes. It is the textual *visibility* of the self that has undergone transformation.

It has become an accepted feature of qualitative research, certainly over the last twenty-five years or so, to produce personal narratives of the qualitative research process—as fables of rapport or confessional tales. However, it is still relatively common practice to separate these personal accounts from the data and analysis proper. Indeed the semi-autobiographical accounts of fieldwork exemplified by Powdermaker and Bowen, with their mixing of experiences, emotions, and data were never adopted as a usual genre for the writing of the personal within the ethnographic. Confessional tales of the field and personal "self" stories are still more usually written as parallel but separate accounts to the research monograph proper (see for example deMarrais 1998; De Soto and Dudwick 2000). Indeed, conventions of writing about the self in the research process continue to reinforce the ethnographer as split personality—the authorial monograph writer and the personal, experiential, emotional self. So while it is increasingly acceptable and even desirable to (re)construct and (re)write the self into the fieldwork, there remains a level of ambivalence about how far such practices and texts should be part of, or divert us from, "telling the story of the field." Collections of confessional tales, such as Hobbs and May (1992) and Lareau and

Shultz (1996), recapitulate some of the general themes of this genre—revealing the personal sides of fieldwork and dealing with problems such as access, immersion, departure, field roles, and so on. Further exemplification is provided by senior anthropologists in *Others Knowing Others* (Fowler and Hardesty 1994), where personal portraits of the discipline are given, through accounts of long-term fieldwork and reformulations of the self through time and place.

The conceptualization of ethnographer as voyager or traveller is a common theme of confessional tales or personal fieldwork stories (Atkinson 1990 and 1996). The researcher here is (re)presented as a naïve explorer or social intruder who learns to live on the margins, engaging in a quest of discovery, and maybe learning something about him- or herself along the way. The confessional allows for self-revelation and indiscretion, but within a recognizable and acceptable format. Whyte's semi-autobiographical account of the evolution of fieldwork for *Street Corner Society* (Whyte 1981) is a classic example of this kind. He admits to a lack of confidence, to incompetence and ignorance. He presents a narrative of learning by trial-and-error, getting by, learning by mistakes, and surviving. He presents himself as human, fallible, and with no exceptional powers. As Lareau and Shultz (1996: 2–3) suggest, confessional tales:

> provide clarity of how methodological goals such as building rapport are translated into action. They provide insight into the kinds of factors other researchers considered when they stumbled into difficulty and the strategies—for example, of reflection and data analysis—that researchers used to extract themselves from their temporary woes. More to the point, they highlight the uncertainty and confusion that inevitably accompany field research.

Despite their increasing acceptance as part of the research endeavor (or its textual representation) these personal tales of qualitative inquiry are still cautious in the ways in which they approach the subject of self. Usually located alongside the ethnographic monograph, these accounts may actually serve to isolate, rather than integrate, the self into the field. They attempt to establish a separateness and distance that is not really there. The confessional genre is one of description rather than analysis, presenting a version of the self as mediating, consequential, or problematic—and hence revealing only a semi-detached or partial self.

Some authors have chosen to take the relationship between research, the text, and the self to different dimensions, locating the self more centrally in the contexts and products of qualitative inquiry. These have taken a number of forms. For example research monographs such as *Crafting Selves* (Kondo 1990) and *Blacked Out* (Fordham 1996) present multilayered texts that challenge the dichotomy between researcher and researched, author and "other". These ethnographers-as-authors frame their accounts with personal reflexive views of the self. Their ethnographic data are situated within their personal experiences and sense making. They themselves form part of the representational processes in which they are engaging, and are part of the story they are telling. Thus the "story" of (in these instances) the Japanese workplace and the African American School are interwoven with personal journeys and narrations.

In other instances, the autobiographical has been used more substantively as a basis for data collection, analysis, and understanding. Early versions of this approach utilized personal life experiences as the basis for modest fieldwork, (re)presented in conventional ways. For example, Delamont (1987) and Beynon (1987) chose to write ethnographic accounts about periods as hospital inpatients, although both were keen to play down the scholarly contributions of their pieces. The paper by Delamont, researched while she was in the hospital having an elective hysterectomy at age thirty-two, is a structuralist analysis of the ways in which "good" women separated themselves from "dirty" women with whom they were forced to share a hospital ward and—worse—baths, showers, and lavatories. Beynon explored how even an admission for an investigative procedure can produce a Goffmanesque feeling of powerlessness, de-individualization, and loss of autonomy. Beynon's "Zombies in Dressing Gowns" and Delamont's "Clean Baths and Dirty Women" are not confessional at all compared with Sparkes's piece quoted below. Neither used them as reflexive writings on the relationships between the self, the field, and the text. Indeed the self is distanced and even apologized for. Both used the collection of fieldnotes as mechanisms for getting through and understanding medical events, and did not undertake to claim more than that. To some extent the distinction is implicitly drawn here between therapy (using fieldnotes as a means of getting through and understanding periods of illness) and ethnography (Ellis and Bochner 2000). Contemporary ethnographic writing on illness and the body blurs normalized boundaries between ethnography and autobiography. For example, Sparkes's ethnographic body narrative is personal and highly reflexive. Using extended diary entries and personal conversations, Sparkes reconstructs his failing body-self over his (auto)biographical career. His body-self is centrally positioned in his text and analysis. This gives a performative quality to the piece, and positions it in terms of autobiographical writing and reflection. The following extract is illustrative of this.

Stopping for a rest I turn toward Kitty, my wife, who is six months pregnant. "Déjà vu" I say to her, "It's happening again." The tears well up in
her eyes and we hold each other close in the corridor. I kiss her on the
cheeks. I kiss her eyes. As the roundness of her stomach presses against
me a wave of guilt washes over me. Kitty is pregnant, so tired, caring for
Jessica our daughter (three years old at the time) and now having to
worry and cope with the stress of me and my body failure. My useless-
ness makes me angry with my body. At the moment I *hate* it intensely.
(Sparkes 1996: 468; emphasis in original)

Sparkes's text presents a rather different and shifting relationship between
ethnography and the self. The personal and the ethnographic are interwoven
and overlapping; distinctions are not only blurred, they all but disappear. This
can be located within a new wave of autobiographical–ethnographic writing
that has taken the self as the focus of inquiry. Much of this writing has focused
on issues of illness and the body. For example, Paget (1990 and 1993) provided
a moving ethnographic account of living (and dying) with cancer; Kolker
(1996) has reflected upon her personal and ethnographic experiences of breast
cancer, and Tillman-Healy has written evocative text on her ongoing relationship with the eating disorder, bulimia.

In the spring of 1986, at the age of fifteen, I invited bulimia to come to
live with me. She never moved out. Sometimes I tuck her deep in my
closet behind forgotten dresses and old shoes. Then one day, I'll come
across her—as if by accident—and experience genuine surprise that she
remains with me. Other times, for a few days or perhaps a week or
month, she'll emerge from that closet to sleep at my side, closer than a
sister or lover would. This is our story. (Tillman-Healy 1996: 76)

These ethnographic texts are not, then, tales of the naïve incompetent,
overcoming adversity and difficulty in the quest for data. They are not simply providing personalized accounts of fieldwork, or the research process.
Rather, the self and the field become one—ethnography and autobiography
are symbiotic. In these instances writing and representing reveals, consolidates, and disrupts the self (or selves).

Representation has become both contested and innovative in contemporary qualitative research practice. Qualitative writing has always
reflected variety—of disciplinary styles, genres, textual conventions,
and subject matter. The work of Zora Neale Hurston in the period
1935–1950 is an early, and important, example (see Hernandez 1995).
Yet in recent years, representation and authorship has been especially

dynamic. This has in part been due to temporal and critical movements such as postmodernism and (post)feminism, but also to the attendant crises of legitimation and representation of qualitative texts (as we outlined above). The authoritative status of the conventional monograph has been questioned and reassessed. The diversification of representation styles has been influenced by the calls to alternative genres and (non)textual styles, and by the rise in ethnographic autobiography.

Despite this recognition that the production of qualitative or ethnographic texts has never been especially static or monolithic, it has only been since the mid-1980s (Denzin and Lincoln's fourth moment) that the production and reading of these texts have been subjected to detailed and critical scrutiny. These critical (re)readings have formed part of more general debates about the (textual) representation of culture and reality (Atkinson 1990 and 1996). Feminist qualitative research praxis, for example, has brought to the fore relationships between the personal, the biographical, and the social (see Clough 1992; Stanley 1992; Stanley and Wise 1993; Olesen 2000). Indeed, as Jennaway (1990) argued, many of the developments embedded in a postmodern ethnography have a basis in feminist ethnographic discourse. Cognizant within these shifts and new directions has been both recognition and critical appraisal of the relationships between fieldwork, representation, intimacy, and the self.

AUTOETHNOGRAPHY AND THE RECLAIMING OF SELF

Alternative forms of ethnographic representation have been particularly well utilized as mechanisms for representing deeply personal (or sensitive) events, emotive voices and stories, and for making the author a visible presence in the text. Moreover, and especially relevant in the context of this chapter, they have been used as representation devices for (re)writing the self (see Ellis and Flaherty 1992). As has already been noted, authors have given ethnographic purchase to their personal experiences of illness and the body (Kolker 1996; Paget 1993; Sparkes 1996; Tillman-Healy 1996). They have also been used to explore deeply personal experiences and relationships (Ellis 1995; Ellis and Bochner 1992; Fox 1996; Quinney 1996; Ronai 1996), as well as the autobiographical processes of writing and representing (Bochner and Ellis 1996; Ely, Vinz, Downing, and Anzul 1997; Richardson and Lockeridge 1991). All of these personal or autobiographical narratives can be located within a broader (new) genre of autoethnography. This term encapsulates many variants on a theme—such as autobiographical ethnography, ethnobiography, and personal ethnography (see Reed-Danahay 1997) and is described by Ellis and Bochner (2000: 739) thus

> Autoethnography is an autobiographical genre of writing and research that displays multiple layers of consciousness, connecting the personal to the cultural. Back and forth autobiographers gaze, first through an ethnographic wide-angle lens, focusing outward on social and cultural aspects of their personal experience; then, they look inward, exposing a vulnerable self that is moved by and may move through, refract, and resist cultural interpretations.

These autoethnographic texts are first-person accounts, drawing on personal experiences of the author. They are autobiographical ethnographic "essays" that can take different representational forms—for example dialogues, scripts, stories, poems, diaries and journals, photographic essays, biographical reflections, and multilayered writing (see chapter 7 of this book). Autoethnography intimately and categorically relates the research process to both the social world and the self. It draws on personal stories and narratives and consolidates the intertextuality between ethnography and autobiography. In their chapter for the second edition of the *Handbook of Qualitative Research* (Denzin and Lincoln 2000), Ellis and Bochner take their readers on a number of journeys in order to trace the history of, explain, and give meaning to autoethnography. Through conversations, social science prose, and accounts of student supervision and department colloquia, Ellis and Bochner defend and expand autoethnographic praxis and writing. They argue for personally meaningful ethnography and the working of the spaces between social science prose and other genres. Thus autobiographical ethnography takes the researcher as subject and troubles conventional genres for (re)presenting culture, thus denying the dichotomies between the personal and the intellectual (Reed-Danahay 2001). This resonates with Gearing's claim to an emotionally aware ethnography.

If weaving the self into the ethnography is a journey (with different routes or texts), then autoethnography represents one possible destination. We do not have to travel there in order to acknowledge that the personal self, the ethnographic self, and the author self are interwoven in complex ways. The myth of the silent author has long been exposed in ethnographic writings. The position adopted by Charmaz and Mitchell (1997: 194) occupies a middle ground here. They argue that just as there is merit in humility and deference to the views of "others," and to reasoned, systematic discourse, so too is there merit in "a visible authorship." While the words of ethnographers are neither magical nor authoritative, neither is the author's voice a biased irrelevancy. They advocate vocal texts where the author is an active and visible participant. This highlights the understanding of voice articulated by Hertz (1997). That is the dilemma of presenting the author self while simultaneously writing and representing the voices and selves of others.

As one moves along the road toward autoethnography, the issue of representing the "other" is both revealed and complicated—as subject and author entwine or merge (Richardson 2000). Some of the criticisms that have been levelled at ethnography and other forms of qualitative research are crystallized in considerations of autobiographical ethnographic practice. For example, the reliance on memory, issues of reliability and validity, and generalization. Some (see Ellis, Kiesinger, and Tillman-Healy 1997) would deny a divide between ethnography and memory, arguing that ethnography and memoir are one—that is experiencing, remembering, and sharing lives. Memories are personal and biographical. They are organized through culturally shared, socially situated, and temporal resources. Memories draw on cultural meanings and language that are biographical and collective. As we are only too aware, reliability and validity are vexed questions in qualitative research generally (see Hammersley 1991), although, as Ellis and Bochner (2000) stress, there are differing and contested definitions of both concepts. There is no reason why autoethnography cannot seek verisimilitude, and reliability checks attempted. Likewise the generalizabilty claims of ethnography are well rehearsed (see Coffey and Atkinson 1996), and can hold fast for autoethnography—observing that all lives are particular, local, temporal, and culturally and historically situated.

A more particular criticism levelled at autobiographical ethnography writing is the potential for romanticizing the self (Atkinson 1997b; Atkinson and Silverman 1997) and engaging in gross self-indulgence. Here the argument is one of balance; between on the one hand the visible authorship of the text, and, on the other hand, texts that engage only in personal narratives and experiences of the author. Mykhalovskiy (1997) has argued that autobiographical sociology *per se* is not necessarily narcissistic or self-indulgent, and that such a charge can actually be perceived as ironic. For it inevitably gives support for "a solitary, authorial voice who writes a text disembodied from the individuals involved in its production" (Mykhalovskiy 1997: 246). Mykhalovskiy argues that personal experience and autobiographical text can be sources of insightful analysis, reacting against the (perceived and real) insularity of academic writing. However, there are those who remain highly skeptical of autobiographical ethnography, dismissing its claims to be social science, and using its potential therapeutic consequences to undermine it. Ellis and Bochner (2000) address these issues, as supporters of the genre(s), and call for "evocative" social science that recognizes the centrality of personal stories. Bochner pleads for:

> A text that functions as an agent of self-discovery or self-creation, for the author as well as for those who read and engage the text, is only threatening under a narrow definition of social inquiry, one that eschews a social science with a moral center and a heart. Why should caring and empathy be secondary to controlling and knowing? Why must academics be conditioned to believe that a text is important only to the extent it moves beyond the merely personal? (Bochner writing in Ellis and Bochner 2000: 746)

Autobiographical approaches to ethnography do not deny that past generations of researchers have experienced fieldwork in emotional, subjective, and personal ways. However recent articulations provide a more recognizable and acceptable environment in which to confront and represent the (auto)biographical. The literary or interpretive turn has made it easier to utilize (auto)biographical and personal narrative genres. In addition, the significant contributions of postmodernism and feminism have encouraged views of the social world in terms of multiple voices and perspectives. Denzin and Lincoln's sixth moment, for example, points to experimental representational styles that disrupt and re-center the self. And in Lincoln and Denzin's (2000) vision of the future of qualitative research—the seventh moment—these themes are recurrent and consolidated. The seventh moment "connects the past with the present and the future" and qualitative inquiry is imagined in the twenty-first century as "simultaneously minimal, existential, *autoethnographic*, vulnerable, performative and critical" (Lincoln and Denzin 2000: 1048, emphasis added). Self/selves, autobiographical ethnography, representation, and performance are all part of their envisaged future of qualitative work. There is an emphasis on "making ourselves visible in our texts" (1053); and on not one future but many, not

> one "moment," but rather many; not one "voice," but polyvocality; not one story, but many tales, dramas, pieces of fiction, fables, memories, histories, autobiographies, poems, and other texts to inform our sense of lifeways, to extend our understandings of the "other," to provide us with the material for "cultural critique" (Lincoln and Denzin 2000: 1060).

Qualitative research in the new century, then, is drawing upon earlier moments, crises, and critiques in order to take stock and move forward. Emergent in this is the affirmation of the personal and ethnographic self as one, and the continuing development of strategies to return the ethnographer to the field and the text.

CONCLUSIONS

In this chapter, we have considered the relationship between the researcher and the researched. This relationship has recurrently been a vexed question for qualitative researchers—faced with concerns about over-familiarity and the realities of intimate relations in the field. More recent engagements with the place of autobiography in ethnography have exacerbated these concerns, though not necessarily providing clearer answers. It is possible to approach this "revealing" of the self in different ways, and to argue that autoethnographic praxis heralds contrastive futures for ethnography. We return to matters of representation, particularly in chapter 7. In the meantime, we offer three of these alternative visions.

Consolidation	*New Ethnography*	*Beyond Ethnography?*
It is not necessary to render the self as the explicit focus of qualitative inquiry in order to recognize the (auto)biographical work that is routinely accomplished. Detailed or prolonged fieldwork inevitably involves the researcher in various kinds of autobiographical practice and rightly so. The self is shaped by relationships and experiences that are not suspended for the duration of a research project. The personal self cannot, nor should not, be separated from the practical, intellectual, and social processes of qualitative research. This is not advocating that	Autoethnography widens/blurs/disrupts the boundaries of qualitative research. It interweaves the personal and the social, moving back and forth between the two. It links pasts, presents, and futures of qualitative inquiry. It redefines old spaces and opens up new spaces. It reworks dichotomies between subjectivity and objectivity, autobiography and culture, the social and the self. It provides a mechanism for extending ethnography beyond the academy and encourages "writers to make ethnography readable, evocative, engaging and personally meaningful" (Ellis and Bochner 2000:	What we are witnessing may be a new form of ethnographic practice, or it may not be ethnography at all. Autoethnography could be accused of producing self-indulgent writings, published under the guise of social research. There is a danger here of providing ample ammunition for critics of qualitative inquiry. It is uncertain whether there are any long-term benefits for the development of ethnographic research and text, beyond the centralizing of the self as omnipresent. In responding to calls for polyvocality and the recognition of multiple voices, there

a/the primary aim of qualitative research is a better or more complex understanding of self. Nor is this a case for purely self-referential or autobiographical fieldwork. But in recognizing the "self-work" that is part of both research and representational processes, there is greater scope for understanding and making sense of social settings and cultural processes. This does not imply an uncritical celebration of the self. But it does imply recognition that the self is part of the field and part of the text. It promotes the intertextuality of biography and ethnography. It argues for vocal texts and a diversity of representational forms, visible authorship, and a reflexive approach.

761). Autoethnography draws on the therapeutic and analytical value of personal narratives and self-stories, and makes visible that which is often dismissed or rendered invisible in qualitative inquiry. The practice of autoethnography is still relatively marginal to the mainstream of qualitative research—and only time will tell what place it holds in ethnographic futures. But we ignore what it has to teach us at our peril.

is a danger of creating monovocal and self-indulgent texts. Autobiographical ethnography (Reed-Danahay 1997) has much to commend it, not least in rendering the self a visible and vocal presence. However it is debatable as to whether utilizing ethnographical strategies to write autobiography really counts as ethnography at all. This may be especially the case where the only "field" researched and represented is the self. Utilizing ethnographic devices to work through life events can have therapeutic and analytical value, but should not detract from the work of qualitative inquiry in observing and understanding the social world.

3

WHOSE SIDE ARE WE ON?

INHERENT TENSIONS

The classic paper "Whose Side Are We On?" by Howard Becker was published in *Social Problems* in 1967, and reprinted in his collected papers, *Sociological Work* (Becker 1970). (Our page references are to this latter source.) The paper was his presidential address in 1966 to the Society for the Study of Social Problems. We have chosen to begin this chapter with Becker's paper precisely because it was such an important contribution to the growing methodological literature of the day. It has been widely cited in the years since it was first published. (See for example Galliher 1995; Hammersley 2000; Murphy and Dingwall 2001.) Here we focus upon three specific issues that arise from revisiting Becker's argument. These are issues of methods and methodology, queries about who is and is not included in the term "we," and a changing feature of the research landscape around which empirical topics are and are not "political." We make Becker's formulations problematic, but in so doing we are paying tribute to the thirty-five-year-old paper. It raises issues that remain pertinent for contemporary social research. Possible changes in the field since Becker's original formulation of the problem help illuminate more general features of methodological development and debate. We should make clear at the outset that we have not embroiled ourselves here in debates with Hammersley (2000) or Murphy and Dingwall (2001) or indeed other writers who have commented on Becker's original paper. Rather, we have concentrated on our own reactions to the 1967 paper as we read and reread it from a contemporary perspective.

Much of the argument in this chapter is about the ethics and politics of doing research on the powerless, the inarticulate, the unvoiced, the muted, the silenced, the stigmatized. There is a smaller, but important, parallel literature on the ethics and politics of studying "up": doing research on people who are richer, more powerful, higher caste, higher class, or more aristocratic than the ethnographer can ever hope to be. Laura Nader (1972) is the classic formulation of this debate for anthropologists, in a paper sparked off by a crisis about the use of anthropology by the Central Intelligence Agency in the Johnson years. There are some landmark studies of elites, such as Gary McDonogh's (1986) study of the old rich families of Barcelona. In educational research there have been some discussions of data gathering from elites (Walford 1994).

Becker started from the position that it is impossible to do research that is "uncontaminated by personal and political sympathies" (1967: 123), and that it is inevitable that all researchers will take sides. Therefore "whose side are we on?" is a crucial question. Becker illustrated his argument with examples from the study of deviance, drawing on his own studies of drug users such as the fieldwork for Hughes (1961) and Becker (1963). Deviance research is contrasted in the paper with ethnographies of health and education, topics on which Becker had also conducted fieldwork. (See Becker et al. 1961: 1968.) Becker addressed the accusations made against sociologists, especially qualitative researchers, that their research is partial, biased, and distorted. Becker chose deviance because sociologists of deviance were frequently told they were "too sympathetic" to the deviants, and that this had in turn distorted and biased research in that field. Becker (1967: 124–25) summarized the charge thus:

1. We fall into deep sympathy with the people we are studying;
2. we believe they are more sinned against than sinning;
3. we do not give a balanced picture;
4. we neglect to ask those questions that would show that the deviant has done something pretty rotten;
5. we produce a whitewash of the deviant; and
6. we produce a condemnation of respectable citizens.

Becker examined the precise circumstances in which such charges are levelled at sociologists and concluded that the accusation of bias is levelled at investigations which give credence to "the perspective of the subordinate group in some hierarchical relationship" (125). In deviance research, the subordinate groups are criminals, prisoners, and "other deviants"; the respectable are police, prison officers, judges, lawyers, and the "law abiding" citizen, especially in the middle classes.

Becker made comparisons between deviance research and educational studies, pointing out that "professors and administrators, principals and teachers, are the superordinates, while students and pupils are the subordinates" (125). In all hierarchies, Becker argued that "credibility and the right to be heard are differentially distributed through the ranks of the system" (127). Researchers who refuse to abide by that "hierarchy of credibility" are actually expressing "disrespect for the entire established order" (127). Thus accusations of bias arise when the researcher has not accepted the established hierarchy of credibility. Given that "we must always look at the matter from someone's point of view" (131), and "we can never avoid taking sides" (132), Becker argued that the real question is whether our work is so distorted that it is rendered useless. The central point of his paper is that good researchers have to try to undertake empirical research that is not rendered useless by their biases. We must ensure that "our unavoidable sympathies do not render our work invalid" (132).

To operationalize this undertaking, Becker (1967: 132–34) outlined a number of strategies for valid research.

1. Do not misuse the techniques of our discipline.
2. Use our theories impartially.
3. Avoid sentimentality.
4. Inspect our methods and theories to ensure they could disprove our beliefs.
5. Make clear the limits of what we have studied (i.e., the vantage point adopted).

Throughout his paper Becker distinguished between research settings that were explicitly political, and those which were commonly held to be apolitical, such as schools, hospitals, and prisons. Accusations of bias were less frequently made, Becker claimed, when explicitly political settings were studied, because the disputed claims of the participants are overt, and the different sides (such as Republicans and Democrats) have spokespeople in the setting. Becker's argument became a classic, and, like many other taken-for-granted references, may be cited more often than it is read. Hammersley (2001: 107) identified over 100 citations to the paper in the *Social Science Citation Index* between the years 1980–2000.

Becker's position was valuable in articulating, in a clear and accessible way, a number of concerns and commitments characteristic of methodological and other writing at a time when qualitative methods were being rendered into canonical accounts. His was among a series of authoritative statements emanating from the Second Chicago School (Fine 1995), and others, that were being incorporated into an emerging orthodoxy concerning field research based on participant observation and interviewing. Those views were anthologised and found currency through secondary sources, graduate-level courses in research methods, and widespread citation.

The argument articulated by Becker had its critics at the time of publication, and it was never unquestionably taken for granted in the way that some other publications of the time became part of a widespread orthodoxy. Among the most powerful of the contemporaneous critiques was that of Gouldner (1973). Gouldner was not arguing from the standpoint of value-free social science. Rather, he argued that Becker's formulation omitted a commitment to *values* in favor of a perspectival commitment. Troyna and Carrington (1989: 207–08) summarize Gouldner's argument—that sociologists must strive for objectivity and give their ultimate commitment to fundamental values—"this demands that the researcher's preeminent commitment should not be to black or white youth, teachers or administrators, but to the fundamental principles of social justice, equality, and participatory democracy."

The tension between partisan or perspectival loyalty and universal values remains a relevant one. Moreover, in the current climate, the epistemological and ethical problems have been recognized as more tangled, more complex, and more pervasive. In this chapter we explore four ways in which the debates have developed, expanded, and changed since 1967. We begin by addressing issues of method and methodology. Second we focus on the notion of "sides." This leads us to an analysis of the changing membership categories glossed by the pronoun "we." Finally we revisit the distinction between political and nonpolitical research settings, taking examples from educational, medical, and science research.

ISSUES OF METHOD AND METHODOLOGY

What appears remarkable now is the fact that Becker treats research methods themselves as relatively unproblematic. His account of perspectival research is a very "cool" one. To a considerable extent, indeed, his reference to "underdog" research is presented as a methodological precept rather than as a primarily moral one. The social world has to be understood from the point of view of particular social actors. In his empirical research of the period (with colleagues such as Hughes, Geer, and Strauss) Becker described the "perspectives" of particular social categories—most notably in educational settings such as the University of Kansas Medical School (Becker et al. 1961). The notion of a "perspective" is perfectly unremarkable in the context of Chicago School interactionist work on institutions, persons, and moral careers. Faced with common situations and problems, groups of actors develop shared modes of understanding that in turn imply particular lines of action. The researcher necessarily examines and documents actors' perspectives, and those perspectives reflect those actors' social positions. In order to research them, then, the social analyst must, if only as a methodological precept, align her or his perspective with that of some social actors:

> We must always look at the matter from someone's point of view. The scientist who proposes to understand society must, as Mead long ago pointed out, get into the situation enough to have a perspective on it. And it is likely that his [*sic*] perspective will be greatly affected by whatever positions are taken by any or all of the other participants in that varied situation. [. . .] Almost all the topics that sociologists study, at least those that have some relation to the real worlds around us, are seen by society as morality plays and we shall find ourselves, willy-nilly, taking part in those plays on one side or the other. (Becker 1970: 131)

Some degree of alignment is, therefore, an unavoidable consequence of research in "the real world." It clearly has implications for the design and conduct of field research, as the researcher must associate and become aligned with social actors. This does not, apparently, impinge directly on research methods themselves. It is noticeable that Becker's own discussion of the topic is concerned with the use of research, not its conduct. Becker's paper is a reflection on how research findings are received by their audience(s), especially the nonacademic audience(s) such as the police, school administrators, or doctors. Reading the paper today it is striking that Becker does not discuss his bias and partisanship issues as they do, or as they might, impact upon the choice of a research problem, the selection of a field setting, access negotiations, data collection, the processes of analysis, the style or content of the "writing up," or the decisions about when, where, and even if, to publish. By the standards of today, the paper is also remarkably free of autoethnography (Reed-Danahay 2001), reflexive engagement, and self-scrutiny.

Throughout his essay Becker is silent about specific methods of data collection. He does not discuss the relative merits of observation versus life history interviewing versus group interviews as ways of gathering data on prisoners, drug users, or Latino school pupils. The investigator's choice from a toolkit of methods is not problematized from the political point of view. (Becker of course considered the relative merits of methods from other perspectives, discussed elsewhere in this chapter.) In this context, Becker implicitly treats the choice of methods as a neutrally technical matter. Because it is not discussed, there is an implicit appeal to trust. The reader will trust the investigator to choose the "best" method to collect the perspective of prisoners, drug users, or Latino high school students. Presented with a life history (for example Hughes 1961) of a heroin addict, the reader will assume that the life-history method was appropriately selected from the toolkit because it was the right tool for the job. The investigator is a technician, who chooses wisely. The choice of methods is emotionally, ethically, and personally neutral. The issues of partisanship arise from either choosing to collect and treat seriously the perspective of the prisoner, drug user, or Latino student, and/or from reporting it to the world as if it were a rational, valid, and worthwhile perspective that readers should try to understand and to recognize, (instead of dismissing it as irrational, invalid, and inherently worthless, like its "owner").

Becker argued elsewhere for a preference for direct observation over interviews in addressing particular kinds of research question, and we discuss that argument from a contemporary perspective elsewhere in this chapter. We stress that the undifferentiated notions of "observation" or "interview" in the original formulation by Geer and Becker and in their exchange with Trow are untenable today. There has been an explosion of books on observational methods. The interview method has not only diversified and has itself been subject to multiple and contested codification, but also the roles of the participants have been subject to critical scrutiny. Researchers are faced with what appears to be a wide range of types of qualitative research, and a variety of theoretical positions underpinning them. So Seale, Gobo, Gubrium, and Silverman's *Handbook of Qualitative Research Practice* (2003) offers the following methods of data collection: in-depth interviews, biographical methods, narrative analysis, focus groups, the internet, visual techniques, secondary analysis of texts, as well as participant observation. The analytic strategies proposed include: grounded theory, discourse analysis, conversation analysis, computer-aided analysis software, and rhetorical analysis. The theoretical and/or ideological approaches include: naturalism, critical theory, ethnomethodology, feminism, and Foucauldian discourse studies. When such an array of data collection, data analysis, and theoretical positions is offered, a researcher cannot see choice of method as a neutral selection from an open toolbox.

The theoretical and ideological approaches in Seale et al. (2003) are by no means a complete list. Queer theory and method (Tierney 1999), antiracist theory and method (hooks 1981 and 1990), and postcolonial (Minh-ha 1989) or subaltern theory and method (Spivak 1988) are obvious possible additions to the list. Feminist, queer, antiracist, and subaltern methods are highly controversial (Hammersley 2000), and they relate to Becker's original question in a concentrated manner. They answer the question of "whose side?" not in the way the data are presented to audiences, but by building an explicit standpoint from the earliest stage of the research (constructing a research question) through all the stages of data collection, analysis, and writing. For example, Virginia Olesen (1994: 158), in a review of the field, argued that feminist researchers:

> Shared the outlook that it is important to center and make problematic women's diverse situations and the institutions and frames that influence those situations, and then to refer the examination of that problematic to theoretical, policy or action frameworks in the interest of realizing social justice for women.

Six years later she had streamlined the definition to "incisive scholarship to frame, direct, and harness passion in the interests of redressing grievous problems" (Olesen 2000: 215). In either of these formulations, the question of sides is foregrounded, explicit, and suffuses all stages of the research. Tierney (1999: 451) provides a similar standpoint for queer methods. Judith Butler (1990 and 1999), a founder of Queer Theory and its associated methods and methodology, works in rhetoric and literature. One of the notable features of feminist and queer methods is their transgression of the academic barriers between sociology or anthropology and traditional humanities fields, such as literature, philosophy, and aesthetics.

The authors promoting antiracist methods and postcolonial standpoints are equally resistant to being confined to traditional disciplines. John Stanfield (1994), commissioned to write on "ethnic" qualitative research, criticized the existing texts and handbooks on methods for ignoring issues of racial diversity, and for being dominated by Eurocentric reasoning, grounded in the ethnic experiences of privileged white intellectuals. He proposed that "ethnic modelling in qualitative research must involve calling into serious question the vast warehouse of knowledge that researchers of European descent have been accumulating and legitimating as ways of knowing and seeing" (183). Complaining that there was little available on how indigenous ethnic models of qualitative research might be implemented in the field, Stanfield argued that what had been published was merely about being sensitive to ethnicity. He wanted a new textbook to show Africans how to study the lifeworlds of the dominant.

Postcolonial theorists, particularly Spivak (1990), have been much stronger in literary theory and cultural studies than in sociology or anthropology, but the general intellectual movement they represent has had a pervasive influence in the social sciences. Anthropologists can certainly not preserve any innocence concerning the colonial past or the implications of postcolonial theory. The processes of translation between cultural idioms are now much more complex, and more overtly contested than they were for previous generations. The publication of Said's *Orientalism* (1978) with its denunciation of dualisms that juxtapose Western rationality, objectivity, and science with Oriental irrationality, subjectivity, magic, religion, and adherence to tradition, was one of several decisive interventions that rendered increasingly problematic the relationship between the researcher and the researched. One does not need to deal specifically with the "orient" (in Said's own work this refers primarily to the Near East and Middle East) in order to recognize the intellectual processes of orientalism at work. In ethnographic work on any culture there are manifest dangers of overemphasizing the exotic, the bizarre, the extreme, and the most alien. There is, moreover, the related danger inherent in analytic arguments that are based on ironic contrasts between "us" and "them," between "mainstream culture" and "subcultures," between the pragmatic and the ritual, or between the rational and the traditional. All such contrasts—and many more like them—risk "othering" the subjects of the research (irrespective of whether they occupy social worlds that are "far" or "near"). As Marcus (2001: 112) points out, Said's questions about representing other cultures are the central issues of anthropology, and the translation across cultural boundaries remains central to the intellectual commitments of anthropology, sociology, and the other cultural disciplines. It is not, after all, the function of social research only to study oneself. The problems that have been highlighted include the desire to study others without rendering their otherness in terms that reproduce hegemonic relationships and representations.

Work on whiteness further problematizes the notion of "sides." Frankenberg (1993) opened up the contemporary discussions of whiteness through her life-history interviews with white women living on the American west coast. The performance of whiteness is an important issue that has been taken up and pursued by others; for instance, Fine, Weis, Powell, and Wong (1997: vii) draw attention to the "silence on questions of whiteness" in their research on men facing the deindustrialization of the cities of the rustbelt. They call for researchers to put "whiteness" in the analytic spotlight, to stop it being "both invisible and dominant" (ix). This is again but one instance of the ways in which taken-for-granted categories and social positions have become increasingly problematic. While race and ethnicity have been self-evident topics for sociological and anthropological research for many decades, the category of whiteness has remained unmarked. It is only recently that whiteness could have become a problematic category, to be treated analytically like any other social category. It is normal for the socially dominant categories to be unmarked and to be relatively invisible. It takes an extra effort of intellectual commitment and will to treat the objects of study with complete symmetry.

The analysis of gender is another case in point. When a topic of scrutiny, "gender" overwhelmingly implied the study of women, while the study of sexual orientation equally readily implied consideration of same-sex relations. It remains a minority commitment to examine masculine identities and the construction of heterosexual behavior with equal urgency. The cultural and analytic relations of identity and difference have, therefore, become increasingly problematic. The distinctions between a white, male Western intellectual and a variety of others have become less clear-cut. One can no longer assume that "we" know who "we" are. Equally, we can no longer feel so comfortable in knowing who "they," the "others" are either. The question of partisanship and alignment is ever more pressing, but its social and ethical configuration is more complex. Social and professional categories are less homogenous and less certain. The lines of authority are more overtly contested.

When Becker published his paper, research methods in themselves were seen as ethically contentious but otherwise inherently neutral. Becker, Gouldner, and Cynthia Epstein all studied employment with different theoretical agendas, but regarded each other's methods as essentially the same: technically different but politically neutral. Our problem today is that many of us no longer believe that. Today the "choice" of method is apparently wider, yet much more problematic. Instead we accept feminist methods, antiracist methods, queer methods, and so on. Even if we reject the wilder shores of Denzin and Lincoln's (2000) fifth, sixth, and seventh postmodern moments, we have certainly abandoned the idea that there are value-free technical methods that can be applied without sentimentality. Becker's dilemma is still with us, but his solution needs a rethink.

The translation of methods into inherently ethical or political issues derives from multiple inspirations, and has a variety of connotations. At the most general level, there are plenty of occasions on which qualitative research methods in general are portrayed as inherently preferable—on moral grounds—to other kinds of research strategies. There are a series of equations that are readily drawn. Quantitative methods are easily identified with

positivist approaches, which in turn have connotations of objectifying research subjects, dehumanizing them, and in the process emptying social life
of its essential meaningfulness. In contrast, qualitative research is identified
with humane values, and a commitment to naturalism in capturing everyday lives. In recent years, such general "political" approbation for qualitative
research has become less clear. Commentators like Denzin and Lincoln have
identified earlier implementations of qualitative research as positivist in
tenor. Given such views, it is difficult for the avant garde to sustain a generalized approval for qualitative research.

The ethical dimensions of research methods have, in any case, become
more specific. They have increasingly included the exploration and celebration of "voices." While ethnographic and other qualitative research has always included examples and extracts of informants' accounts, the voices of
social actors have become increasingly prominent in their own right. In this
context, attention to voices means more and carries much heavier ethical
connotations than simply letting informants' own words appear in life histories or as extracts in conventional ethnographies. The celebration and representation of voices, rather, implies endowing speaking subjects with a special significance. Giving voice to subjects includes the representation of
individuals and groups who have been muted and marginalized. It implies
the expression of their unique experience, usually through the reproduction
of personal testimony and narrative.

In turn, this involves a particular treatment of data collection and a distinctive style of analytic representation. Data collection is represented as "dialogic," or such a mode of work is advocated as the ideal. This stands in contrast to the supposedly hegemonic approach to observation and
interviewing characteristic even of earlier forms of qualitative research. The
dialogic mode is allegedly egalitarian: it departs from a supposedly more in-
quisitorial style of conventional research methods. Moreover—rather like
Becker's reversal of mainstream values, it places special significance on the
ability of silenced minorities to be "heard" (that is, read).

The qualitative representation of voices is thus congruent with the intentions of various standpoints, and similar, epistemological positions that
explicitly align research strategies with the experiences and interests of
specific groups—feminist, queer, and subaltern stances among them. The
equation of feminist commitments with qualitative work—interviewing in
particular—is not especially recent. The notion that women interviewing
women, aligned with a distinctive sensibility for women's lives and experiences, confers an especial affinity between feminism and qualitative research
is a relatively long-standing one. Oakley's commentary on interviewing

women was but one early and influential example (Oakley 1981; see also Oakley 1998 for her current, and very different, position).

These approaches render research strategies and methods themselves more political than Becker's kind of formulation. They all imply that the research process itself is ideologically implicated. Research methods cannot, it is argued, be neutral. There are no politically or interpretatively neutral standpoints from which the social world can be scrutinized and analyzed. Furthermore, these arguments apply to the strategies used to represent the social world and the research process. We discuss contemporary perspectives on representation much more fully in chapter 6, and we do not need to recapitulate them in full now. Here we simply point out that writing up qualitative research and the construction of the written account ("the ethnography" for instance) is also far from neutral. "I" too has become politicized, with ethical implications. Just as commentators advocate a research process that is dialogic, so they commend representational devices that are polyvocal, and that are faithful to a fractured and multiperspectival social reality. The politicized text is, therefore, a polyvocal one, inhabited by different voices.

When Howard Becker asked whose side we are on, then, he did not automatically involve research methods in that question. Of course, he included a general approach to research. He was talking about the interpretation of field research, not the analysis of official statistics, and his remarks implicitly referred to the interpretation of field data. But it is apparent in that original essay, and in other methodological work of the same period, that the entire process of research was not perceived as being as thoroughly interested and political as it has become subsequently. The discussion of research ethics was undoubtedly visible in the classic period of papers and anthologies. For the most part, however, they were confined to discussions of overt and covert research and the ethics of research access. The ethics of research were a fairly restricted set of concerns. By contrast, contemporary perspectives treat all aspects of the research and representational process as inherently implicated in moral and ideological matters.

SIDES

In recent years commentators on qualitative field research have contributed to two parallel processes. First—as we have just seen—they have treated research methods as being increasingly problematic. They have problematized them from various points of view, including moral or ethical commitments.

Secondly, they have endorsed a variety of ethical commitments that are themselves more complex than the dichotomies on which Becker based his account. We are no longer free to think simply in terms of the powerful and the powerless. It becomes increasingly difficult to discern "sides," while increasingly acceptable to be committed to taking sides of some sort. The methodological and ethical terrain has become more fragmented. While it has become more overtly politicized, the lines of political commitment and affiliation have become less distinct. Research methods themselves have become increasingly politicized. Those commitments have in their turn been challenged and resisted, as sociologists and others have sought to reaffirm a distinction between research methods and ethical standpoints. The contemporary position reflects the wider multiplicity of standpoints that characterize the current state of play. This intellectual context and the ferment that appears to characterize it represent a state of the intellectual field that Lincoln and Denzin, among many others, have associated with a late, postmodern phase (or "moment") in the development of qualitative research.

The last decade of the twentieth century saw a number of publications arguing that qualitative research is in turmoil. Lincoln and Denzin (1994: 581) provided a typical claim of this type, describing the particular juncture in terms of "A messy moment, multiple voices, experimental texts, breaks, ruptures, crises of legitimization and representation, self-critique, new moral discourses, and technologies." Six years later they remained convinced that:

> The sixth [post experimental] and seventh [the future] moments are upon us. Fictional ethnographers, ethnographic poetry, and multimedia texts are today taken for granted. Post-experimental writers seek to connect their writings to the needs of a free democratic society. The demands of a moral and sacred qualitative social science are being actively explored. (Denzin and Lincoln 2000: 17)

Note that their comments are actually about representation, not the collection and analysis of data, and that their viewpoint could be regarded as ethnocentric: both points we return to below. But it is certainly the case that when Becker wrote his original paper, the representation of the groups and individuals being researched seemed to be relatively unproblematic. Becker's discussion is free of any angst about how a white male could or should represent the worldviews of others. It is not foregrounded as the most fundamental of methodological problems.

The issue of "sides" has been complicated by the success of qualitative research in many subspecialisms. Since 1967 there has been such a growth in ethnographies in such a range of diverse settings that the deceptive simplicity of treating prison officers and prisoners, or teachers and pupils, or doctors, nurses and patients, or scientists, technicians, and students as undifferentiated sides has become untenable. In the literature on the socialization of medical students that followed Becker, Geer, Hughes, and Strauss (1961) for example, the "sides" of medical faculty and students have been disaggregated. The original Chicago study treated the dynamics of medical education in terms of two relatively undifferentiated collectivities—the medical students and the medical faculty. With very few female medical students, they did not even have to consider gender as a topic, apparently. They treated the world of medicine and medical faculty members as a relatively undifferentiated one. Atkinson (1981 and 1997a), for instance, stressed the segmentation of the staff, echoing Bucher and Stelling's (1971) analysis of differentiation within the profession of medicine. Sinclair (1996) draws attention to racial and religious divisions within the body of medical students. A range of feminist work on medical education and occupational socialization has explored gender divisions as disruptions of a unitary student perspective (Lorber 1984; Cassell 1998).

Becker's other intellectual field—the study of deviance—has certainly become more complex, and the "sides" involved have become more complex (Hobbs 2001). There has, for example, been a refocusing of work from police versus deviants onto victims, especially those living in inner city high crime areas, and on women, gays and lesbians, and the elderly. Here the researchers have been explicitly and firmly on the "side" of those who fear crime and are or have been its victims (Hanmer and Saunders 1984). Studying the residents of a street where street prostitutes ply for trade, who "experience" the messier aftereffects of crime, the policing and the deviance, changes the idea of "sides." A supposedly "victimless" crime, reclassified as deviance by work taking the view from the prostitutes and their clients, becomes once again a negative phenomenon when the neighborhood residents are recast as victims. The research field has thus become more fragmented and diverse, traversed by the ethical and political connotations of gender, generation, or sexuality.

Even for those skeptical of the linear model of ascent into polyvocality, there is no doubt that methods and methodology are more problematic and more contested in 2002 than they (apparently) were in 1967. This heady mixture of crises and differences is shot through with moral problems and contestations. It is no longer a question of asking whose side we are on: we now have to ask ourselves who "we" are, who "they" are, how we represent ourselves and others, and even what methods we employ. We may no longer feel able to choose sides, and we may find that we study ourselves as much as we study others. Perspectives certainly seem less clearly drawn than they did for Becker, the moral imperatives more urgent and yet less sharply defined.

The moral imperatives, and the moral confusion, arise from a multiplicity of tendencies within the traditions of qualitative research. They include the influence of feminist scholarship, the commitments of postcolonialist and antiorientalist thinking, the influence of critical ethnography, the rise of "autoethnography," and the various crises of representation among ethnographers. These have all, often in complementary ways, reinforced a variegated and contested terrain of ideological and ethical discourse concerning the conduct and representation of ethnographic research. Equally, they have given a renewed urgency to debate concerning the proper relationship between research and ideological commitments. These do not occur in a social vacuum. There are multiple institutional and personal frameworks that influence researchers' values and perspectives. The "we" of Becker's original formulation now seems a much less obvious category than it might when it was first published. In the next section of the paper we therefore explore what "we" might have meant when Howard Becker was writing, opening up issues of ethnocentrism, sexism, orientalism, and of personal stigma.

WHO ARE "WE"? WHO CAN BE "WE"?

Becker did not overtly reflect on who was and was not included in the term "we." We do not attribute to Becker who he intended to include in his taken-for-granted "we," or who he would have added or excluded if challenged on the topic in 1967. Our point here is first that an equivalent scholar today, in a presidential address to a learned society, or in a methodological reflection, *would* address the question of "we" more overtly and in more complex terms. Any author's understanding of who "we" are is, today, problematic, demanding explication and justification. Additionally, of course, there is an important distinction between an objective "we" and a subjective "we" in 1967, between the "we" of 1967 that is remembered or recreated for reminiscences, autobiographical reflections, or reports for a work such as Fine (1995), and how our "we" might have changed in the years since 1967. Our point here is that Becker's "we" of 1967 cannot be read off simply either as a description of 1967 or as a useful category today. Community glossed as "we" has changed and appeals to "we" have become complex. Moreover the objective and subjective "we" have coalesced and diverged.

Becker delivered his paper originally to the Society for the Study of Social Problems (SSSP). The paper discussed research on deviance, and Becker is an expert on qualitative methods in sociology. His "we" in the address, and the published version that followed, is drawn from those three overlapping sets of professional colleagues. Becker had come out of the Second Chicago School and was best known as a researcher on deviance (Galliher 1995), although he had also studied school teachers, medical students, and liberal arts undergraduates. Gusfield (1982, cited in Platt 1995: 93) summarized the shared culture of the graduates produced by the Second Chicago School as "a methodology that held the student firmly to what he/she could see, hear, and experience at first hand. . . . Abstractions and concepts ungrounded by the experience with concrete observations were suspect." The sociologists likely to share Becker's ideas about taking sides in 1967 were those who valued making concrete observations; they were the implied hearers or readers of his subjective "we."

There was also an objective "we," of course, made up of members of the SSSP in 1966, of qualitative researchers in American sociology, of tenured sociologists in research universities, and the graduate students and junior faculty who aspired to join them. Abbott and Gaziano's (1995) historical study of the Chicago faculty shows that Chicago sociologists were prominent in the foundation and running of the SSSP. (Fifteen of the fifty-three office holders up to 1995 had Chicago doctorates, for example.) So objectively, the SSSP and the Chicago School of Sociology were drawn from the same population, committed to the same paradigm of empirical research, grounded in concrete observation. No women and no ethnic minority representatives held tenured posts in Chicago Sociology between 1945 and 1960, although there were women and minority members among the 200-strong body of graduate students, and among the research associates, including of course Blanche Geer, Becker's coauthor on several key methodological papers as well as empirical monographs. Deegan (1995) has studied the women who were "trained or employed in marginal positions" (322) in the relevant era. About 15 percent of the graduate students were women, and those who responded to Deegan's research reported an intellectual egalitarianism and companionship.

Given the nature of research-led sociology departments in top universities in the 1950s and 1960s, however, we can be confident about who the objective "we" were. The objective "we" of Becker's era excluded many of the categories of people who have, since 1967, clamored or demanded to be heard in sociology. Some have been more successful and influential than others, some have challenged the discipline more fundamentally than others. When Becker wrote "Whose Side Are We On?" the dominant culture of American sociology assumed "we" were straight, white, American Protestant or Jewish men. Gays and lesbians, people of color, non-Americans, Catholics, Muslims, Hindus, Buddhists, and women were all implicitly *not* "we." Nothing Becker wrote in the paper challenged the dominant culture, or embraced sociological outsiders. This is certainly not because Becker was deliberately setting out to exclude such people from the sociological elite or to exclude their perspectives from the dominant worldview of sociology. It arose because first the standpoint(s) of the researchers were not seen as relevant to or implicated in the investigation except in a few unusual and specific circumstances (a Negro researcher could mix more easily in a black neighborhood); and second because the elite sociology departments *were* staffed by such men who monopolized appointments, tenure, and the intellectual climate. The tenured faculty were white men, sexual orientation was private, and America was in an isolationist era.

The third "we" of 1967 is that remembered or recreated for (auto)biographies and/or scholars researching the history of American sociology. The Chicago School has exercised a particular fascination for scholars, and there have been many opportunities for the great men, such as Becker, to talk and write about their lives and work there. As Deegan (1995) has angrily pointed out, women are "forgotten," "written out," or ignored by men in these autobiographical accounts. Galliher's (1995) story of deviance research in the Second Chicago School does not mention a single woman. Thirty men produced self-reports for Gary Fine (1995), and the women are almost invisible. These men had been specifically asked to reflect on gender as a feature of their student life and subsequent professional career. They chose to ignore the request. Their important recollections of who had been significantly part of the "we" led them to stress an all-male community. The interview Erving Goffman gave Jef Verhoeven in 1983 (published in 1992) is the same: Goffman recollects only male coevals; only men are highlighted as intellectually significant. Lyn Lofland's (1997) memories of the founding of the Society for the Study of Symbolic Interaction also support this view of the relative marginalization or invisibility of women.

Becker's address to the SSSP predated the explosion of "outsiders" demanding to be included in the sociological "we" that began in 1968. The political movements of women, blacks, Hispanics, gays, lesbians, Native Americans, and the physically impaired that grew up after 1968 led, over the following two decades, to new caucuses and pressure groups inside the academy. Groups such as Sociologists for Women in Society had a double agenda within sociology. They were campaigning both to change the content and focus of the subject, and to obtain tenured posts for women in elite universities. So African Americans challenged the validity of conventional sociological research on the black family, and the neglect of sickle-cell anemia as a topic in medical sociology, while promoting the need for African Americans to get doctorates and tenure-track jobs. Many of these outsider groups also worked to set up new disciplines or interdisciplinary areas, such as Women's Studies or Chicano/a Studies, and chose to locate their sociological research in that new context. Along with these campaigns came new journals, new book series, new conferences, and new intellectual networks. Such movements challenge the unitary voice of the "we," and encourage a critically reflexive set of multiple "we's."

The content and personnel of American qualitative sociology have changed. There are many women, in tenured posts, whose research is cited and known. When Millman and Kanter (1975) edited *Another Voice*, an early collection of feminist papers, many of the chapters focused on the products of ethnography. The authors in that collection showed how male sociologists had produced an androcentric view of many topics in the public domains of American life. The sociologies of deviance, health and illness, urban life, education, work and politics, drawn from ethnographic work, were male accounts of men's lives and perspectives. The mass entry of women into qualitative sociology, and their insistence upon feminist perspectives, has created a second "we": women sociologist ethnographers. There is an issue about whether the women are now part of the same "we" as the men, or indeed contribute to and work within different standpoint theories (see Hekman 2000; Hartsock 2000; Collins 2000; Harding 2000; Smith 2000; and chapter 6 of this book).

Sexuality and sexual orientation were, when Becker wrote in 1967, private matters. Disclosure of anything other than heterosexuality would have been a discrediting stigma, and there was no public acknowledgement that sexuality or sexual orientation was relevant to research at any of the stages of project design, data collection, analysis, or writing. Today, while there are still social contexts in which sexuality and sexual orientation have to be kept secret for fear of imprisonment or discriminatory practices, qualitative sociology in developed Anglophone countries is not one of them. Researchers who wish to self-identify as gay or lesbian, as transsexuals or as bisexuals can do so, and do so in their research-based writing.

The most problematic case here is that of Harry Wolcott and the Sneaky Kid. Here issues of a very powerless informant, a very senior and established scholar, gay identity, and research ethics are entwined to make a very difficult case (Wolcott 1990a and 1990b). In 1984 a young man,

"Brad," burnt down Wolcott's house in an attempted murder, only averted by Wolcott's longtime companion, "Norman," who interrupted the attack. Both Wolcott and Norman lost everything they owned. In the paper, Wolcott told of his physical relationship with Brad in addition to revisiting his academic research on Brad's life story. The latter, as told to Wolcott, bore many similarities to Shaw's classic *The Jack-Roller* (Shaw 1930). Since this publication, Wolcott has received much criticism. Our point, however, is that the criticism is not levelled at his sexuality and long-term relationships with Norman. The reservations concern the relationship with Brad, who was much younger (his age range was nineteen to twenty-one) than Wolcott, was vulnerable because he was trespassing on Wolcott's land, and because Wolcott conducted life-history research on, with, and about Brad. The anger provoked by audiences for Wolcott's confessional accounts is provoked by his infidelity to Norman, the possible exploitation of Brad, and his failure to confess that he had the physical relationship *before* he did the research, so that his hearers and readers could judge the project in the light of that personal relationship. Wolcott's homosexuality is *not* the issue: research ethics, openness, and integrity are.

Of course there are still discreditable and discrediting forms of sexuality. It is unlikely that any academic sociologist would choose to come out as a pedophile, an Internet porn producer, or a rapist. Few would want to self-identify as a rubber fetishist or a sadomasochist. We are not arguing that coming out to funding bodies, employers, and audiences as gay or lesbian is unproblematic. However, successful scholars such as Tierney in the United States or Mac an Ghaill in the United Kingdom have used their identities as gay men to develop nuanced ethnographic writing (Tierney 1993; Tierney and Dilley 2002; Mac an Ghaill 1994). Similarly, lesbians, such as Krieger (1983 and 1991) and Stanley (2001) have discussed how their lesbian identity interacts with their research. It is very unlikely that these scholars could, or would, have written in these ways in 1953 or 1967.

When Becker wrote in 1967, the majority of tenured sociologists were white, especially in the elite universities. Since then there have been three developments that make the "we" problematic. First, there are now tenured sociologists from many races in elite universities. Second, celebration of racial identity is now recognized and indeed encouraged. A sociologist from a Chicano or Vietnamese background is able to belong to a caucus, and be proud of *not* being a WASP. Thirdly, ethnic identity is now seen as a potential resource for research insight(s). The American Educational Research Association annual conference program for 2001 illustrates this. There are caucuses of the following groups featured on the program, in sessions that help build career (Brothers of the Academy, Up and Coming Black Scholars Earning our Way in Higher Education) and focus on themselves as research objects (Biliteracy, Learning Styles, Parent Expectations, and Academic Achievement of Asian American Students). Other caucuses included: Disability Studies; Hispanic Research Interest; Indigenous Peoples; Lesbian and Gay; Black; Asian and Pacific; and Women. Parallel examples can be found from equivalent meetings of the American Sociological Association.

The exclusions from the "we" of 1967 have mostly been brought into the public identity of researchers. Ethnicity, gender, and sexuality certainly have. Religion has not. When Becker wrote "we," he meant men reared as Protestants or Jews. Today sociologists have been reared in many different faiths, but in general sociologists do not celebrate their religious identities or backgrounds as a research resource. The most famous Catholic sociologist, Andrew Greeley (1990), is a partial exception to this. He is an ordained Catholic priest who is not only a sociologist but also a bestselling novelist who finances his empirical work with the royalties from his novels. He has written movingly of the resentment and censorship he faces within the Catholic Church because his professional research "violated the rules of amateurism and mediocrity" which are "at the core of clerical culture" (139). He also reports meeting anti-Catholic prejudice from sociologists: "I would no more permit that man in our department . . . than I would a card-carrying Communist, for the same reason" (138). Because he is a quantitative, positivist researcher, Greeley does not use his Catholicism as a standpoint or a research resource as a contemporary qualitative investigator well might. It is striking that Catholicism and other mainstream Christian denominations are not deployed as authenticity markers in qualitative sociology or anthropology with the same frequency that ethnicity, sexual orientation, or gender are.

In contrast to the relative lack of invocation of mainstream religions, qualitative researchers have explored how they were changed by studying religious, magical, or paranormal phenomena in "other" cultures (Young and Goulet 1994). In this collection Guedon (1994) discusses how she learned to share the dream culture of the Dene. Swartz (1994) explains how she acquired a Native American guardian spirit, and came to believe it was protecting her. Favret-Saada's account of witchcraft beliefs in modern France is a dramatic example (Favret-Saada 1980). Her research on witchcraft practices demonstrated that there was no position of neutrality within the discursive system of witchcraft victims, witchcraft diagnosis, and processes of unwitching.

There is, however, a fervor equivalent to the religious fervor that sociologists generally eschew. Just as Becker's "we" were Protestant or Jewish, but saw religion as private, so too their health status, mental or physical, and their experiences of "victimhood" were largely private troubles, kept separate from the research processes. In the past decade, this reticence has totally vanished. There is celebration of a formerly private characteristic—health status. Today's researchers frequently invoke their health status or stigma and/or that of family and friends to claim research insight. Papers at conferences rarely start "As a Baptist," but frequently begin "As a cancer survivor," or "As a carer" or "As a recovering alcoholic/bulimic/domestic violence victim" (see for example Paget 1993; Tillman-Healy 1996). In a typical example of this sort, Margot Eyring (1998: 141) writes: "My interest in well being began after having a debilitating illness after living a life with few physical problems. Developing a case of mononucleosis motivated me." Alongside health-related survival claims many other personal qualities are routinely invoked.

The contributors to the anthology edited by deMarrais (1998) produce typical confessional tales of difficulties in data collection and analysis, and of embarrassing or disruptive incidents in the course of fieldwork, such as falling into deep mud or being hoaxed by informants. However, alongside these orthodox confessions (see Atkinson 1996 for an analysis of the genre) many of the contributors offer individual, personal qualities to give authenticity to their accounts. *Inter alia* they reveal themselves as part Choctaw, an activist for the Navajo in court cases, a Puerto Rican, an African American, a bluegrass musician, a trade union activist, and a conscientious objector. Such identities stand both as a source of authenticity and as a distancing mechanism from the older and unitary "we" of the academy.

Behar (1999: 478), for example, gives a list of current students doing ethnographies who are "overwhelmingly expressing a strong need to understand their own sense of emotional, ethical, political, and historical connections to the intellectual projects they are taking on." The personal qualities she celebrates in her list include class of origin, Latino identity, Irishness, devotion to a father, gender, Jewish identity, African American identity, Holocaust survival, legacies of slavery, and issues of backgrounds in Catholicism and Protestantism, plus enthusiasm for the Santeria religion (derived from Yoruba beliefs in Cuba). Not all these will produce published ethnographies, of course, but if they do, it is likely that the personal diversity Behar celebrates will be foregrounded by their authors.

There are two aspects to this fragmentation and contestation of the "we." It is important to ask whether the original white male American "we" have actually recognized and accepted the many other races, sexes, and nationalities joining, or trying to join the "we." Many women commentators in sociology and anthropology have noted that the white male elite are still remarkably unenthusiastic about recognizing any valid membership claims from women or other outsider groups. Behar and Gordon (1995) assembled their collection *Women Writing Culture* because when, in 1986, Clifford and Marcus produced an edited collection (*Writing Culture*), which opened up to widespread debate the problematic nature of textual representation in anthropology, there was only one woman author (Mary Pratt, a literary critic), and none of the scholars whose texts were analyzed was a woman either. Justifying this, Clifford stated that women were excluded because their writing was not both feminist and textually innovative. As Behar (1995: 5) summarized it: "To be a woman writing culture became a contradiction in terms: women who write experimentally are not feminist enough, while women who write as feminists write in ignorance of the textual theory that underpins their own texts."

Catherine Lutz (1990) wrote of the continuing male domination of "the process of academic gatekeeping" leading to a continued "marginalizing or failing to publish the work of women." Chafetz (1997) levels similar accusations at male sociologists, while bell hooks (1989) and Delgardo (1984) have made similar claims that work by black and antiracist scholars is undervalued. In the 1970s, feminist sociologists and anthropologists highlighted the omission of women as both creators of knowledge and as the topic of research. They went on to conduct research on women, and create new forms of knowledge. Yet thirty years later it is still the case that such "outsider" knowledge has not been taken into the malestream. Jo Eadie (2001: 575) writes: "There seems something oddly old-fashioned about assessing the contemporarity of a critical text by the number of women writers that it recognizes—but then there are times when only the bluntest of tools will do." Having searched for a "core text" to use on a social theory module, Eadie concluded that: "reading the most recent surveys of the field, one could be forgiven for thinking that gender played a negligible role in the functioning of contemporary society." Eadie reviewed six texts, and concluded that most of them: "construct feminism in ways that effectively exclude it from what purports to be a coherent and comprehensive overview of social theory" (2001: 576). For example, Bauman's (2000) *Liquid Modernity* makes no mention of feminism, and has only six women in the bibliography. The power in American sociology is probably still with Becker's original "we." Within qualitative sociology, the original "we" may still have the power but be more self-conscious about how their race, sex, and sexuality are interwoven with their research practices. Among positivists, there is still a total refusal to accept that the personal has any relevance to the processes of empirical research. That is a question for the discipline as a whole. For the purposes of this chapter, the important question is: Does the fragmentation and contestation of "we" change "our" methods and "our" ethics?

It is ironic that for all their expressed sensitivity to marginalization and cultural subordination, social scientists retain major blind spots. For instance, American ethnographic sociology has changed in many ways since 1967, but it would be a mistake to think that many contemporary American ethnographers would include any non-Americans in "we." Adler and Adler (1999) for example describe a party they gave during the ASA in New York in 1980, attended by 150 ethnographers. They imagined an equivalent event in 1999, and explored the different guests who would be present. Not a single person mentioned is a non-American. The two volume *Journal of Contemporary Ethnography* celebration of Ethnography at the Millennium's Turn contains twenty-six papers. Four are by non-Americans. The twenty-two American chapters are remorselessly ethnocentric. Fifteen cite nothing by non-Americans. Three cite a foreign theorist or novelist (Sartre, Foucault, Levi-Strauss, Wittgenstein, Zola). Three cite *one* non-American researcher each (Silverman, Connell, Mann). Only Preissle (1999) cites multiple non-Americans (nine of them, all united by another American author in a single book). The second edition of Denzin and Lincoln's (2000) *Handbook of Qualitative of Research* is equally remorselessly American. The two editors are American. The International Advisory Board has twenty-four members; only six are based outside the United States. There are forty-one chapters by sixty-one authors, of whom forty-seven are Americans. For Denzin and Lincoln "we" are American. Similarly, Ellis and Bochner's (1996) innovative collection of confessional papers has fourteen chapters—all but one by Americans. Similiarly Jessor, Colby, and Schweder (1996) has twenty-one chapters, all by Americans.

One could also point to a similar process of ethnocentrism and elective attention among anthropologists. Anthropologists—both British social anthropologists and American cultural anthropologists—have increasingly turned their attention to the study of fractions of their "own" culture. They have begun to assemble published works on the anthropology of institutions and organizations such as hospitals and clinics, schools and college, businesses and the like. One might have thought that this would imply a high degree of explicit convergence between such anthropology and the traditions of sociologically-inspired ethnography of just the same types of social settings. Oddly—though characteristically—many anthropological authors maintain the disciplinary boundary by ignoring the existence of sociological ethnographic fieldwork and similar kinds of research. They happily pro-claim that anthropologists have not studied settings like complex organiza-tions, and pay no attention whatsoever to virtually identical approaches and publications that anticipate the work by decades. The collection edited by Gellner and Hirsch (2001) is a case in point, as we pointed out in chapter 1. In the long term, of course, this is a trivial matter. Academic disciplines are defined as much by what they ignore as by what they acknowledge, and what they actually study. It does, nevertheless, help to illustrate that the frag-mentation of "we" among social scientists—even among those who seem to share common methodological perspectives—is not straightforward. More-over, the proliferation of qualitative research methods across a variety of sub-stantive domains means that the older disciplinary certainties can no longer be taken on trust. We certainly cannot assume an implicit "we" of fellow anthropologists or sociologists.

POLITICAL AND NONPOLITICAL RESEARCH TOPICS

There is a third issue arising from Becker's original paper that merits fresh consideration. He operated with a clear distinction between political and nonpolitical research settings. In 1967, Becker felt able to claim that research on crime and deviance, health and illness, and education were "nonpoliti-cal." That is, there were areas in which accusations of bias were frequently made. He contrasted these areas with research on party politics at state and federal levels, and studies of the Los Angeles riots of the 1960s. In these ex-plicitly political areas, Becker argued, it was obvious that there *were* sides and that these sides had their own spokespeople. Qualitative sociologists today working in crime and deviance, health and illness, and education would be unlikely to recognise Becker's description/categorization of these areas as nonpolitical.

In contemporary Britain or the United States, it is easy to see that ed-ucation has moved into the same discursive space as was occupied by prob-lems of race in the 1960s. In the United States, Berliner and Biddle (1995) argue, the Reagan and Bush presidencies saw education become politicized in unprecedented ways, which drew educational research into the explicitly political arena. Three different right-wing political movements have, for twenty years, campaigned against American schools, universities, and initial teacher training institutions. Sharing a conviction that all three sectors are be-ing run by a coalition of left-wing intellectuals to favor the interests of eth-nic minorities, feminists, gays, lesbians, atheists, and communists, to prevent white heterosexual patriotic Americans from learning facts about proper subjects in a Protestant context, these groups have spent a great deal of money. Much of this has been spent on funding dubious research, which is then publicized as "scientific" fact. Berliner and Biddle's book is a systematic demolition of the most famous "studies," showing how they are not, in fact, as simplistically "factual" as the right-wing groups want their fellow Americans to believe. (For a more detailed discussion, see Delamont 1999 and 2000.) In the United Kingdom, the conservative governments of 1979–1997 were equally determined to politicize education and educational research. In a long period when state education was subjected to a discourse of derision (Ball 1990), educational research was accused of being both political and biased.

The attacks on British sociology of education by Tooley and Darby (1998) and Woodhead (1998) were targeted at ethnographic work and took two forms. First, researchers were accused of bias, in that they favored the views of working class, female, black, Asian, and gay students in their complaints that schools were oppressively bourgeois, male, white, or heterosexist, and preferred those views over those of teachers and government. Secondly, the researchers were attacked for showing that issues of class, race, sex, sexuality, or sexual orientation were inherently part of schooling, when the government was demanding that nothing but mastery of basic skills was a relevant topic for research (see Ball and Gewirtz, 1997, for a response to these accusations). The attacks by Tooley and Woodhead on British educational research were a comprehensive reprise of the bias accusations that the SSSP faced in the United States in the 1960s.

Medicine has also been drawn into the overtly political arena. In 1967 the medical profession's view of all aspects of health and illness could plausibly (though not necessarily accurately) be seen as dispassionate and objective. In the subsequent era, its expertise has been challenged: by the women's health movement (Olesen 1993), and by AIDS activists (Epstein 1996), among others. A similar process of politicization has characterized the study of science. Campaigns by ecological and antinuclear social movements, coupled with the scholarly work of the post-Kuhnian historians, philosophers, anthropologists, and sociologists of science have dethroned the universalistic and decontextualized objectivity of science. Women, gays, and ethnic minorities have challenged the ways in which science has constructed them. When Gross, Levitt, and Lewis (1996) published their polemic about "higher superstition" they were the forerunners of the "science wars" of the late 1990s (see also Gross and Levitt 1998). Subsequently, Sokal's notorious hoax and the books that followed it (Sokal and Bricmont

1997; Koertge 1998) were attempts by a few scientists to regain the moral high ground of objectivity by discrediting the imputed beliefs of social scientists. The work of scholars in Science, Technology and Innovation Studies owes its origins to Fleck (1935/1979), popularized in English by Kuhn (1962). Central to its concerns has been the investigation of the social organization of scientific work, the significance of social networks among key scientists, the construction of plausible scientific arguments, the discourse of scientific disputes, and the social production of scientific facts and texts. Ethnographies of laboratories (see Knorr-Cetina 1995) do not in themselves produce hostility to science, but they do undermine naïve perceptions of lofty detached "super-brains" discerning truth in a social vacuum. Rather, science emerges as work, like any other productive activity, and as thoroughly dependent on socially shared conventions or assumptions.

The research domains of the social sciences—irrespective of the methods deployed in their study—have therefore become thoroughly "political." We certainly cannot think in terms of the kind of distinction Becker invoked in the 1960s. The various research communities are now more likely to endorse the view that the personal is political, and that the everyday world is therefore inescapably "political" in some sense, than to excuse some research topics from political consideration.

CONCLUSIONS

We have seen a series of linked developments in the recent conceptualization and conduct of qualitative research. We have seen that the dimensions of partisanship have become more complex than they once were. While researchers have increasingly endorsed ideological positions explicitly, the positions themselves have also become diverse. Simple distinctions between researchers and researched or between the powerful and the powerless have been replaced by a multiplicity of standpoints. Those changes have been productive in some ways—leading to a lively engagement of qualitative researchers with a wide variety of social phenomena.

These moves have not been entirely welcome, however. The proliferation of standpoint and similar orientations to research does not always lead to open debate on research and its commitments. This reflects the extent to which the politicization of research too frequently reflects a form of identity politics rather than the expression of more general values. In the United States research communities in particular, research has been increasingly justified in terms of the identity of the researcher herself or himself (see chapter 2, this book). It is warranted on the basis of the researcher's own biography, orientations, or origins. Moreover, the equation of epistemology or methodology with such personal qualities renders research all but immune from criticism and scrutiny. If the validity of research is rendered in terms of personal identity, then it becomes impossible to engage in criticism and controversy without appearing to resort to *ad hominem* argument. Principled methodological critique may too readily be treated as a matter of personal attack and defense. Alternatively, research and research methods may become unimpeachable precisely because of advocates' personal-political identities.

The proliferation of methodological commitments associated with feminism, queer theory, or ethnic heritage render the disciplined discussion and practice of practical research methods especially difficult. Particular research strategies and research problems may arise among a particular intellectual segment or movement. Feminism, for example, may inspire particular kinds of research approaches, but the potential value of those methods is by no means confined to research by, for, and about women. If feminist researchers find an affinity between their research commitments and styles of research interviewing, the analytic value of that interviewing is of more universal application. In other words, it is unnecessary and unhelpful to identify research methods with particular ideological or personal commitments. It is even less helpful to assume that qualitative research methods are or ought to be inherently superior to other research methods on ethical or political grounds. Ethics are not inherent in any research method, independently of occasions of research practice and interpretation. We certainly do not think that the conduct of qualitative research is in itself more laudable than the use of other research strategies.

Equally, we are skeptical of claims that qualitative research is inherently desirable by virtue of "giving voice" to the underdog, the muted, or the disempowered. Qualitative research strategies allow us to study social action and social organization in a multiplicity of social settings. Those social worlds are themselves highly fragmented, and are characterized by a multiplicity of interests and commitments. The value of ethnographic exploration, or the conduct of extended interviews, lies in the capacity they give us to explore the complexities of everyday social life. The question "Whose side are we on?" is as relevant today as it was when Becker posed it in the 1960s. However the assumptions that implicitly lay behind the question have been subject to critical challenge, both within social science, and qualitative research more generally.

4

PARTICIPANT OBSERVATION
AND INTERVIEWING

EVENTS AND ACCOUNTS

Comparison between participant observation and interviewing—as methods of data collection—has been part of the discourse of qualitative methodologists for over four decades. The starting point for our reexamination of this comparison is the paper published by Howard Becker and Blanche Geer in the 1950s (Becker and Geer 1957a), where they outlined the relative merits of participant observation and interviewing. The paper and its ensuing debate were reprinted in the collection edited by William Filstead (1970), and our page references in this chapter are to that anthology. That paper was, and has remained, an influential reference point for scholars engaged in field research. The subject matter and arguments presented in the paper remain valuable in their own right, as well as providing a means of tracing significant changes in how the conduct of field research is conceptualized.

In the first half of this chapter we reread the paper by Becker and Geer through a contemporary lens, as a step to rethinking the relationships between participant observation and interviewing. We consider briefly the use of the notion of triangulation to mediate the relationships between participant observation and interviewing. We then move on to propose a possible approach to ethnographic data that subsumes participant observation and interviewing. Developing our argument initially through a reconsideration of the classic position exemplified by Becker and Geer, we argue that as field researchers we must not assume that what is done should enjoy primacy over what is said, and that therefore observation and interviewing stand in opposition to one another. Actions, we argue, are understandable because they can be talked about. Equally, accounts—including those derived from interviewing—are also social actions. Social life is performed and narrated, and we need to recognize the performative qualities of social life and talk. In doing so we should not find it necessary to juxtapose talk and events as if they occupy different spheres of meaning. We thus propose an analytic stance that transcends some of the methodological puzzles that have appeared to confront qualitative methods for several decades.

Becker and Geer's original paper compares the relative strengths and applications of participant observation and interviewing. It deals with both the relationships between them, and the possibility of complementarity. While it would be quite unwarranted to accuse Becker and his colleagues of naïveté, from today's perspectives (and one uses the plural here advisedly) one is struck by the extent to which the data-collection methods are treated as relatively unproblematic in themselves. A closer reading of Becker and Geer is worthwhile, not merely for historical purposes, but in order to unpack some of the implicit assumptions that informed the original paper and understandings of field research that stemmed from them. It is helpful to reread the paper in conjunction with Martin Trow's reply and the rejoinder by Becker and Geer (Trow 1957/1970; Becker and Geer 1957b/1970). We do so not in order to belittle the contributions of Becker and Geer or their contemporaries. On the contrary, we think that the issues they raised remain worthy of fresh consideration. We would pay them least respect were we merely to treat their ideas as part of a stock of taken-for-granted ideas.

REEXAMINING BECKER AND GEER

A specific advantage for participant observation over other kinds of data-collection strategy was advocated by Becker and Geer, based in part on their own research on medical students (Becker et al. 1961). Becker and Geer suggested that:

> The most complete form of the sociological datum, after all, is the form in which the participant observer gathers it: An observation of some social event, the events which precede and follow it, and explanations of its meaning by participants and spectators, before, during, and after its occurrence. Such a datum gives us more information about the event under study than data gathered by any other sociological method. Participant observation can thus provide us with a yardstick against which to measure the completeness of data gathered in other ways, a model which

can serve to let us know what modes of information escape us when we use other methods. (Becker and Geer 1957a/1970: 133)

Trow's response challenged this apparent claim for participant observation's status as a gold-standard method for sociological data collection. Trow reiterated the commonplace assumption that the choice of research methods should be dictated by the research problem, rather than the unchallenged superiority of one kind of strategy:

> It is with this assertion, that a given method of collecting data—any method—has an inherent superiority over others by virtue of its special qualities and divorced from the nature of the problem studied, that I take sharp issue. The authoritative view, and I would have thought this the view most widely accepted by social scientists, is that different kinds of information about man [*sic*] and society are gathered most fully and economically in different ways, and that the problem under investigation properly dictates the methods of investigation. (Trow 1957/ 1970: 143)

Here is not the place to divert attention to unpacking the value of this particular theme—except to note that in the world of real research, social scientists do not dream up "problems" to investigate out of thin air, divorced from concerns of theory and methodology, and only then search for precisely the right method. Clearly, problems and methods come as part of packages of ideas—whether or not one chooses to call them "paradigms." The notion that one can simply apply the best method to an independently derived problem is at best unrealistic. However, the rebuttal by Becker and Geer clarifies their original argument, and helps sharpen our own focus. They point out that theirs was not a sweeping claim for the superiority of participant observation over all other methods in all cases. On the contrary, they stress their original emphasis on the observation and understanding of events:

> It is possible Trow thought we were arguing the general superiority of participant observation because he misunderstood our use of the word "event." We intended to refer only to specific and limited events which are observable, not to include in the term such large and complex aggregates of specific events as national political campaigns. (Becker and Geer, 1957b/1970: 151)

Contrary to some possible, glib readings of their paper, then, Becker and Geer were certainly not advocating the wholesale superiority of participant observation over interviewing, nor proposing participant observation as the only valid method for sociological fieldwork.

Becker and Geer claim that the significance of participant observation and its superiority over interviewing rests on the "completeness" of the data. The observation of events in context is proposed as yielding a more complete record and understanding of events, than reliance on interviewing about those events alone. The comparison between participant observation and interviewing was not wholesale, therefore. Becker and Geer made specific claims. In some ways, the original argument—especially as clarified by Becker and Geer—is unremarkable. Indeed, as formulated it is virtually unassailable. It is hard to quarrel with the assertion that the study of observable events is better accomplished by the observation of those events rather than by the collection of retrospective and decontextualized descriptions of them. Clearly, Becker and Geer were advocating a holistic approach to data collection and its interpretation. They believed that the sociological understanding of a given social world was optimized by the deployment of participation, observation, and conversation (in the form of field interviews). What is remarkable, however, and what strikes us from a contemporary vantage point is the extent to which Becker and Geer treat "events" as self-evident and the extent to which they assume that the observation of "events" is a primary goal of participant observation. In turn they also seem to assume that interviews are primarily "about" events.

Becker and Geer's own illustration of the phenomenon is telling, and it bears reexamination. Their remarks on research methods were informed by their recent fieldwork with medical students at the University of Kansas (Becker et al. 1961). The example they give from their fieldwork is illuminating about the general perspective from which they wrote. They give an extract from their field materials in which they discuss medical students' perceptions of their teachers. Being in a subordinate position, the students, it is argued, are likely to develop a kind of mythology about their teachers, and so to interpret their actions in a particular way: "Any such mythology will distort people's view of events to such a degree that they will report as fact things which have not occurred, but which seem to them to have occurred" (Becker and Geer 1957a/1970: 138). In comparing participant observation and interviewing, therefore, Becker and Geer suggest that observation can be a corrective, allowing for adjudication of what "really" happened: "The point is that things can be reported in an interview through such a distorting lens, and the interviewer may have no way of knowing what is fact and what is distortion of this kind; participant observation makes it possible to check such points" (Becker and Geer 1957a/1970: 138).

The actual example Becker and Geer use to demonstrate this assertion strikes a false note with the contemporary reader. The medical students had, apparently, formed the view that particular resident physicians on the teaching staff would regularly humiliate the students. The extract of field notes reproduced in the paper shows either Becker or Geer (the author of the data extract is not specified) reflecting on his or her observations of a particular teaching episode and students' reflections on it. Following a particular encounter with one of the residents, a student reported to his fellow students that the resident had "chewed him out." The observer felt able to intervene and say that the resident had actually been "pretty decent." Another student disputed the observer's description and affirmed that such behavior by a resident was always "chewing out," no matter how "God damn nice" they might be. In evaluating this episode Becker and Geer conclude:

> In short, participant observation makes it possible to check descriptions against fact and, noting discrepancies, become aware of systematic distortions made by the person under study; such distortions are less likely to be discovered by interviewing alone. (Becker and Geer 1957a/1970: 139)

The authors add a caveat to this point, distinguishing between the descriptive content and the process of the interview:

> This point, let us repeat, is only relevant when the interview is used as a source of information about situations and events the researcher himself has not seen. It is not relevant when it is the person's behavior in the interview itself that is under analysis. (Becker and Geer 1957a/1970: 139)

Notwithstanding that last proviso—to which we shall return later—Becker and Geer's argument may strike the contemporary reader as naïve, schooled now in the complexities of accounts, actions, and interpretations, and at home amid the ambiguities of postmodern analysis (Gubrium and Holstein 1997; Silverman 1993; Atkinson 1996). They seem to be operating with a strangely unproblematic view of "events," and thus of the social world. They strongly imply that there are "events" that are amenable to definitive description and evaluation by sociological observers. Consequently, the observer can adjudicate between a true description of events and a distorted one, and can therefore evaluate degrees of "distortion" in such descriptions. It is, incidentally, instructive to read the data extract used in the paper and to which we have referred here—a passage from processed fieldnotes in narrative form, incorporating short verbatim quotes. It does not contain a description of the events that are under consideration and that are the subject of the disputed interpretation. The "events" that are described are the students' comments about the resident and the subsequent conversation between the observer and the students. The original interaction between the resident and the student, on which the latter's claim of being "chewed out" was based, is summarized in the most cursory fashion. Strikingly, it is totally impossible to reconstruct the original interaction from the data provided. Any adjudication as to the reasonableness of the student's complaint, the observer's corrective intervention, or the second student's reaffirmation of the student perspective—their "mythology" as the authors describe it—is not possible. In principle, this treatment of data is congruent with the general analysis that is enshrined in *Boys in White* (Becker et al. 1961). They do not actually base their account on "events" in the sense that they report and analyze much of what medical students or their teachers actually do. Their analysis is concerned with the development of students' perspectives rather than with, say, their embodied skills or their actual encounters with hospital patients. To that extent, Becker and Geer are consistent: the published monograph and their methodological prescriptions are congruent. The problems we raise, by contrast, reflect their treatment of observation, interviewing, accounts, and events as all rather unproblematic.

One might argue in defense of Becker and Geer that the data extract is only being used by way of illustration: that the general argument is important rather than the details of a particular example. Yet this is not just an isolated incident or a minor discrepancy. It is thoroughly characteristic of the wider research project from which it is taken, which is in turn representative of a lot of work based on some combination of participant observation and interviewing, of a kind typical among the generation of researchers represented by Becker and Geer. Any reading of *Boys in White* (Becker et al. 1961), other than a most cursory one, will emphasize the problem. Although the Chicago research team spent a considerable amount of time engaged in participant observation with the medical students and their teachers, the book does remarkably little to report what these social actors actually did. We gain few glimpses of, say, the actual work with patients on hospital wards or in clinics. The "data" consist primarily of what the students themselves said about their lives and work. The primary data, in practice, therefore seem to be conversations about events and actors' perspectives on events and happenings. At least, it is those data that are reported directly in the monograph. The subsequent project by Strauss, Schatzman, Bucher, Ehrlich, and Sabshin (1964) in state and private mental hospitals displays the same style of ethnographic research and reporting.

From our own point of view, the example from Becker and Geer is especially pertinent, as Atkinson (1997a) observed and documented similar phenomena in his own ethnography of a medical school. The degradations that clinical teachers sometimes engage in are a part of a wider repertoire of actions that clinical teachers engage in. Not for nothing are some of them known as "prima donnas" by students (and some of their colleagues). Some of them can act quite flamboyantly—including reenacting patients' presenting symptoms. They can tell stories about themselves, their patients, dramatic "cases" they have treated or witnessed. The ethnography included multiple occasions when teaching clinicians made students feel small, or humiliated them in front of their peers. Indeed, there were numerous occasions when consultants in medicine or surgery gave their students a hard time. Some could be abusive, even personally insulting; others could be sarcastic; others could use mimicry. Students would compare notes about how they had been treated by their clinical teachers, how they'd been called "an idiot" or "thick" by an apparently irate clinician. But these were among several different genres of performance that such clinical teachers could engage in. They frequently engaged in flamboyant and self-dramatizing behavior. In other words, "showing up" or (in the American case) "chewing out" students is just one aspect of a whole variety of performances that clinical teachers can enact. They are in turn aspects of a much wider repertoire of pedagogic devices that they deploy in order to render clinical medicine—the "lesson of the hospitals"—visible and memorable. In doing so, some clinicians can construct themselves as equally vivid and memorable. They become "characters."

Equally, the actions and characters of clinicians are a recurrent and significant part of student culture. Culture is not something "out there" that one invokes as an explanation for action. Culture is what is enacted. Student culture is what students talk about—what they treat as memorable, remarkable, tellable (amongst many other things). So students also render their own "experiences" in terms of what can be narrated to other students. Being humiliated by a senior hospital consultant is just such a biographical topic—which is possible because it can become one among a fund of stories and recollections—assisting at one's first operation, putting up one's first drip, solving a particularly difficult diagnostic puzzle, doing something embarrassingly awful at a viva voce examination. In some of these stories the teller (the student or young doctor) is a kind of hero; in many others the story is told at one's own expense.

So we can think about Becker and Geer's "events" in a slightly new light. And it is one that starts to dissolve their unhelpful distinction between events and what is said about those events. When residents or attendings, registrars or consultants, engage with medical students in clinical instruction, there is a repertoire of spoken and unspoken enactments or performances that they engage in. Clinicians perform clinical medicine, and enact clinical medicine. Indeed, it goes beyond that, and becomes more complex. In clinical medicine, patients themselves perform their illness. So clinical instruction is a complicated array of performative acts. In the course of those encounters, the participants—most notably the clinicians—perform their own characters. Likewise, medical students enact themselves as medical students, and construct their own biographical trajectories, through their own performances—through their biographical narratives and dramatic reconstructions.

In Becker and Geer's original formulation, then, their evaluation and denial of the medical students' version is a cardinal error. They fail to recognize that any encounter with a clinical teacher is potentially tellable in accordance with the shared understandings of what constitutes an experience. Being dealt with rationally, reasonably, and undemonstratively by a clinical teacher does not count as a tellable experience—except when used as a contrastive device to highlight the unreasonable behavior of someone else, or to highlight how extreme this particular event was. What Becker and Geer were actually documenting was something about the oral culture of medical schools. That oral culture includes—as we have said—repertoires of performances and narratives on the part of clinicians. It also includes stocks of stories and reminiscences about characters, blunders, successes, and so on. So, a radical distinction between "events" and "accounts" of those events seems (at best) to be more difficult than Becker and Geer's original formulation. Events are far from things that just happen. They are made to happen. They are enacted. They are also comprehensible as "events" because they can be described and narrated. Likewise, the tellings or narratives about events are themselves performances (or social events). They too are enacted.

A reexamination of the original formulation of the problem by Becker and Geer highlights some significant issues and problems. As we have seen, their argument was a very specific one that was extremely plausible. Even within its restricted scope, a strong case for the value of participant observation seemed to have been established. On closer inspection, however, the argument seems less straightforward, and raises some potentially intriguing issues that we shall attempt to address afresh in the final sections of this chapter.

RETHINKING THE RELATIONSHIP(S)

Radical criticisms of the interview can treat naturally occurring social action as primary, and talk about action as but a poor substitute for the observation of action, echoing the original argument by Becker and Geer. From that perspective, we cannot take the interview as a proxy for action. Hence we cannot rely on it for information about what people do, or what they have done, rather only as a mechanism for eliciting what people say they do. From this perspective, the interview inhabits a quite different universe from the observation of social action. One can readily move to the position that grants primacy to the recording of naturally occurring social interaction, and relegates virtually everything else to the periphery of sociological interest. This particular view is sometimes accompanied by appeals for primary reliance on the analysis of permanent recordings of spoken activity, such as conversation analysis (Atkinson and Heritage 1984; Boden and Zimmerman 1991; Sacks 1992).

This is one possible position, but is perhaps an unnecessary and unhelpful one. It is unduly insensitive to the variety of social action. It is also in danger of endorsing a particular kind of naturalism; the endorsement of one sort of action or activity over another implicitly attributes authenticity to one, while denying it to others. It runs the risk of assuming that some sorts of actions are "natural" while others are "contrived" (Hammersley and Atkinson 1995; Silverman 1985 and 1993). A more productive way of thinking about these relationships is to start from a more symmetrical perspective, rather than trying to privilege one source, or method, over another. This approach is, in one respect at least, more in keeping with contemporary epistemology. It is also antipathetic to the excesses of some recent enthusiasms that have rejected the study of action in situ in favor of an almost exclusive focus on interviews, narratives, and accounts (see Atkinson and Silverman 1997). We can fruitfully begin to think of what we observe (and the work of observing) and the contents of interviews (and the work of interviewing) as incorporating social actions of different kinds, and yielding data of different forms. We can thus be released from trying to combine them to produce information from them about something else, in order to concentrate more on the performance of the social actions themselves.

Indeed, we know enough about the performance of everyday social action to be thoroughly suspicious of methodological formulations that even appear to attach particular kinds of authenticity to it. All of Goffman's work, for instance, is—with varying degrees of explicitness—concerned with rendering problematic such a naïve view. Erving Goffman's entire sociological output explores the conditions under which social actors accomplish social encounters and enact social selves (see Burns 1992; Ditton 1980; Drew and Wootton 1988; Manning 1992; Smith 1999). His most famous early work on "the presentation of self" (Goffman 1959) established his dramaturgical perspective on everyday life. Goffman describes an ideal–typical social actor who is constantly giving off messages and creating a personal front. Goffman provided vividly recognizable descriptions of how our self-awareness or self-consciousness leads us to try to maintain our "face," while our attentiveness to the rituals of tact help us to maintain the "face" of others. Our selves are, therefore, carefully managed, and are collaborative undertakings. The social self is fragile, or as Goffman put it "ritually delicate": it can be threatened or undermined by the adverse judgments or reactions of others (Goffman 1963a and 1963b). Goffman's prototypical social actor is inescapably (if not always consciously) engaged in the production of social selves. Moreover, the self is contextual—far from being an essential property of the individual, it is a product of social encounters and social situations (Goffman 1961a and 1971). Goffman's work is a stark reminder that we search in vain for a private self anterior to the social processes, and conventions that render the very idea of a self possible in the first place. Admittedly, some of Goffman's key insights might seem to suggest the contrary. His famous essay on role distance, for example, seems to imply a dichotomy, not a continuity, between an ironic distance and a wholehearted commitment (Goffman 1961b). Likewise, some accounts that are thoroughly or partially indebted to Goffman, such as Hochschild's *The Managed Heart* (1983)—an account of the self-conscious management of emotional work among workers like airline flight attendants—seem to imply a contrast between authentic and insincere social actions. Hochschild distances herself from Goffman's vision of the social self. Her analysis depends on the presence of a deep self that preexists and authors authentic and inauthentic performances. But if we take full and serious account of the performativity of social life (the dramaturgical metaphor) then it clearly makes no more sense to assume any action as inherently authentic, and thus to grant it priority. We need to remain theoretically and methodologically vigilant in order to avoid slipping into the ready assumption that we are studying private experience rather than socially shared actions and resources.

Part of the reported comparison between participant observation and interviewing has revolved around the ironic contrast between what people do and what people say that they do. This has also fed into the equally hoary question posed to and by field researchers: "How do you know if your informant is telling the truth?" (see chapter 5). These related problems equally reflect the position we have characterized as naïve: the contrasts between actions and accounts, and between truth and dissimulation. This approach to interviewing as action can be illustrated with reference to the topic of memory. One way of thinking about interviews and the data they yield is to think about informants producing descriptions of past events. In part, therefore, the interview is aimed at the elicitation of memories. Viewed from a naïve perspective, it also follows that one of the main problems of this kind of data collection concerns the accuracy or reliability of such recollections. Such a perspective certainly presents pressing problems if—to return to the preoccupations of Becker and Geer—one is using the interview to gather information about "events." The same is true of the elicitation of "experiences." It is possible to view the interview as a means for the retrieval of informants' personal experiences—a biographically grounded view of memories and past events.

The analytic problems of memory and experience are equivalent from our point of view. It is possible to address memory and experience sociologically, and it is possible to address them through the interview (and through other "documents of life"). But it is appropriate to do so only if one accepts that memory and experience are social actions in themselves. They are both enacted. Seen from this perspective, memory is not (simply) a matter of individual psychology, and is certainly not only a function of internal mental states. Equally, it is not a private issue. (We are not denying the existence of psychological processes in general, nor the personal qualities and significance of our memories—ours is a methodological argument about the appropriate way of conducting and conceptualizing social research.) Memory is a cultural phenomenon, and is therefore a collective one. What is "memorable" is a function of the cultural categories that shape what is thinkable and what is not, what is counted as appropriate, what is valued, what is noteworthy and so on. Memory is far from uniquely (auto)biographical. It can reside in material culture; for instance, the deliberate collection or hoarding of memorabilia and souvenirs—photographs, tourist artifacts, family treasures or other bric-a-brac—is one enactment of memory. Equally, memory is grounded in what is tellable. In many ways the past is a narrative enactment.

At this point we return to the original formulation offered by Becker and Geer. They refer to the study of "events," arguing that observation provided access to events in a way that interviews cannot. In one sense, that is self-evidently true. We can observe, and we can make permanent recordings of events. On the other hand, we need to ask ourselves what constitutes an "event." Clearly an event is not merely a string of unrelated moments of behavior, nor is it devoid of significance. In order to be observable and reportable, events in themselves must have some degree of coherence and internal structure. An "event" in the social world is not something that happens: it is made to happen. It has a beginning, a middle, and an end. It is differentiated from the surrounding stream of activity. Its structure and the observer's capacity to recognize it are essentially narrative in form. In that sense, therefore, a radical distinction between "events" that are observed and "accounts" that are narrated starts to become less stark, and the boundary maintenance more difficult to sustain.

Does this mean that we still acknowledge the primacy of particular kinds of social actions? Not necessarily. By acknowledging that accounts, recollections, and experiences are enacted, we can start to avoid the strict dualism between "what people do" and "what people say." This is a recurrent topic in the methodological discourse of social science. It rests on the commonplace assumption that there may be differences or discrepancies between observed actions and accounts about action. (This may be proposed as a rather vulgar counterargument against simplistic articulations of "triangulation.") They are different kinds of enactments, certainly, but we would argue that the specific dualism that implicitly asserts an authenticity for what people (observably) do and the fallibility of accounts of action is both unhelpful and "untrue." By treating both the observed and the narrated as kinds of social action we move beyond such simple articulations, and instead reassert a methodological principle of symmetry.

We therefore bracket the assumption of authenticity, or the "natural" character of "naturally occurring" action, and the contrasts that are founded on that implicit dualism. If we recognize that memories, experiences, motives, and so on are themselves forms of action, and equally recognize that they and other mundane routine activities are enacted, then we can indeed begin to deal with these issues in a symmetrical, but nonreductionist way. In other words, it is not necessary to assert the primacy of one form of data over another, nor to assert the primacy of one form of action over another. Equally, a recognition of the performative action of interview talk removes the temptation to deal with such data as if they gave us access to personal or private "experiences." We need, therefore, to divorce the use of the interview from the myth of inferiority—the essentially romantic view of the social actor as a repository of "inner" feelings and intensely personal recollections. Rather interviews become equally valid ways of capturing shared cultural understandings and enactments of the social world.

We have thus far said very little about the positions of the researcher within these different kinds of research "event." One of the distinctions between participant observation and interviewing has pivoted on the relationship of the researcher to the field of study. In the case of observational work the claims have been made that this enables the researcher to participate first hand in the happenings of the setting, countered of course by warnings of the researcher affecting (contaminating) the setting, or becoming too much of a participant, and thereby losing the capacity to critically observe (see the introduction and chapter 1). In contrast, the interview has been perceived as an artificial enactment, with unequal relations but potentially less contamination, and more recently as a site for collaboration and the genuine sharing of experiences.

Here we would wish to stress again the symmetry of the two broad approaches. This does not necessary imply complementarity nor sameness, but recognizes the complexity of research experiences and relationships. Through both participant observation and interviewing there is the potential for "contamination," although as we have already argued, this is a paralyzing and unhelpful way of characterizing the research process (and can actually render all research inadequate). Rather, through active reflexivity we should recognize that we are part of the social events and processes we observe and help to narrate. Myerhoff's study of elderly Jews in Los Angeles is a classic example illustrating the importance of such reflexivity (Myerhoff 1978). It is noticeable that Myerhoff's interview-based study is very different from the types of research interview detailed by Becker, Geer, and Trow. Myerhoff was not collecting data on "events." Rather, she was seeking to capture the dying world of a generation of elderly Jews and convey it through an interpretation of their talk. Kaminsky (1992), in his editorial introduction to Myerhoff's posthumous papers (Myerhoff 1992), stresses her insistence on interpreting the words of the informants. She used the idea of a "third voice," which she explained as "neither the voice of the informant nor the voice of the interviewer, but the voice of their collaboration" (Kaminsky 1992: 7).

To overemphasize our potential to change things artificially swells our own importance. To deny our being "there" misunderstands the inherent qualities of both methods—in terms of documenting and making sense of social worlds of which we are a part (either through participant observation, or the facilitator of shared accounts and narrative strategies). It is also worth noting the (auto)biographical work which is common to both approaches. Again, in digressing from Becker and Geer's assertion of the primary goal of describing events, we should recognize that the process of undertaking research is suffused with biographical and identity work (Coffey 1999). The complex relationships between field settings, significant social actors, the practical accomplishment of the research and the researcher–self are increasingly recognized as significant to all those who engage in research of a qualitative nature (whether that be participant observation, interviewing, some combination of the two, or other forms of data collection).

We began this chapter with a retrospective evaluation of Becker and Geer's original observations concerning the respective merits and weaknesses of participant observation and interviewing. We did so for two reasons. First, it is a locus classicus in the corpus of methodological writing in qualitative sociology. Secondly, it helps us to identify a particular constellation of assumptions concerning observation and interviewing characteristic of that period in which many aspects of qualitative fieldwork were being codified. We repeat our acknowledgment that this generation of scholars was responsible for the demystification of qualitative methods, providing practical advice manuals for the research community as well as acting as methodological advocates. Their contribution should not be underestimated, and it was never our intention to do so. However, we have reached a point that suggests a position very different from that articulated by Becker and Geer. This difference reflects a good deal of methodological change and development over the intervening years, not least in the burgeoning of qualitative methods texts and the increased acceptance and innovative use of the whole variety of qualitative research strategies.

By the same token, actions or events, even observed firsthand, are not inherently endowed with meaning, nor is their meaning unequivocally available for inspection. The kinds of "events" that Becker and Geer discussed are recognized as such precisely because they are describable and narratable by participants and by onlookers, including ethnographers or other observers. After all, the "data" of participant observation are the events as narrated (written down, often retrospectively) by observers, and hence rely on the same culturally shared categories of memory, account, narrative, and experience. In retrospect it seems odd that Becker and Geer felt able to legislate for "what really happened" and to discount the tellings of medical students. From our point of view, they could have paid much more attention to several things. For example: how the "events" were performed; how the medical students narrated and evaluated them; how certain events or classes of events were endowed with significance through the medical students' own tellings; how they themselves, as observers, recorded and described the "events." They might thus have found themselves dealing with classes of performance and rhetoric, in different contexts, in different modes, rather than incommensurable kinds of phenomena. And once articulated in this way, their particular distinction between participant observation and interviewing, and primacy of the former becomes untenable. This does not deny the different qualities of these as data-collection strategies. Rather in emphasizing their commonalities in terms of social action and performance (and extinguishing the false dichotomy), we may actually be in a better, and certainly a more informed, position to "choose."

A RETURN TO PARTICIPATION

We have suggested that the terms of long-standing comparisons between participant observation and interviewing were unnecessary. A sensible attitude toward the sociological analysis of action dissolves some of the differences and boundaries between the two. This does not, however, imply that Becker and Geer's original formulation was completely irrelevant. In this concluding section of the chapter we turn to a rather different—and contemporary—sense in which the proper relationship between participant observation and interviewing demands consideration.

It is arguable that in some quarters the original position articulated by Becker and Geer has become reversed. Where once they proclaimed participant observation as the yardstick for researchers to understand events, many contemporary researchers have all but lost sight of participant observation. Interviews, focus groups, the analysis of texts—these often seem more attractive and more prominent in the contemporary array of research methods and in the published research literature.

There has never been such an emphasis on the conduct of interviews as there is now. Indeed, it is noticeable that the terrain of research methods has become dominated by qualitative interviewing in various guises. While it is not readily documented in explicit methodological advice, in the practical conduct of research in many of the main substantive areas, "qualitative research" seems often to be equated with interviewing. As Silverman (1997) and Atkinson and Silverman (1997) have argued, social science interviewing has become implicated in the "interview society." They argue that the biographical interview and the resulting character-work it gives rise to have become a pervasive technique through which selves and identities are constructed in contemporary society. There are multiple sites at which these technologies of the self are deployed. Celebrity is enacted through the multiple performance of interviews; they are the stuff of print and broadcast media. Likewise, the same media create interview–identities from the extraordinary experiences of ordinary people. There are various prominent genres that are dependent on the methods of the interview society. They include various kinds of "chat shows" in which a predictable array of public figures are constructed for a mass audience through equally predictable repertoires of questioning. These exercises in interviewing are often part of the round of managed publicity surrounding a new film or a new book. The interviewers themselves—the "hosts"—can also become celebrities in their own right. The encounter between chat-show host and guest thus becomes a collaborative act of mutual identity construction. Through these discursive acts, the participants can create public selves, characters, moral categories, and varieties of experience. There is a public discourse of the private self. Or, to put it another way, the interior world of private experience is a public construct.

This general perspective has been discussed most recently by Gubrium and Holstein (2002) in the course of a major and sustained review of contemporary interview-based research. They point out that the interview pervasively mediates contemporary social life. They, too, note the significance of an interview culture in the sphere of mass media and entertainment. They also point out that "chat" is now the medium of expression through the Internet, so that the sharing of biographical information—if not always in the format of the interview—is possible on a global scale. Gubrium and Holstein also suggest that the interview has become increasingly significant in professional practice. The people-oriented professions—such as medicine, psychotherapy, or social work—deploy the discursive resources of the interview in order to transmute clients' interests or problems into "stories." The interview in such institutional domains is a device for the translation of personal narratives into professional cases (Mishler 1984).

The interview society thus involves the circulation of biographical information, derived from popular and professional sources. These are in turn aspects of a cultural system whereby social actors invent and affirm personhood. The interview society and its cultural forms are predicated on the existence of a private self, and an interior life of personal experience. These are not naturally given entities and processes. The technologies of the self reflexively construct the nature of the selves and experiences that are to be uncovered and explored. As Rose (1990 and 1997) has demonstrated, the "private" selves that are the topics of revelatory investigation are themselves the products of modern technologies of the self. In that sense, therefore, the social sciences must recognize themselves and their own work. They, too, are among the disciplines that construct actors' selves and experiences. They are not simply "there" to be revealed through the investigative technique of the interview: they are created through the shared discourse of the interview and similar kinds of encounter.

The implication of contemporary social science in the interview culture has meant a noticeable reliance on interviews as a preferred method of data collection. In some quarters at least "qualitative research" is in practice equated with interview-based research. This has in turn led to a heavy reliance on biographical and experiential kinds of information being treated as data. If we return to our starting point in this chapter, then there seems to have been a material and substantial shift in qualitative research over recent generations. At the time when Becker and Geer were writing, it was certainly not remarkable to assume that there was a distinct approach to "field research." While Becker and Geer might have felt that the merits of participant observation might need affirmation, the research that they themselves and their Chicago colleagues promoted and carried out was firmly rooted in a tradition that treated participant observation seriously. Whether or not one regarded participant observation as the "gold standard" in understanding, there was a clear understanding that participant observation was central to the overall project of field research—what is more commonly termed ethnography in contemporary parlance (Atkinson et al. 2001). Given the preponderance of interview research, it is perhaps necessary to reaffirm the value of participant observation.

We have argued that the simple distinction between participant observation and interviewing, paralleling a duality between deeds and words, between what people do and what people say they do, is not productive. It makes spurious distinctions between different kinds of social action. This is, however, no reason to overlook the value of participant observation. It is certainly no reason to emphasize interview-based research at the expense of other kinds of social inquiry. Moreover, we must not forget that Becker and Geer's classic statement assumed that "interviews" would be conducted in the course of field research, and not that interviews would be conducted in a social vacuum, and in the absence of participation and observation.

The real issues here reside in the fact that participant observation is not merely a data collection technique. Perhaps research interviewing is not either, but it seems to have a rather more restricted scope. The role of participant observation is not merely to gather "data" about observed actions. We need to broaden our shared commitments when it comes to social research. We need to reaffirm that participation and observation mean much more than simply seeing what is done, as if sociologists and anthropologists need only concern themselves with a behaviorist emphasis on observable conduct. We are committed to much more than that. We are persuaded that the proper understanding of social life is derived from the interpretation of social action. That is: the interpretation of meaningful and intentional social action; an understanding of the social organization of concerted social activity; an analysis of the local realization of generic social processes. These commitments are fundamental to the interpretative social sciences, whether they be labelled as anthropology, or sociology, or associated with a substantive domain of social life, such as education or health.

From this point of view, therefore, we take exception to versions of social research which imply that its primary subject matter is a mixture of actors' experience, and an understanding of the social actor's "point of view." This is a dilution and distortion of the ethnographic enterprise. It ignores the significance of the collective and the truly social, by rendering social life primarily in terms of individual actors' perceptions and personal experiences. We need, therefore, to remind ourselves that the stuff of social research includes social encounters and collective performances (whether they be practical, aesthetic, or ritual in nature). We need to affirm some of the assumptions that underpinned classic formulations of research method: that self and society are both aspects of the same social processes, as are mind, memory, and experience. (We elaborate on some of these specific observations in the next chapter.)

Moreover, the ethnographic imagination implies a commitment to understanding the forms of life that constitute a social and cultural world. This does not have to imply a romantic and subjective surrender to exotic and new social worlds. But it does imply a commitment to the complexity of the forms of social life, its detail and the slowness of its unfolding. This was exemplified by, for example, Suttles (1968) on the social order that actually exists in the apparently chaotic slum, or Lofland (1973/1985) on the interaction order of apparently random behavior in public spaces, or Heyl's theorized analysis of the moral career of the madam (Heyl 1979), or Fine's fine-grained account of life and work in restaurant kitchens (Fine 1996). It is not captured in one-off personal accounts and recollections. Such a commitment involves a proper understanding of the sort of analyses that Geertz glossed in terms of "thick description" (Geertz 1973). This is a dreadfully misunderstood and misrepresented term—indeed it might have merited a chapter-length discussion elsewhere in this book. What it clearly does not mean is a sociological or anthropological account that simply has a lot of "detail," or that is "richly illustrated" with vignettes and illustrative material. Rather, it means a disciplined appreciation of the over-determination of cultural phenomena and of social forms. In other words, social life is densely coded and performed through multiple frames of reference. There are multiple forms through which the social is enacted and accounted for. It is rendered through actions, narratives, texts, visual representations, and material artifacts. These do not cumulate to convey one simple set of cultural "messages," but they constitute multiple semantic domains, multiple arenas of action, and multiple sources of significance. It is the task of the participant observer to make sense of actions that are constructed and interpreted through these multiple forms. It is, moreover, important to understand and to document how social actions are enacted. This requires a commitment to the domains of social action. It requires the temporal commitment that encompasses the unfolding organization of sequence, tempo, and coordination. In terms used by Schutz (1967), it involves "growing old together" with the social actors we want to understand.

Without a commitment to the naturally occurring settings of social action, and without the concomitant commitment to understanding their indigenous forms of organization and representation, then social scientists will not produce the "thick descriptions" of social forms and social processes to which they aspire. They will produce "thin" accounts that do not do justice to the complexities of social organization. We certainly do not need social sciences that rely on interviews and accounts to the virtual exclusion of a more complete ethnographic understanding. Participant observation is significant not just because the researcher can "see" things happen. It rests on something much more fundamental: it is possible by virtue of the human and social capacity we have—as ordinary actors—to engage with our fellow men and women, and through practical and symbolic transactions with them to acquire some degree of understanding of them. It rests on the capacity we have, as a basic precondition of everyday life, to take the role of the other, in achieving at least a partial perspective on the social world and on ourselves from the point of view of others. It also rests on our ordinary (but extraordinarily skilled) capacity to learn from the social world about us: to learn languages and other symbolic forms, to acquire abstract knowledge, and to develop practical skills. It also depends on our ability to reflect upon ourselves as objects of knowledge. We are, therefore, able to engage with other actors and in new social settings with reflective self-knowledge. These capacities are ordinary aspects of our everyday competence as social actors. They are equally fundamental to the conduct of social research. Without the capacity and the willingness to commit ourselves to social worlds, and to "participate" in them—albeit to a limited and temporary degree—then we shall never bring to bear those intellectual, symbolic, and emotional competencies to a disciplined understanding of the social world about us.

These observations on ethnographic engagement and the proper attitude toward interviews raise further questions concerning the analysis of interview data. Our observations so far suggest that the accounts gathered from interviewing need to be analyzed from a perspective that emphasizes their functions—the actions that are enacted through them—and hence the discursive forms that are used to achieve those ends. We obviously cannot treat them as proxy data for information about events that are otherwise unobservable, nor can we treat them as transparent windows on informants' personal feelings and memories. This does not imply that phenomena like "emotions" or "memories" remain locked away in an inaccessible and ineffable realm of interior personal experience. On the contrary, it means that from a social science perspective we ought to regard such things as constituted through shared resources. They are rendered visible to ourselves and to others through socially shared and culturally specific resources. Those resources include narrative formats, rhetorical tropes, and vocabularies of motive and sentiment. In the chapter that follows, therefore, we turn to yet another classic problem and use it as a starting point to consider some of the ways in which informants' accounts might usefully be addressed.

CONCLUSIONS

As we have tried to display, a consideration of participant observation and interviewing raises more than purely technical issues about data collection. It raises more fundamental questions about what we are trying to achieve when we undertake field research using qualitative research methods. While we have not endorsed the original formulation of the issues by Becker and Geer, we think that a careful consideration of their arguments, and of the subsequent directions taken by methodologists, is fruitful. We took issue with Becker and Geer over their unduly facile characterization of "events" and the distinction between events and talk about events. On the other hand, we think that too many of our contemporaries and younger scholars turn to the research interview as an easier alternative to the harder work of prolonged immersion in a social world. Even when interview data are not used as surrogate data about "events," they are too readily deployed as information about social members' "experiences." Indeed, the documentation of experience—the reconstruction of the social world from an actor's point of view—is often promoted as the goal of qualitative sociological or anthropological research. We do not favor that view for two reasons.

First, the emphasis on experience and biographically grounded stories overlooks a more fundamental goal of social research—the analysis of social action. While conventional distinctions between "what people do" and "what people say" are often overdrawn, we should not lose sight of the importance of what people do. The practices of everyday life, the performance of social selves, or the conduct of social encounters will not be documented through the collection of interview data. If we wish to understand the forms of life and the types of social action in a given social setting, then we surely cannot escape the kind of engagement that is implied by participant observation. We might, in addition, need to record the recurrent patterns of social action by other means as well, but we certainly cannot rely solely on data generated by interviews, of whatever sort.

Secondly, we also have to recognize that forms of talk—including narratives and interview accounts—are themselves examples of social action. People do things with words, and they do things with narratives. They use biographical accounts to perform social actions. Through them they construct their own lives and those of others; they justify and legitimate past, current, and future actions; they formulate explanations; they locate their own actions within socially shared frames of reference. Such accounts are certainly not private, and they do not yield accounts of unmediated personal experience. If we collect spoken (and indeed written) accounts of "events" or "experiences," then we need to analyze them in terms of the cultural resources people use to construct them, the kinds of interpersonal or organizational functions they fulfill, and the socially distributed forms that they take.

5

HOW DO YOU KNOW
IF YOUR INFORMANT
IS TELLING THE TRUTH?

BELIEVING INFORMANTS

In the last chapter we revisited the vexed question of the proper relation-ship between participant observation and interviewing. We suggested that some classic formulations of the problem were unhelpful. The problems were partly a result of misplaced assumptions concerning the relationships between "what people do" and "what people say they do." The issues can be resolved in part by thinking about the connotations of "doing" in such a context. We pointed out that *action* has multiple forms, and in addition to observed doings, there are also the spoken actions and performances that include the enactment of "interviews" in research settings, and informants' spoken actions in accounting for and describing what they and others "do" or have done.

In this chapter we develop these arguments further, by revisiting a closely related question. For many years a recurrent question for qualita-tive researchers—irrespective of whether they conducted participant observation—was: how do you know if your informant is telling the truth? Indeed, that was precisely the question posed, as the title, in one of the most widely cited and anthologized of the "classic" papers (Dean and Whyte 1958); it is reprinted in McCall and Simmons (1969), and our page references are to that reprinting. If we take that paper as our starting point, then, we must be careful—as with the other classic questions and debates —not to caricature the positions of an earlier generation. We certainly do not wish to imply that authors in the 1950s and 1960s put forward naïve views on methods and the relationships between them. Indeed, it is a re-current theme in this book that the excesses of contemporary writers are to be avoided as strenuously as the particular shortcomings (of any) of their predecessors. We take this as a point of departure, not as something to demolish gratuitously.

Dean and Whyte noted that doubts concerning the credibility of informants seemed to be a recurrent trouble for social scientists. Interviews are a frequently used means of data collection, and therefore the truthfulness of informants could be seen as a major problem. As Dean and Whyte pointed out as early as 1958, there was a sense in which the question was inappropriately framed in the first place. They pointed out that informants were not simply reporting factual matters, and rather than simply asking "how do I know if the informant is telling the truth?," one should more fruitfully ask what an informant's statements reveal about his or her perspectives, perceptions, or feelings. The question never was, therefore, whether the informant being interviewed could ever be a transparent reporter of some independent domain, and could—even in principle—be a "truthful" witness of a world independent of her or his interpretations of it.

In stressing the inescapably perspectival character of what informants say in an interview, Dean and Whyte were clearly *not* guilty of providing a naïve answer to their own question. They emphasised the extent to which an interview account gives insight and information about an informant's perceptions and emotions. They suggested, indeed, that there are matters that are comprehensible as more or less objective, more or less subjective. Clearly, they argued, reports of informants' feelings and emotions are not susceptible to "objective" criteria, and are bound to be perspectival.

In evaluating informants' statements, we try to distinguish the subjective and objective components. But no matter how objective an informant seems to be, the research point of view is: *The informant's statement represents merely the perception of the informant, filtered and modified by his* [sic] *cognitive and emotional reactions and reported through his personal verbal usages* (Dean and Whyte, 1958: 105–6, emphasis in original).

There is no doubt that the early formulations of this issue give us a useful starting point. Far from being oversimplified, the Dean and Whyte paper suggests a relatively sophisticated approach to the topic, recognizing that any and all accounts are going to reflect the personal interests and perspectives of informants. On the other hand, we can subject their original paper to a more thoroughly critical reading, and use that as a starting point for a more detailed consideration.

Notwithstanding Dean and Whyte's general standpoint, it is clear that their interest lay in *evaluating* informants' accounts. Indeed, the word is used quite explicitly in their paper. They distinguish between subjective and objective matters and discuss them separately. They therefore ask themselves what factors are likely to "influence" an informant's report in the interview. Subjective issues, they suggest, can be influenced by an informant's *motives*. This is treated as a matter of ulterior motive, or self-interest: informants may wish to present themselves in an especially favorable light, for instance. Similar interests may bar spontaneity, leading to guarded responses, especially if they bear on negative or critical issues. In a similar vein, Dean and Whyte suggest that the informant may have a desire to please the interviewer in the attempt to be well thought of. Further, there may be idiosyncratic factors, such as recent personal experience of something being explored in the interview. Dean and Whyte proposed these factors as problems for the analyst: "Unless they are taken into account, these various factors that influence the interview situation may cause serious problems and misinterpretations of the informant's statements" (108). The authors go on to suggest various interview strategies that may be used to minimize the effect of such factors, or to contrast expressed sentiments with observed behavior.

In a similar vein, the authors dealt with threats to the reliability of an informant's account of "objective" topics. They did so because, as they put it: "Frequently the research worker wants to determine from an interview what actually happened on some occasion pertinent to the research" (110). Dean and Whyte argued that the interviewer clearly couldn't take all accounts at face value. And they went on to enumerate possible sources of "distortion" in the interview. They include the possibility that the informant did not actually observe what is reported, or cannot recall what was observed, and therefore reports conjecture. Alternatively, the informant may report a selective memory, despite any effort at accurate recall. Or, the informant may unconsciously modify a report because of defense against emotional aspects. Finally, the informant may deliberately modify the facts in order to create a "distorted impression."

Throughout their discussion, then, Dean and Whyte are interested in evaluating informants' reports and trying to establish the grounds on which distortions and inaccuracies can occur. Their distinction between objective and subjective phenomena, and the analytic problems they enumerate, demonstrate that they retained a commitment to remedying the "distortions" and other "filters" that intervene between events or experiences and informants' verbal accounts of them. It is, therefore, no great surprise that they recommended procedures to detect distortion and correct for it. For instance: "the major way in which we detect distortion, and correct for it, is by *comparing an informant's account with the accounts given by other informants*" (111). They explicitly compare this strategy with the forensic treatment of competing accounts from witnesses in the courtroom.

More recent empirical and methodological approaches to interviewing have diverted from those earlier perspectives. The forensic approach to the reliability of accounts has given way to a more complex and multiple array of analytic strategies. Significantly, most of those approaches have abandoned the possibility of any correspondence between informants' accounts and the reported events or phenomena themselves. (Indeed we shall suggest later that some contemporary accounts have inadvertently introduced a new version of correspondence.) In general terms, most of the recent methodological accounts have stressed various kinds of perspectival analytic strategies. That is, they have stressed the importance of understanding accounts to embody and reflect informants' own definitions, reflecting their particular social positions and interests. Informants' accounts have been examined from essentially biographical perspectives. In recent years, the research interest in interviewing has been given a renewed lease on life by a major renewal of life history research, the collection of biographical and autobiographical narratives, and the reporting of various kinds of "documents of life" (Plummer 2001).

CREDIBILITY AND PLAUSIBILITY

If we accept that "truth"—in the conventional sense—is not the right topic to begin with, does that mean that we are left with nothing but personal accounts, from informants in interviews or from elsewhere, that are incommensurate, and that are not really susceptible to further systematic analysis? Are we committed only to the collection of accounts that have no referential value, and that will only illuminate the private experiences of their tellers? We argue that these are not the logical outcomes. They are certainly not the desirable outcomes. If we accept that informants are not providing us with proxy evidence about events and actions, that they are not in that sense objective accounts of the "truth," then we would do well to start by asking more sensitive questions about truth and objectivity. Having done so, we can then go on to ask similar questions about aspects such as experience and subjectivity. We would wish to argue that they can all be treated in a similar fashion—being analytic problems or topics, and not interpretative resources that can be brought to bear unproblematically. We begin our discussions with a discussion of "truth."

It is surely a far more productive research question to ask ourselves, not "how do I know she or he is telling the truth?," but rather, "how does he or she try to persuade me of the truthfulness of this?" If the perfect "truth" of an account is ultimately unknowable, there being no neutral gold standard against which accounts can be evaluated, there is greater analytic advantage to be gained from examining the kinds of plausibility and credibility devices that an informant uses. Such issues are undoubtedly susceptible to systematic and empirical investigation. Indeed, there are plenty of examples of analytic work to draw on here in addressing the plausibility and credibility of accounts—examining their discourse structure rather than comparing them with the external world. It must be emphasized that we are not dealing here with the "plausibility" of accounts merely in terms of whether they seem plausible to us as interviewers or as analysts. That would be to conflate once more the subjective and the analytic—by examining our own credulity rather than inspecting the properties of accounts for their mechanisms of producing recognizable descriptions, credible characterizations, plausible motives, defensible justifications, and so on. Far from being just matters of personal experience and subjective interpretation, these are managed by means of socially shared resources of language and common stocks of everyday competence. They can be analyzed as matters of language and culture. We do not need, therefore, to treat the interview as a biographically unique event, concerned with private meanings and unique biographies. We can approach it with clear analytic intent, and with genuinely sociological or anthropological commitments.

We can, for example, inspect informants' accounts for their *evidential* contents and structures. Whenever we find ourselves with a tricky, even insurmountable, problem (such as "is the informant telling the truth?") it is worth performing a particular kind of transformation of the topic. If it is a major problem for the analyst to determine such matters, then maybe we could more fruitfully ask ourselves if it is an equivalent problem for social actors. If we cannot unequivocally decide if an informant is telling the truth, then maybe credibility and plausibility are matters that any and every "informant" and hearer need to pay attention to. If the truth or otherwise of an account is at issue, then we must have ways of inspecting accounts in order to judge (however tacitly) how much credence to put on them. Moreover, it is not the case that all "informants"—whether in the course of social research or in everyday social interaction—produce unvarnished or unmarked factual accounts that hearers and analysts simply have to evaluate in the absence of relevant discourse features. On the contrary, there are culturally shared resources in accordance with which informants construct accounts with more or less faith in their credibility, and which hearers can also draw upon in order to evaluate them.

There are, for instance, perfectly well-documented analytic issues concerned with *evidentiality*. This is a term applied by some linguists and discourse analysts to describe devices—lexical and others—that are used to convey the degree of belief that a speaker has in the factual or truthful nature of what is being reported. This is not in itself a matter of "truthfulness" in contrast to deception and dissimulation. Rather it refers to the faith or certainty expressed by the speaker (see Chafe and Nichols 1986 for a series of papers discussing the linguistic marking of evidentiality). Speakers can use a variety of language devices to demonstrate the degree of credence they attach to particular information—either imparted by them or reportedly imparted to them. They can employ devices such as those of "hedging" to accomplish uncertainty or tentativeness in expressing an opinion. Equally, they can proffer "factual" accounts that are unmarked, and are provided as straightforward accounts of what is reported. Equally, factual accounts can be framed with discourse markers that convey their reliability as eyewitness statement, with local color and detail that furnish internal narrative evidence as to their validity. From this discursive point of view, therefore, the credibility of an account is something that is accomplished through shared discursive methods. They are, therefore, susceptible to systematic analysis *independently of a gold standard of truth.*

Of course, evidentiality is not the whole story. For when we ask if the informant is telling the truth, and even when we turn the question into the plausibility of informants' accounts, we are interested in more than the degree of certainty he or she expresses. We are also interested in the structures of plausibility that form part of the structure of the informant's accounts. Plausibility here must refer to a number of features. They necessarily draw on the culturally shared resources that establish issues of motive and causation. We can, again, turn to well-established—classic—modes of analysis to address some of these phenomena. For example, we can do no better than to return to C. Wright Mills's characterization of "motive" as a sociological topic (Mills 1940). Over fifty years ago, Mills proposed a view of motive that was quite remarkably prescient. It foreshadowed modes of discursive analysis that are only now being fleshed out by analysts of language, including the recently emergent specialism of discursive psychology. Mills proposed what was a thoroughly socialized view of "motive," in a manner that was a direct and worthy successor of founding classics of sociology—such as Durkheim's attempts to demonstrate the essentially social character of many phenomena that might otherwise be regarded commonsensically as "mental" matters of individual psychology. In seizing on the topic of motive, Mills was tackling just such a theme, apparently a problem for social psychology, but demonstrably susceptible to a sociological or anthropological analysis. Mills suggested that motives were best approached as shared resources rather than internal mental states or dispositions. He gave us the idea of "vocabularies of motive" to capture this mode of analysis. He suggested that motivation is a linguistic resource that speakers and hearers draw on in interpreting descriptions and explanation of social action. In proposing an account of doings and events, a speaker is constrained to locate such an action within a shared frame of reference. Action only "makes sense" insofar as behavior is related to a comprehensible frame of relevance. Any event or act can be accounted for by reference to a number of alternative social codes, domains, and intentions. An act can be accounted for simultaneously by reference to religious motivation, economic interest, political ideals, or personal ambition, for instance.

The construction of motives through situated vocabularies and the invocation of frames of relevance are not the only way of understanding some of these issues. A classic study by Margaret Voysey provides a complementary perspective. She demonstrates how informants can enact the interview encounter in order to create "normal appearances" (Voysey 1975). Her informants were a series of mothers who had a disabled child. Voysey points out that most research up to that point had started from the a priori assumption that families with a disabled child necessarily experienced "problems" of family living. Consequently family members' accounts of their everyday lives were expected to provide evidence for such problematic experience, or to deny them through processes of "normalization" (akin to the processes of "deviance disavowal" reported by criminologists and deviance researchers). Voysey's informants' accounts and her treatment of them suggest a subtly but significantly different analytic perspective. Voysey emphasizes that in their autobiographical accounts, the mothers were constructing normal families and normal parenthood. They did not experience a "real" problem and then "deny" or "normalize" it. Rather, their biographical work constructed normality as an achievement in its own right. Consequently, the distinction between real underlying problems and the possibility of them being acknowledged or denied becomes an inappropriate one. The interview becomes one site in which the moral agency of mothers is enacted—as competent and good parents.

When social scientists implicitly or explicitly ask themselves "is the informant telling the truth," it is clear (although largely unacknowledged) that they evaluate vocabularies of motive for what counts as an acceptable account. It is abundantly clear that—whether we like it or not—there are hierarchies of credibility. We do not seem to like any or all vocabularies equally. We are always in danger of accepting some kinds of accounts as sociologically well formed while implicitly rejecting others as being

incompatible with social science. We say this not to endorse it, but in order to alert us to a range of analytic possibilities.

This issue can be illustrated by Robin Bunton's research on trainee
psychiatrists (Bunton 1986). Bunton spent a protracted period of time undertaking participant observation with young doctors who were undergoing specialized postgraduate training, rotating through various training posts
in different kinds of psychiatric practice. The trainees were, therefore, exposed to a variety of psychiatric therapeutic ideologies and practices. In addition to participating with them on their various rotations, Bunton also
conducted interviews with the trainees. In itself, the act of interviewing psychiatrists was not wholly straightforward. They tended to regard themselves
as the professional interviewers, and consequently repeatedly evaluated
Bunton's own performance. Moreover, they implicitly assumed that the purpose of the interviewing was to discover and discuss "personal problems."
Among other topics, Bunton explored with them their motives for entering the specialty of psychiatry. Psychiatrists are among a wide range of types
of actor who have expertise about their own work and conditions. All actors are, of course, knowledgeable about all sorts of things, but they do not
all have explicitly theorized ways of providing psychological or sociological
explanations of themselves. Psychiatrists do. Motives and intentions are
among their stock-in-trade. The same would be true of a range of professional experts in the management of human affairs—psychologists, counsel-
lors, social workers, and human resource managers among them. They are
among those "new middle class" professionals who are responsible for the
cultural manipulation of our individual and shared self-understanding.

So, when you ask a psychiatrist why she or he entered that particular specialty, you are likely to evoke a range of different kinds of response.
They may well include explanations that are couched in terms of a set of
psychological or psychiatric categories. Indeed, when asked to account
for their own motivation, Bunton's psychiatrists sometimes did so in
terms of psychodynamic explanations, and "analyzed" their own motives
in terms of psychological needs and dispositions. As Bunton himself puts
it:

> When, for instance, I asked if trainees "identified" with anyone, they
> spoke of identity and identity formation as distinct psychological con-
> cepts. Though my question was intended to elicit which types of work
> they had preferences for, I received a response which told me about their
> projected identity. In a similar manner, "type of person" became "per-
> sonality type." Or again, my notion of problems, by which I meant

something of a practical nature, was received often as meaning some kind
of psychological or personality problem. (Bunton 1986: 122)

Likewise, when accounting for career choices, the young psychiatrists included accounts based on personality types as being especially predisposed
to psychiatric work.

Our point is that when given an answer like "In order to cope with
my own unresolved Oedipus complex" or "Because I'm a rather manipu-
lative personality type," the average social scientist is quite likely to have a
bit of a problem. On the whole, these kinds of explanation do not form
part of our own analytic frames of reference. We do not construct our own
explanations in terms of such psychological predispositions. We shy away
from anything that smacks of psychoanalyzing our informants, or claiming
to identify personality types, or identifying character weaknesses. So when
a psychiatrist gives a psychiatric self-analysis in response to a motivational
question, there is a very ready temptation to dismiss such a response as unhelpful or unacceptable. This does not have to be a conscious decision. Analysts do not consciously set about pre-judging what is going to "count"
as an adequate response. But some kinds of accounts seem to fit analysts'
frames of disciplinary reference better than others. To take the case of the
psychiatrists once more, there are many sociological analyses for which a
preferred kind of motivational account would be about, say, women's preference for specialties that could be combined with family-building; or
going into subspecialties where there is a shortage of recruits and it would
be easier to get a job (as would have been true for a specialization like
psycho-geriatrics); or accounts based on a life-changing event or person,
such as a charismatic teacher and role-model. These seem to fit the bill better than self-descriptions in terms of the informant's own neuroses.

The argument here is not a negative criticism of Bunton (who was
well aware of the analytic issue himself), or to criticize other sociologists
who may have reproduced the motivational accounts of psychiatrists or
other professionals. The point is to raise the question: Do we accept any and
every such account as equally valid? Or do we not secretly think that sometimes we have hit upon a personal account that seems more or less "authentic." We find it easier, perhaps, to accept and deal with accounts that are
in tune with the sort of analytic categories we are already familiar with. Professionals are, as it were, allowed to be motivated by career contingencies,
rewards, and mentors.

It certainly is not our concern to admit only accounts that we judge
to be sane or even reasonable. If it were permissible so to do, then accounts

of religious phenomena or of what we categorize as supernatural experiences (such as witchcraft and magic) would be problematic. In the last analysis they might rest on the religiosity or credulity of the individual analyst. It is, of course, not easy to demonstrate this in a positive fashion. Few contexts offer us the same contrasts as did Bunton's work with psychiatrists. When we do encounter overtly strange or unusual vocabularies of motive and cultural frames of reference, it is easier if we can treat them as anthropologically strange. We can then accept that our informants "genuinely" believe them, while separating them off from our anthropological explanations. In fact, social and cultural anthropology are replete with indigenous frameworks in which informants' accounts are granted rationality, without necessarily being treated as "true" motivational accounts—so that other explanatory frameworks are sought that are less true to the indigenous viewpoint, but are more faithful to our accepted modes of analytic thought. This is manifestly so when we are dealing with belief systems that are different from those of the cosmopolitan European-American observer.

Think, for instance, of the classic study—often used to exemplify the ethical and analytic complexities of covert participant observation—by Festinger and his collaborators, reported in the monograph *When Prophecy Fails* (Festinger, Riecken, and Schachter 1956). It will be recalled that the social scientists infiltrated a group of people who believed that they were in receipt of messages from extraterrestrial intelligence, and were receiving warnings about impending doom. They had many attributes of the ideal-typical doomsday cult, believing that they would be saved, and taken up from the earth's surface in time to escape the coming cataclysm. When the predicted disaster did not occur, the group did not abandon their beliefs as having been demonstrably falsified. They redoubled their efforts to get the messages correct, and to hold the group together. Hence the analysts used the study to exemplify the topic of cognitive dissonance, illustrating how strenuously actors may strive to bring incongruent beliefs and perceptions in line with other experiences. It is clear, and manifest from the textual devices used by Festinger and his co-authors, if from nothing else (cf. Atkinson 1990), that of the available motivational accounts available from the group members (admittedly they were not "informants" in the conventional sense, since the research was covert) Festinger and his team did not regard the descriptions of the voices and the extraterrestrial messages as true in any literal sense. Equally, they clearly preferred, as a "better" motivational account, not the urgency imposed by the impending terrestrial disaster, but the "cognitive dissonance" experienced by the group members after the world did not come to an end on the predicted day. So if we ask ourselves whether informants could ever be telling us the "truth" that we would be prepared to "believe," we soon find ourselves amongst rather difficult interpretive questions.

Today we could certainly ask much the same sort of questions—and with just the same problems—of informants who reported abduction by aliens. There are now very many documented first-person accounts of such abductions, freely given by adults who give vivid descriptions and concrete details about their own abduction, the extraterrestrial beings who took them, the craft in which they travelled, and (from many of them) details of the scientific investigations they were subjected to. These are not accounts like Dean and Whyte's most "subjective" kinds. Certainly, there is a strong evaluative element in them: one could hardly report such dramatic and alarming events without a strong element of emotion and without the account being strongly colored by one's own personal experience. Equally, however, these are undoubtedly *factual* accounts. It is entirely characteristic of abduction experiences that informants report them *not* as incomprehensible or hallucinatory experiences, but as (to repeat Dean and Whyte) "objective" matters of report. The experiences are narrated as matters of fact, with concrete detail, firmly rooted in time, place, and circumstance. Autobiographical accounts of abduction may be marked to suggest that "this may be hard to credit," but they are also evidentially marked to assure the reader that they are accounts of the plain facts of the case (see for example Smith 2001; Hough and Kalman 1992). The same is true of other autobiographical accounts of apparently extraordinary phenomena, such as encounters with angels (Sutherland 2001). The analysis cannot start from the assumption that such accounts are inherently unbelievable, however they may be at odds with our own mundane experiences. We do not proceed fruitfully if we assume the authority and the means to legislate between accounts. We are not, after all, placing ourselves in a position to adjudicate as to the legitimacy of one or other view of the world. We need to maintain sufficient cultural relativism to enable us to approach these matters as analytic topics rather than as issues that demand our implicit evaluation.

In many analytic contexts, indeed, we certainly cannot appeal to apparently self-evident criteria from our own everyday experience. There are indeed many types of accounts that escape such ready categorization. It is precisely their contested nature that may give rise to their anthropological or sociological interest. In the recent history of Western societies, for instance, there have been several genres of personal account, the status of which have been treated as highly contentious. They include accounts relating to "recovered memory syndrome." These involve adults' previously suppressed memories of sexual abuse in childhood that may be invoked to account for emotional problems in adult life. These personal accounts are in turn adduced as evidence for the prevalence of child abuse. They can be used as evidence in complaints against parents or other individuals on the part of the abused individuals. Similar remarks can be made concerning stories of satanic ritual abuse. There are many personal accounts that provide plausible narratives from the victims of such accounts (LaFontaine 1998). Like recovered memory accounts, these can furnish highly emotional, but factual narratives. It is noteworthy that one cannot describe these accounts in a way that does not implicitly deny or affirm their factual status. In these brief references, we have left the descriptions unmarked—and so presented them as "factual," if contested. Any other description marks them as less than straightforwardly factual—descriptors such as "alleged" bracket and calls into question their veracity.

ANALYZING ACCOUNTS

As analysts we are not constrained to assume that accounts are always entirely consistent. Indeed, it is a commonplace that personal accounts, if not internally inconsistent, draw on different frames of reference simultaneously. Again, we do not have to endorse any one frame of reference and discount one or more others in order to analyze them successfully. On the contrary, a thorough analysis needs to take account of the different frames of explanation and justification that may be in play. Let us return to the example of Bunton's psychiatrists. They remind us that an informant may be able to generate more than one frame of reference in her or his accounting. Social actors are perfectly capable of producing plausible and reasonable accounts that contain apparently incompatible—or at least perceptibly different— kinds of explanation or motivation. On reflection, we should be able to cope quite comfortably with the idea that a psychiatrist might *simultaneously* hold at least two versions of her or his professional motivation. We might, after all, find little difficulty in understanding that a social scientist might express her or his motivation to conduct and publish research in terms of a disinterested commitment to learning, a desire for social amelioration, and a desire to gain tenure in a good university. As Bunton in fact reports, the psychiatrists had several accounting repertoires or registers to describe their careers and career contingencies. For instance, they produced various kinds of "conversion accounts" that explained things in terms of a personal epiphany or transformation. They also used "pragmatic" accounts that explained the career choice of psychiatry in terms of family and domestic commitments. They also invoked "long-term commitment" accounts, suggesting that they had been personally committed to the specialty of psychiatry from a relatively young age.

The coexistence of different registers is aptly illustrated by the study of natural scientists' discourse. Gilbert and Mulkay (1980) collected, by means of interviews, scientists' accounts of scientific discoveries. Amongst other things, they show that scientists can account for the process of discovery using contrasting "repertoires" of accounting device. On the one hand, scientists employ what the authors call "the truth will out" device. Drawing on this mode of accounting, scientists account for discovery in terms of the inexorable revelation of the natural world—the inevitability of discovery following proper scientific method. This is the kind of account that scientists themselves tend to endorse explicitly when challenged by sociologists or anthropologists of science and when they engage in the so-called "science wars."

Equally, however, they are able to account for scientific breakthroughs in terms of more "contingent factors." They talk in terms of the personal qualities of individual research scientists, and they account for discoveries in terms of factors like luck. These two repertoires of accounting device do not compete in scientists' accounts: they coexist. Viewed from one point of view they seem to suggest a profound inconsistency in the scientists' accounts. But in the very fact of their simultaneous existence, we can see that they are not so much inconsistent as alternating, or as palimpsests that are equally available to perception and interpretation at the same time.

A parallel case of scientists' accounts is provided by the study of a genetic discovery (Batchelor, Parsons, and Atkinson 1997). In documenting the accounts of scientists who had been responsible for the discovery of the gene incriminated as the causal factor in the disease myotonic dystrophy, these authors also show the ways in which the scientists explained, in the course of interviews, how the specific discovery was made. They employ rhetorical repertoires of predictable science, craft skills, *and* chance. Again, they do not do so in a way that suggests that these are "really" incompatible; the accounts co-exist in the scientists' personal narratives of the research process. In just the same way, the same genetic scientists describe processes of collaboration *and* competition between research groups and between individuals as part of the same accounts.

It is, in fact, perfectly possible to "rationalize" these simultaneously expressed repertoires. Evans-Pritchard did exactly the same for Azande witchcraft beliefs. Evans-Pritchard (1937) suggested that the witchcraft system allowed the practical logic of Azande culture to interpolate a personal factor within the causal chain. When misfortune strikes, Evans-Pritchard suggested, Azande actors are quite capable of recognizing the physical agents and their actions that injure them or damage their goods. But the invocation of what we might call the witchcraft and sorcery repertoire provides a way of accounting not just for the misfortune in general, but accounts for the specific affliction of the individual person, at a specific time, and in a particular place. In the same vein, the scientists' accounts simultaneously affirm the epistemological status of natural science, and account for why a breakthrough that was inevitable in the general order of things actually occurred in a particular laboratory, at a particular time, attributable to one or more individual actors. What is different between our perspective and Evans-Pritchard's classic anthropological understanding is this: we do not try to domesticate Azande thought by making it appear more "rational," any more than we exorcise laboratory scientists' thought by making it appear "subjective." Rather, we recognize that any collectivity may have different registers of interpretation available to them simultaneously.

In interview-derived accounts like these, then, "telling the truth" is a far from simple matter. Equally the proper analysis of such materials is far from straightforward. It is clear that we cannot really separate out matters of fact from matters of affect, nor can we inspect accounts in order to remedy the problems of distortion and bias. As we have tried to illustrate up to this point, however, it does not altogether mean abandoning the question of "truth." We cannot coherently adjudicate the truth of an account by comparing it to a different account, or by juxtaposing it with what really happened. That way lies the infinite regress of kaleidoscopic versions. "Truth" needs to be translated into researchable topics. These may include investigating how informants construct various kinds of persuasion: how they chronicle facts and evidence; how they represent their own motives and feelings; how they attribute motives to others; how they display the rationality of their own and others' actions. Truth, credibility, facticity, rationality—these are all *achievements* on the part of social actors. There are various contexts in which they are performed. The interview is one such site.

We have shown and exemplified how the "objective" view of informants' accounts is flawed, and how Dean and Whyte's original formulation of the issue was limited and partial, even when they tried to be sensitive to its complexities. From what we have suggested so far, it might be tempting to veer to a different extreme. One might argue that far from revealing the objective truth, interviews can only—and should only—be deployed in order to explore informants' "subjective" experiences. If accounts are inescapably perspectival, then perhaps we can recuperate them for social research by studying only the personal experiences of our informants, collecting their personal biographies and recollections, allowing them to speak freely about their emotional responses, their dreams, hopes, and fears. The informant here becomes primarily an informant about herself or himself. The purpose of the interview is not to gain referential information about some anterior events, but rather to gain access to the interior world of the private and the personal.

There is no doubt that the pendulum has shifted among sociologists and others. While reliance on informants for proxy access to events and actions has reduced, there are now more interview-based studies than ever before. The rise in qualitative research has really been a rise in the number of interviews conducted. The character of the interview and the rationales for its use have also changed. The emphasis has clearly shifted from the referential to the biographical. Interviews are conducted in terms of the elicitation of personal narratives, and analyses have been increasingly oriented to the representation of "subjective" states. Ortner's (2002) recent educational research, Thierry Texeira's (2002) study of African-American women in law enforcement, Ortiz (2001) on athletes' wives, and Coles (2002) on African-American men all exemplify this trend. Coles gathered narratives of single-parent fathers, Ortiz says his interviews "became therapy," Thierry Texeira writes of "consciousness raising." Only Ortner uses interview data to build an analysis of a social phenomenon. In the hands of many researchers and methodologists the interview has become transformed into something more akin to a confessional, in which the object of the exercise is the elicitation of personal experience rather than shared culture, social structure, or organized social action.

This has accompanied a perceptible shift of research interest from the "public" to the "private." In itself, this change in perspective is not a bad thing. There is no reason why sociologists and anthropologists should not investigate the domains of biography, memory, desire, love, anger, or hate (see chapters 2 and 7). We would not endorse a return to a social science in which all actors were over-socialized and over-rationalized. A bloodless and emotion-free social world in which we encounter only disembodied and disengaged informants is not an option. The impacts of feminism, postmodernism, postcolonialism, subaltern studies, and the like have transformed the face of social and cultural studies radically and profoundly. The consequences are not all perfectly sensible, however, and the effects are not all equally conducive to good research.

The problem is equivalent to the sociological treatment of "motives." We have seen how C. Wright Mills (1940) transformed the issue into one of culturally shared vocabularies or repertoires. We have seen more recent applications of such an inspiration in the analysis of scientists' discourse, for instance. Let us return to that kind of example once more. We have already referred to the study of genetic scientists by Batchelor, Parsons, and Atkinson. We have summarized how they describe scientists' narratives of skill and chance in success in chasing a scientific breakthrough. Those authors also draw attention to the fact that, notwithstanding the growth in social research on science and technology, most of it still implicitly endorses an over-rationalized view of scientists as social actors. They are largely devoid of feelings and emotions. The literature focuses almost obsessively on the intellectual work of science. Little attention is paid to social relationships (as opposed to networks of scientific collaboration) and even less attention to the expressions of emotion on the part of scientists. The interviews with geneticists involved in the discovery of the myotonic dystrophy gene included a number of expressions of emotion. The initial announcement of the discovery—simultaneously by three research groups in the journal—led initially to excitement and elation. Congratulatory telegrams and other messages came in. But the scientists described how after that initial excitement, things started to feel distinctly flat. The interviews included expressions of disillusionment, even of bitterness, as scientists—especially more junior members of a research team—said they felt that there was no longer-term advantage to them from the discovery they had helped to make. The interviews contained accounts of emotional highs and lows in the months after the initial publication of the research group's discovery claim. The point here is not the fact that scientists' narratives include emotional expressions. Rather what is at issue is how one is to treat these episodes. It would be easy to make a simple ironic contrast. We could compare the "scientific" discourse of the discovery process with the "emotional" discourse of the scientists' response to its consequences. We might be tempted to go further, and make another contrast—say between the "public" face of scientific work and the "private" face of the scientists' feelings of joy, emptiness, betrayal, and the like. We might like to think that the expressions of feeling were in some senses more authentically frank. We might even think that we had revealed a domain of private and personal experience that was qualitatively and phenomenologically different from the less personalized expression more characteristic of the data of the sociology of science. These latter temptations should be resisted, however.

Methodologically speaking we have no warrant for privileging one register of talk over another. If we find one repertoire that is relatively devoid of emotion, couched in terms of the logical progress of scientific discovery and diligent skilful work, another expressed in terms of luck, and a third that is expressive of emotional response, then we should not start to privilege one over another. Whatever may be our commonsense attitudes toward these matters, it is unsound to confuse them with analytic principles. If we examine, say, scientists' accounts of scientific work in terms of culturally shared and conventional repertoires of accounting device, then we should do exactly the same for other repertoires as well. The principle of analytic symmetry applies here as in any other analytic context.

So we must avoid prior assumptions that lead us to believe that we have private experiences available to us through our interviews. We should certainly not value such accounts over others, in the belief that they are somehow more profoundly or honestly felt than other kinds of expression. In the case of scientists, we need to recognize that we have no warrant for priviliging one register of expression over another. We may have grounds for attempting some such contrast as the distinction between a public discourse and a private one. But that is acceptable methodologically speaking only if we accept that these can only be treated as differences in *context*. We should not assume that the private domain has greater authenticity over the public, as if public expressions were acts of bad faith while private expressions were more honest. The public and the private (if we accept such a distinction for the sake of argument) are equally social contexts. There are conventions for intimacy just as there are conventions for public comportment. Frontstage and backstage are both social domains. Informality and formality are equally susceptible to the constraints of cultural convention.

Cornwell's account of health and illness among a series of families in East London illustrates some of the complexities of public and private discourses. Cornwell (1984) suggests—plausibly—that the interview data she collected contain accounts of illness of different kinds. She suggests that they embody public *and* private accounts of the causation of illness. The public accounts are typically elicited by questioning specifically about illness and its etiology. The explanatory accounts they contain include reference to what the medical professions know and say. The private accounts, by contrast, are normally embedded in concrete biographical accounts, not necessarily produced directly in response to questioning about health and illness. Cornwell suggests that these accounts have different discursive features—but does not offer a systematic analysis that explores those features. Up to that point her treatment of the interview data is productive. We should not be at all surprised to find contrasting registers or genres of accounting in the accounts constructed by Cornwell's informants. Indeed, it would be remarkable were they to have but one frame of reference. What is problematic, however, is the attribution of them to the realms of the public and the private. This is not just an accident of terminology. Cornwell explicitly claims that the private accounts "spring directly from personal experience and from the thoughts and feelings accompanying it" (16). These private experiences contrast with accounts and explanations that are available in order to satisfy the requirement to furnish socially acceptable accounts to others. The public account is, as it were, directed to the generalized "other," while the private account is directed to the self or an intimate other. While it is incontrovertible that different accounts are provided for different actual or potential audiences, and address different frames of rationality or morality, it is dangerous to attribute one particular register to the expression of personal experience. This move is dangerously close to the invocation of private experience and its expression in personal narratives. It takes insufficient account of the extent to which the genres of account *constitute* experience, rather than reproduce it. The substance of Cornwell's analyses avoids the worst pitfalls that her own dualism sets up. Nevertheless, the contrast between public and private is an inherently dangerous one. It glosses over the extent to which the personal, the private, and the intimate are enacted through accounting mechanisms.

Plummer (1995) has documented the "public" and conventional formats of intimate and personal experience with outstanding force and clarity. He analyzes the narrative formats through which people narrate various kinds of sexual stories. These include "coming out" accounts and narratives by rape victims. There is no need to be cynical or dismissive of the actors who have such narratives to relate in order to recognize that there are narrative styles and formats through which the most "intimate" and emotionally charged of phenomena find expression. Discourse is as thoroughly dependent on cultural conventions as is the syntax of language. It is self-evident that if the notion of "personal experience" means anything, then sexual stories are intensely personal. They are by definition concerned with intimate matters. Equally, there is no doubt that such experiences are of special significance to the informants. We can acknowledge that such sexual stories have considerable biographical force, therefore. But, as Plummer demonstrates in some detail and with considerable elegance, the personal significance of such accounts does not mean that they are purely individualized. On the contrary, personal stories of those genres are constructed in accordance with culturally shared narrative formats. We have *shared* resources for the meaningful expression of the personal.

Of course, the use of cultural repertoires for the expression of personal experience is hardly a dramatic revelation. Everything we know in the traditions of anthropology and sociology leads us to stress the cultural components of the personal. Durkheim's original work on suicide—established as one of the first warrants for a distinctive discipline of sociology and an equally distinct analytic level of the social—is a classic exemplar. Equally, the anthropology of religious experience makes the same point over and over again. Ecstatic religion and devotees' possession provide repeated exemplars. The individual worshipper, convert, or cult member is transformed by the intensely personal experience of religious revelation or possession. He or she may be translated into an altered state of consciousness. It is an intensely personal experience. Equally, it is manifest that each of those personal conversions or possessions is enacted through the idiom of the culture or the religious community in which it is experienced. Inside Brazil, there are three types of ceremonies at which different spirits manifest themselves. White, middle-class Brazilian adherents of Kardecism might receive Gandhi or Confucius or Freud (Hess 1994); believers in *condomblé* receive the spirits of Amazonian indigenous "Indians" and former African-Brazilian slaves (Brown 1986), while *umbanda* ceremonies are visited by Yoruba and other West African gods and goddesses—*orixas* (Leacock and Leacock 1972). The "same" possession experience and resolution of problems—such as marital discord or migraines—will be performed in different idioms depending on the cultural context. Elsewhere in the world, of course, religious conversion and possession will be expressed in altogether different idioms again, such as physical shaking and *glossolalia* ("speaking in tongues") among Christian groups. In consequence, informants' accounts of their religious experiences will be expressed through the culture–specific repertoires of such expressive action.

This is not to deny or to gloss over the intensity of the reported experiences, nor of the authenticity of the accounts. We do not have to assume that informants have not in fact felt what they report, or have not had a moment of religious conversion, or have not felt themselves to be possessed. We do have to recognize, however, that our analytic task lies in understanding how cultural idioms provide shared and comprehensible interpretative frameworks. We cannot "have" the experiences in the absence of the cultural categories in the first place. It is difficult to think of anything as personal as a near-death experience. But narratives of near-death experience by individuals who have been resuscitated display very obvious cultural genres of expression. Buddhists report being welcomed by shining Buddhas, while Christians report Christian iconography. The point is obvious. It does not necessarily imply that such accounts are bogus. It does not even mean that the accounts are based on self-delusion. It does mean that it is impossible to conceive of an intimate experience that is independent of shared cultural and public categories of representation. In just the same way, we do not have to explain away the nature of ill health and physical suffering in order to recognize that there are culturally specific idioms of suffering and socially shared formats. Illness narratives are among the most widely collected, analyzed, and documented of the "documents of life." Their treatment is also the most diverse of genres of biographical analysis. Some prominent authors are clearly motivated by the desire to use narrative analysis in order to recuperate the personal experience of illness, and to promote insight into the reality of that experience.

Social analysts commit major methodological blunders if they assume that some narratives are more authentic than others, or that some are more personal than others, or that some are more revelatory of experience than others. What counts as experience—like memory—is organized through a variety of conventional resources and repertoires. There are undoubtedly different accounting registers, and there are different contexts of narration. It makes sense to talk of "public" and "private" only if they are confined to the description of particular kinds of social occasion, and only if we recognize that they are recognizable *as* private or public precisely by virtue of the kind of activities—including narratives and accounts—that are socially acceptable.

All of these observations would go without saying were it not for the fact that a certain amount of contemporary practice and an equal amount of contemporary advice seems to imply that it is the task of social research to gain access to a realm of intimate biographical experience. Indeed, this is sometimes cited as the most powerful justification for qualitative research— and most notably for qualitative interviewing. Biographical research methods such as life-history interviewing and the conduct of long interviews are all too often justified in terms of their capacity to provide researchers with data of an intimate nature. It is often claimed that the task of ethnographic or, more often, qualitative research is to gain access to the "lived" or personal experience of the actors or respondents whose accounts are being reproduced and reported on. Now it is, as we have already illustrated, perfectly proper for analysts to examine how social actors organize and report their personal experiences, and how these are grounded in different domains of everyday life. Equally, it is perfectly proper to examine how they construct themselves as particular kinds of persons. Consequently, it is necessary to maintain methodological vigilance. It may make everyday sense to think of some stories being more credible than others, or more appealing, or more satisfying emotionally. But the *analytic* tasks are different from those commonsense predispositions and preferences. There are matters of empirical, analytic significance to be addressed in exploring *how* such performances are enacted, how plausible they are to other social actors, and the interactional consequences of such performance.

To return to the original question, then, and to rephrase it: How do social actors give credible accounts of themselves? Viewed from this perspective, credibility or plausibility is a property of situated talk. It draws on the cultural conventions shared by tellers and hearers. It also draws on the discursive resources of evidentiality, the vocabularies of motive, the narrative formats, and the accounting repertoires of given groups of actors. These are different kinds of issues than the analyst's attempt to adjudicate the truth of a given description or narration.

Equally, differences or discrepancies are not simply opportunities to test accounts in a quasi-forensic manner. Notwithstanding the appeal of the metaphor, the social researcher is *not* operating like a detective. We are not trying to piece together fragments of evidence, testing the veracity of informants, exposing some of them as liars—all to establish the truth. To do so is to miss out on most of the analytic opportunities that data offer. Whereas the forensic mentality is to seek out the one single, truthful account that can reconstruct one single set of facts (and account for the self-interested lies or self-deceptions that informants tell), the analytic mentality of the sociologist or anthropologist is to explore the complexities of the context. We need to understand the multiple contexts and perspectives that bring into play different accounts; different notions of truth and falsehood; competing versions of "the same" phenomena.

CONCLUSIONS

It should be apparent from the preceding discussion that there is a potential danger in the contemporary treatment of interviews and narratives. On the one hand, vulgar realism is no longer promoted by methodologists, and the notions of "truth" have been rendered more problematic and more complex. On the other hand, there is a danger of an equally unsatisfactory position. There is, indeed, the danger of assuming, and then searching for, a different kind of "truth" that is equally untenable. That is, the assumption that life histories, oral testimonies, and autobiographical narratives can give analysts access to personal "experience." This alternative quest for truth is grounded in a rather naïve romantic position. It implicitly seeks to explore not the truth of reported events, but the authenticity of personal or private experience. It explores the interiority of experience. It seeks to uncover the inner world of the person. There is no place within a social science for such an un-social view of the person. We certainly cannot oppose the public with the personal, the external with the interior. The expression of "experience" never escapes the shared cultural frameworks of idiom, register, and genre.

There is therefore no methodological need for us to "believe" narrative accounts such as those derived from interviews, any more than we are enjoined to reject them out of hand. Equally, there is no methodological justification to believe in narrative as a form in itself. We are not justified in privileging narratives as providing privileged kinds of insight. This is a perspective that a number of commentators seem to have tried to justify. In a recent essay, for instance, Bochner (2001) has represented the sorts of critiques voiced by Atkinson and Silverman (1997) as an attack on narrative—as if narratives in themselves needed defending. We do not think that any form of social action merits attack or defence; nor does the principled analysis of such materials. What is at stake is the proper analytic stance to be adopted toward them. There is no methodological justification for treating personal biographical accounts as special. They certainly do not escape the need for principled analysis.

Since the questions were posed by Becker and Geer (that constituted the starting point for the previous chapter), and Dean and Whyte (with which we started this chapter), the terrain of qualitative method and research practice has changed. The shared assumptions concerning subject matter and method have shifted. In some ways those changes make the original questions even more relevant and more pressing. The precise form of the questions may have changed, and the form of the answers has certainly been transformed. As we have demonstrated in this chapter, the proper response to informants' accounts has become more interesting, more contested, and more complex than it was for previous generations of commentators. However the underlying issues remain current.

6

FROM INFERENCE TO DIFFERENCE

INFERENCE AND PROOF

The conceptual history of analytic strategies for qualitative or ethnographic research is variegated. It mirrors the more general history of qualitative research. One can trace various trajectories from a preoccupation with conventional notions of "inference," "proof," and "validity," to a more diverse array of interests. The criteria for what "counts" as proper analyses and conclusions have thus been subject to a number of transformations. Where once analysis corresponded to a set of procedures and inferences based on consensual values, broadly congruent with more widespread ideas in the academy, contemporary scholars celebrate a much more divergent set of strategies. We do not mean to imply in this treatment that there was ever just one approach to analysis in qualitative research. In addition to the sociological discussion we take as our point of departure, there were American anthropological statements about analytic principles, especially Spradley (1979 and 1980), who argued forcibly for a semantically oriented domain analysis of field data.

Our starting point is another of the classic papers in the earlier methodological canon. Becker (1958/1969) wrote what became an influential paper on "problems of inference and proof," with particular reference to participant observation. The paper was reprinted in McCall and Simmons (1969), and our page references refer to that version; it was also incorporated into Becker's *Sociological Work* (1970). Becker outlined one of the recurrent issues facing participant observers:

> Observational research produces an immense amount of detailed description; our files contain approximately five thousand single-spaced

pages of such material. Faced with such a quantity of "rich" but varied data, the researcher faces the problem of how to analyze it systematically and then to present his [sic] conclusions so as to convince other scientists of their validity. Participant observation (indeed, qualitative analysis generally) has not done well with this problem, and the full weight of evidence for conclusions and the processes by which they are reached are usually not presented, so that the reader finds it difficult to makes his [sic] own assessment of them and must rely on his faith in the researcher. (Becker 1969: 246)

In attempting to tackle these issues, Becker identifies a number of key aspects of the sequential development of the research: the identification of research problems; the development of concepts and indices; checking on the frequency and distribution of phenomena; and the incorporation of findings into a general model.

We are conscious that this is an extremely early paper of Becker's, that he continued to reflect on analytic strategies over the next thirty years, and his more recent work (e.g. Becker 1986 and 1989) shows key differences. We are using the paper to exemplify a style of thought at the time of its publication, not to criticize Becker himself. In any case, Becker's remarks on the definition of research problems are illuminating. He takes as axiomatic that the researcher identifies concepts and topics that will "give the greatest understanding of the organization he is studying" (247), looks for indicators of "facts which are harder to observe," and selects concepts to develop prior sociological theory. Evidence is thus evaluated in the light of the credibility of informants (see chapter 4 in this book) and whether participants' statements have been volunteered or are in response to direct elicitation—with a preference for evidence "spontaneously" given. The interest here is in the assessment of evidence in support of more general statements about social organizations.

Underlying the propositions Becker enunciates is a desire to establish credible evidence, and to locate it within an analysis of social organization. One of Becker's procedures for establishing the credibility of field data is through mapping the distribution of phenomena. Commending the use of quasi-statistics, and taking a cue from sociology's statistical colleagues, Becker suggests that field researchers can estimate the accuracy of their conclusions by mapping the distribution of observations; by seeing if the events they recorded are typical and widespread. In a more fine-grained way, the analyst should map the distribution of events or statements in terms of their distribution across social groups and social contexts. Likewise, the analyst's confidence in findings is increased not only if there is an accumulation of cases, but also if there are many kinds of different evidence that can be brought to bear on the same topic.

ANALYTIC INDUCTION

The systematic analysis of data and the generation of theory were also captured in the classic, standard methodological literature under the rubric of analytic induction. Like several of these principles, it seems to have resided primarily in the methodological literature itself rather than being followed closely in practice by the majority of researchers. Like the pronouncements by Becker, Zelditch, and others, however, it helps to capture the methodological temper of earlier formulations. It was originally formulated by Florian Znaniecki, but given more popular currency by Denzin's incorporation of it into his text. The steps of analytic induction, as summarized by Denzin (1978: 192) are:

1. A rough definition of the phenomenon to be explained is formulated.
2. A hypothetical explanation of that phenomenon is formulated.
3. One case is studied in the light of the hypothesis with the object of determining whether the hypothesis fits the facts in that case.
4. If the hypothesis does not fit the facts, either the hypothesis is reformulated or the phenomenon to be explained is redefined, or the case is excluded.
5. Practical certainty may be attained after a small number of cases have been examined, but the discovery of negative cases disproves the explanation and requires a reformulation.
6. This procedure of examining cases, redefining the phenomenon, and reformulating the hypothesis is continued until a universal relationship is established, each negative case calling for a redefinition or a reformulation.

This general model of analytic induction was given further methodological approval by Manning, in an essay that sought simultaneously to affirm the value of analytic induction in guiding inquiry, and to offer a critique of its limitations as a guiding principle epistemologically or methodologically (Manning 1982; see also Vidich and Lyman 1994). It is noteworthy, however, that by the time he wrote his own essay on the topic, Manning himself was clearly ambivalent about the epistemological claims for analytic induction and procedures akin to it. He was led to conclude that analytic induction derived from a positivistic inspiration (Manning 1982). Katz (1982/2001) used analytic induction in a study of legal assistance lawyers, and has decribed in meticulous detail how he tested and discarded hypotheses:

> Analytic induction ought to be evaluated in the same way in which field researchers practically gauge the value of their work. The test is not whether a final state of perfect explanation has been achieved but the *distance* that has been traveled over negative cases and through consequent qualifications from an initial state of knowledge. (Katz 2001: 33, emphasis in original)

It is clear that the ideal–typical formulation of analytic induction represented an attempt to place the classics of American sociology—especially those from the Chicago School—within a framework of epistemological respectability. It sought to establish a canonical framework within which the inferential procedures of practical field research could be constituted in properly systematic terms. It was thus intended to provide one way for establishing the validity of ethnographic inferences.

TRIANGULATION

Threats to the validity of qualitative research were also countered in the classic methodological literature with reference to the *combination* of methods of data collection. One of the key areas in which a claim was made for the productive combination of data-collection methods was in the methodological discussion of *triangulation*. While authors like Denzin (1970) certainly never intended to promote a naïve or vulgar view of research methods and their proper relationships, the rhetoric of between-method triangulation clearly implied for many enthusiasts the possibility of combining participant observation and interviewing so as to capitalize on their respective strengths, or to counteract the perceived limitations of each. Denzin's own summary of methodological triangulation captures the essence of this approach:

> In organizational studies, for example, it is extremely difficult to launch large-scale participant–observation studies when the participants are widely distributed by time and place. In such extractions, participant observation may be adapted only to certain categories of persons, certain

events, certain places, or certain times. The interview method can then be employed to study those events that do not directly come under the eyes of the participant observer. (Denzin 1978: 303)

Here interviewing is treated as a potential proxy for direct observation: it is implied that data about events and actors can be gleaned by indirect means in order to supplement the method of direct observation.

It is clear that Denzin's formulation of the relationships between methods is actually addressed to a slightly different issue from that discussed by Becker and Geer in their treatment of participant observation and interviewing (see chapter 3 in this book). But in his early methodological writings, Denzin too treats the methods themselves as relatively unproblematic. His early views of triangulation assume that research methods should be determined by research problems, while they can also be combined in terms of their respective strengths and weaknesses: "methodological triangulation involves a complex process of playing each method off against the other so as to maximise the validity of field efforts" (Denzin 1978: 304). Denzin emphasizes the degree to which the combination of methods is a matter of strategic decision-making, and that research design and choice of methods are emergent features of concrete projects: "Assessment cannot be solely derived from principles given in research manuals—it is an emergent process, contingent on the investigator, the research setting, and the investigator's theoretical perspective" (1978: 304).

Subsequent editions of Denzin's text reflect the changing character of methodological thinking, and make explicit reference to potential, and actual, criticisms of this approach to triangulation. Denzin acknowledges that his account of the relationships between methods such as interviewing and observation were open to the interpretation, and the accusation, that they were unduly positivistic (see Silverman 1985 and 1993 for critiques of the early Denzin approach). Indeed, Denzin did seem to imply that research problems are prior to and independent from methods, and that methods can be brought to bear on research problems in unproblematic ways. While Denzin himself was clearly no naïve positivist in intention, the implications of his text certainly seemed to suggest an easy accommodation between methods, and between methods and problems. The rhetoric of research problems driving the choice of methods too readily implied an independent and prior "list" of researchable topics divorced from the theories and methods that constructed those topics. The answer seems to be that Denzin originally formulated the principle of triangulation as a heuristic principle. Clearly, ideas can be generated from data of different types, and the ideas so produced can be brought to bear on new data or new aspects of the research design. We do not need to endorse a mechanistic view of triangulation in order to glimpse some value for considering different methods and different data types. The danger arises when we regard such an approach as a procedural guarantee of methodological rigor and adequacy.

The simplest view of triangulation treats the relationships between methods as relatively unproblematic, and those methods themselves as even more straightforward. More sophisticated versions of triangulation may treat the relationships between methods in a less straightforward fashion—stressing the differences between them rather than complementarity—but more sophisticated versions of triangulation can still be predicated on unproblematic views of the methods themselves. Current perspectives on methodology and epistemology incline toward a quite different view. Treatments of participant observation and interviewing should not try to privilege one over the other, nor attempt to seek out ways simply to integrate them or treat their outcomes in an additive way. Indeed, contemporary perspectives on field research are more likely to treat different methods of data collection and analysis as incommensurable rather than complementary, let along additive. Consequently, notions of adequacy, accuracy, and validity are transformed—though certainly not abandoned. We explore these contemporary perspectives in the second half of this chapter.

There is a consistent theme running through the classic formulations we have summarized and discussed briefly. There is a recurrent emphasis on principles of *convergence*. Becker's principles include the search for different kinds of evidence that converge on the same phenomenon. The search for appropriate concepts and indicators also depends on the convergence of evidence upon stable categories, as does the enumeration and mapping of events and cases. The strategy of analytic induction likewise implies a convergent process whereby phenomena and relationships are progressively stabilized through the refinement of concepts and the elimination of anomalies (or deviant cases). In the case of triangulation, different kinds of data are brought to bear on the "same" topic in a similarly convergent way. The identity and stability of phenomena themselves are guaranteed through these analytic strategies. There is, moreover, a convergent principle at work at a more epistemological level. The different approaches we have described already seem to cohere around a consensual set of ideas concerned with notions of adequacy, such as reliability and validity. Attempts to stabilize concepts and phenomena through progressive re-formulation, the enumeration and mapping of cases, and the combination of different evidence types, are all predicated on stable social realities that are independent of the specific methods used to document them. The partial documentation of cases and events can be amplified and completed through the addition of complementary materials. The supposed relationship between research methods illustrates this general point.

The "classic" methodological literature we have been dealing with frequently sought to juxtapose different kinds of data collection, comparing them in terms of the most appropriate kinds of research questions that they could address. In an often-cited and reproduced argument, for instance, Zelditch (1962) attempted to match different kinds of research methods to different kinds of "information." The underlying assumption here is that there is a limited array of kinds of research questions. Zelditch divided the domain of social phenomena in three ways. He suggested that one could describe as many properties of the same object, thus describing an *incident*, which could be elaborated over time into a series of incidents, or a *history*. Secondly, one can describe a property across a series of units—so deriving a numeration or distribution. Third, one can derive general properties of a given social system, such as norms and social statuses. Hence, research designs based on enumeration and samples were identified as most appropriately suited to the description of frequency distributions, and participant observation quite inappropriate; informant interviewing was seen as the most appropriate way of getting at institutionalized norms and statuses, while participant observation was offered as the most appropriate way of studying incidents and histories.

Similarly the underlying problem with the simple or "optimistic" version of triangulation is that it treats the nature of social reality as unproblematic, and the relationships between the social world and the methods of investigating it as transparent. But we cannot assume a unitary and stable social world that can simply be viewed from different standpoints or from different perspectives. Rather, we have to pay due attention to the principle of *reflexivity*. Reflexivity is a term that is widely used, with a diverse range of connotations (and sometimes with virtually no meaning at all!). Here we use it in a specific way: to acknowledge that the methods we use to describe the world are—to some degree—constitutive of the realities they describe (Hammersley and Atkinson 1995; Gubrium and Holstein 1997). In other words, the research methods we use imply or depend on particular kinds of transactions and engagements with the world. Each kind of transaction therefore generates a distinctive set of descriptions, versions, and understandings of the world. These are not arbitrary or whimsical. They are generated out of our systematic and methodical explorations of a given social world; they are not private fantasies. Equally, they are not purely contingent. There are systematic relationships between methods and representations. But they cannot be washed out or eliminated through simple-minded aggregation. Rather, we have to address what "social reality" such methods *do* construct, and what sense we can make of those constructions. Such a perspective gives rise to a contested and divergent sense of what counts as validity or adequacy for the research enterprise.

GROUNDED THEORY

One of the most enduring sets of ideas concerning the conduct of research and the relationship between research and ideas is captured by the notion of "grounded theory." There are several introductions to and overviews of grounded theory, which is often written about in an over-reverential way, as if it were the ten commandments rather than one set of practical suggestions. Melia (1996) and Charmaz and Mitchell (2001) are both thoughtful and balanced essays. In the next few paragraphs, we have set out our understanding of what Glaser and Strauss (1967) intended, and what, just as importantly, they did not intend. We deal with it in this context because it has been used—despite the apparent intentions of those who coined the term—to establish a kind of procedural orthodoxy for the conduct of field research and the analysis of the data that result from it. To that extent, therefore, the codification of grounded theory represents another version of the convergent mode of thought in this domain. Moreover, the acrimonious dispute in more recent years between Glaser and Strauss themselves concerning the proper understanding of grounded theory represents one microcosmic example of the kind of tension and movement that we are attempting to capture throughout this chapter—and indeed throughout the whole book.

When Barney Glaser and Anselm Strauss conceived and published their methodological monograph (Glaser and Strauss 1967) they had a number of purposes in mind—not all of which seem to have remained obvious to their readers and followers in the succeeding years. Their work has often been (mis)represented as promoting an inductivist exploration of distinctively qualitative data. It has been invoked to justify the various ways that analysts read their textual data in the attempt to derive general patterns of thematic coherence, recurrent patterns of action, and schemas of cultural relevance or meaning. In its original inspiration, however, grounded theorizing was far from being a primarily inductivist approach. The starting point for Glaser and Strauss was the paradox generated by an epistemological emphasis on theory *testing* as the goal of empirical research. Formulations such as those made famous by Karl Popper, that stressed the role of data in testing—and falsifying—hypotheses derived from preexisting theory, clearly had major flaws as guides to practical research, whatever their logical cogency. If the role of research was to test theory, then one needed some principled sense of where that theory was to come from. If theory comes from theory, then there is little need ever to investigate the world—social or natural—as there can be no practical guidelines as to what sort of theory is to be entertained sufficiently seriously to be tested. Clearly, scientists of any persuasion are not given to formulating and testing hypotheses derived from any old theory, however implausible or whimsical it may be. Indeed, it is part of the skill of the researcher to identify ideas that are likely to prove fruitful and productive. But the strict logic of theory testing and falsifiability seems to leave little or no room for epistemological explanations or practical guidelines concerning the development of plausible ideas. Sociology in particular clearly needs a regular engagement with the changing social world about it in order to ensure a constant flow of pertinent ideas and theories. There needs to be a constant dialectic between the social world and the world of sociological ideas. Equally, a purely inductive approach is inadequate. Even at a purely practical level, the repeated accumulation of facts, or observations, or cases will not in itself lead to the formulation and systematic development of novel ideas. It is likely to lead to voluminous collections of materials illustrating existing ideas, and not the development or new ideas, or even the extension of existing ones.

The solution was the deployment of pragmatist thought, derived from Peirce. The guiding notion was that of "abductive" reasoning. This represents a sort of "third way" between the Scylla of inductive reasoning and the Charybdis of hypothetico-deductive logic. As the Latin derivation implies, abductive reasoning involves the analyst in "drawing out" possible abstractions from observed cases, and using those to formulate working hypotheses that can in turn be tested against new cases and observations. This model of data and ideas provides a way of capturing the dialectical shuttling between the domain of observations and the domain of ideas. It is clear from a reading of the original text that grounded theorizing is not intended to be restricted to qualitative research. On the contrary, although Strauss himself later disowned the references to quantitative research, the book attempts to capture a general heuristic approach for any and all varieties of social research. The crucial idea that lies behind it is the problem of where theory comes from. The virtue of the pragmatist approach, translated into a set of practical precepts for researchers, is that it allows a place for "experience" in the formulation of working hypotheses. Preliminary observations, everyday experience, single cases—these can all be admitted as parts of the discovery process. Furthermore, grounded theory is not a description of a kind of theory. Rather it represents a general way of generating theory (or, even more generically, a way of having ideas on the basis of empirical research). When Glaser and Strauss discuss such issues as the "constant comparative method," they are describing one mode or variation of practical research reasoning.

Unfortunately, the general principles of grounded theory have, in the intervening years since the book's first publication, become translated into a rather stultifying set of procedural orthodoxies. Moreover, the results of the general heuristics have been repeatedly misidentified as grounded theory, as if it were a school of sociological theory in its own right. In many ways this translation into a convergent procedural orthodoxy owes much to the work of Anselm Strauss and his collaborators. The principles of grounded theory have become associated with some basic procedures for the analysis of qualitative data—field notes and interview transcripts, in particular. Moreover, those processes of analysis have themselves become equated with formulae for "coding" of data. The connotations of data coding capture the essential tensions we are exploring in this chapter, and throughout the book. The coding of data can mean a number of different things. In the original formulations of grounded theory, it clearly refers to a process of thinking with the data in order to interrogate it, and to generate working ideas and emergent concepts from them. In subsequent formulations, however, the principles of grounded theory have been translated, and to some extent distorted, into a mechanistic set of "coding" operations. To some extent, this has been the result of Anselm Strauss's own activities. He turned the discovery heuristics that he promoted and reproduced in his graduate seminars into two books—one an "advanced" text that included extended transcripts from his classes (Strauss 1987), the other, with Corbin (Strauss and Corbin 1998), a core introductory text. Unfortunately, the process of translation and simplification meant that the general and heuristic principles that Glaser and Strauss had originally proposed became somewhat distorted. They became interpreted as a rather sterile and rigid set of formulae and prescriptions, largely devoted to mechanisms of data coding. In the hands of Strauss, coding data was essentially a way of expanding on the data: given an observation or small series of observations, or indeed, given the cultural competence of an informant, one could "code" the data by asking sociologically informed questions about the data or of one's informant. How could it be otherwise? What would be the consequences? In the hands of less experienced and more limited authors, however, and in the simplified version enshrined in Strauss's own work with Corbin, the emphasis too readily shifts to a form of data *reduction* through more conventional and more restricted views of data coding.

For these reasons we have considerable sympathy with the strictures leveled by Barney Glaser (Glaser 1992). We do not altogether agree with the manner of his protests, and his impassioned pleas to Strauss to withdraw the book with Corbin. In addition, his patronizing remarks about Corbin herself were inappropriate. Nevertheless, the general thrust of his argument was correct. He argued that the original inspiration for grounded theorizing was the search for what he himself had called theoretical sensitivity. His ideas seem to have affinity with Herbert Blumer's notion of "sensitizing concepts" (Blumer 1954; see also Glaser 1978). Here, sensitizing concepts are intended to be ideas that indicate useful lines of inquiry, which provide directions for inquiry. They are not intended to be what Blumer called, by way of contrast, "definitive" concepts. The precise difference between the two is not easy to specify, and the usage is itself a sensitizing sort of idea. It is metaphorical. But it helps to capture the sense that some ways of proceeding are not intended to be represented in terms of algorithms or formulae; and theories and ideas are not always intended to be tightly defined. We cannot always ask for concepts and data to be perfectly congruent. The same is clearly true in Glaser's use of grounded theory, in what he himself would see as a defence and a restatement of its original inspiration. Glaser believes that Strauss ended up by producing a travesty of grounded theorizing, by translating its heuristic inspiration into a formulaic approach. His restatement of the original version—as he sees it—has been unnecessarily shrill and his attacks unnecessarily *ad personam*. Nevertheless, the tension between the heuristic and the formulaic in this context is illustrative of a greater tension within the intellectual field of qualitative research. Melia (1996) is a finely balanced account of the differences between the two protagonists, and gives the reader a more detailed account than we can provide here.

Grounded theory should, therefore, not be thought of as a particular and limited kind of theoretical exercise. It is not a technique for the analysis of qualitative data. It is a description of how productive research is conducted, and how productive ideas may be generated. It is certainly as much about the strategic design and conduct of empirical field research as it is about techniques for data analysis. Of course, Glaser and Strauss do discuss various particular procedures. But these should not be regarded as constituting a hard-and-fast set of recipes. Many of the recent and contemporary uses of grounded theory, and the statements made about it, imply the latter. They present grounded theory as one of the convergent tendencies within qualitative research, tending towards orthodoxy in research and data analysis strategies. These centripetal tendencies have been reinforced in some treatments by the marrying of grounded theory modes of data reduction through coding, with the uses of computer software for the management of textual and other qualitative data.

COMPUTING AND CODING

An emerging orthodoxy is being adopted globally by key members of the qualitative research community. This links coding, grounded theory, and the use of computers for the management and analysis of qualitative data. This is largely, though by no means exclusively, linked to the growth of Computer Assisted Qualitative Data Analysis Software (CAQDAS) as a subfield of expertise (Fielding and Lee 1991). Software packages aimed at analyzing qualitative data are now widespread, and it is a fast-growing field. We do not intend to review all of that literature, or all of the existing software. That has been done elsewhere (Burgess 1995; Tesch 1990; Weaver and Atkinson 1994; Weitzman and Miles 1995; Kelle 1995; Fielding and Lee 1998). It is, however, important that we draw attention to the area in general, and some specific issues within it. We note, in particular, the convergence of most computer applications on a general model of data marking and retrieval. Many of the software packages may most accurately be described as computer-based applications for the storage and retrieval of data. While there are additional facilities and sophistication involved, the general notion of coding remains fundamental to such CAQDAS.

The computer-based approaches of this sort depend on procedures for coding the text (interview transcripts, fieldnotes, transcribed recordings, documents). This means marking the text in order to tag particular chunks or segments of that text. Code words are thus attached to discrete stretches of data. The purpose of the software is, at root, twofold. First, it facilitates the attachment of these codes to the strips of data. Second, it allows the researcher to retrieve all instances in the data that share a code. Such code-and-retrieve approaches are exemplified in programs such as *The Ethnograph*, one of the most widely disseminated and used of all the applications. The underlying logic of coding and searching for coded segments differs little, if at all, from that of manual techniques. There is no great conceptual advance over the indexing of typed or even manuscript notes and transcripts, or of marking them physically with code words, colored inks, and the like. In practice the computer can add many advantages. The speed and comprehensiveness of searches is an undoubted benefit: the computer does not search the data file until it comes up with the first example that will "do" to illustrate an argument, nor will it stop after it has found just one or a couple of apposite quotes or vignettes. The software has an additional merit that definitely marks an advance on the practical value of manual coding and searching. It can cope with multiple and overlapping codes; it can conduct multiple searches, using more than one code word simultaneously. Software like *The Ethnograph* and *Nud*ist* allows the analyst to combine code words, in an approximation of Boolean logic, to facilitate complex searches. The co-occurrence of codings can be an important issue; finding them can be a useful tool. Since the software can handle very large numbers of codings and separate code words, in purely mechanical terms the computer can help with more comprehensive and more complex code-and-retrieve tasks than can be achieved by manual techniques.

Many of the software packages allow the researcher to do much more than just code textual data. We return briefly to a consideration of alternative uses of information technology at the end of this chapter. Here we are not concerned with developing a review of the current software, or with mounting a systematic critique (Coffey, Holbrook, and Atkinson 1996). Rather, we are discussing some uses of computing software in the broader context of convergent and procedural approaches to qualitative data handling.

A similar view of the convergence of (versions of) grounded theory and CAQDAS has been outlined by Lonkila (1995). Lonkila suggests that some aspects of grounded theory have been overemphasized in the development and use of qualitative data analysis software, while, in comparison, other approaches have been neglected. There is, therefore, a danger that researchers may be led implicitly toward the uncritical adoption of a particular set of strategies as a consequence of adopting computer-aided analysis. The emphasis on coding data is a central feature of this process of convergence. Having summarized key features of two programs (*Atlas/ti* and *Nud*ist*), Lonkila (1995: 48–49) writes:

> It seems clear that the development of the two programs mentioned has been strongly influenced by grounded theory. But it does not follow from this that they can only be (or actually are) used in an analysis in line with grounded methodology. However, nearly all of the programs developed specifically for qualitative data analysis tell us: if you want to do qualitative research with the computer, you have to code your data. How you do it, is basically up to you (even if some of the programs and many

of the articles written on computer-assisted qualitative data analysis suggest that the researcher get acquainted with grounded theory.) It may be that at least some kind of coding is needed in most qualitative research, but it is also possible that coding is overemphasized, given the fact that a large part of the qualitative researcher's work consists of interpretation and a fine-grained hermeneutic analysis.

In other words, the point is not to deny the relevance of grounded theory, or the potential value of coding qualitative data. One is certainly not denying the value of CAQDAS for such work. The danger that we, endorsing Lonkila's caveats, wish to indicate, is the unnecessarily close equation of grounded theory, coding, and computer software. Grounded theorizing is more than coding, and software can be used to do more than code and retrieve textual data. The point here is not about the full potential of CAQDAS, nor about the true nature of grounded theorizing. Rather, the danger we identify lies in the glib association between the two, linked by an emphasis on data coding procedures.

Given the widespread use of CAQDAS and its undoubted value for the management and retrieval of textual (and, increasingly, visual) data, it is easy for a taken-for-granted mode of data handling to develop. This is not necessarily an inherent feature of software itself: it resides in the uses to which such software is put. In our view, the association of CAQDAS with a simplified grounded theory justification can be misleading to students and researchers to whom it is introduced. CAQDAS offers a variety of useful ways of organizing data in order to search them, but coding data for use with computer programs is not *analysis*. It is important to avoid the misapprehension that coding and computing lend a scientific gloss to qualitative research. The growing "respectability" of qualitative methods, together with an adherence to canons of rigor associated primarily with other research traditions, can lead to the imposition of spurious standards (Fielding and Lee 1998). The categorization of textual data and the use of computer software to search for them appear to render the general approach akin to standardized survey or experimental design procedures. In our view, qualitative research is not enhanced by poor imitations of other research styles and traditions. Analytic procedures that appear rooted in standardized, often mechanistic procedures are no substitute for genuinely "grounded" engagement with the data throughout the whole of the research process. It is worth noting that the "usefulness" of such computer programs implies that you have collected and put in all of your data, and this suggests that data collection and data analysis are discrete and linear.

DIVERGENCE

Recent and contemporary perspectives have introduced an array of different perspectives on issues of adequacy and validity. Moreover, the recurrent theme is one of *divergence*. Not only are there different conceptualizations, but the classical assumptions concerning the convergence of analytic strategies on stable entities and conventional notions of validity have been—if not abandoned altogether—thoroughly revised. For instance, Altheide and Johnson (1994) identify a bewildering array of terms and ideas. They summarize these and other positions in terms of broad themes. Validity-as-culture, validity-as-ideology, and validity-as-gender all stress the culturally or socially specific notions of research validity. These are not alternative formulations of validity in the traditional sense. Rather, they provide critiques of them—stressing that validity is always constructed within specific interpretative traditions, ideological positions, and with reference to competing interests. From such critical perspectives, then, the adequacy of research is inescapably framed from within the constraints of language, the conventions of text and representation, and prevailing notions of authority. Summarizing these alternative formulations, Altheide and Johnson (1994: 488) suggest:

> Common to most formulations is an abandonment of any pretense of linkage or adequacy of a life world within a broader context. Rather, the general model seems to be that validity should be relevant and serviceable for some applications of knowledge: Is knowledge useful? Does it, for example, liberate or empower?

In other words, criteria for the adequacy of research and the analysis of data are widely represented as situationally specific and contextual. As a consequence, criteria of adequacy are treated as diverse and grounded in interests, rather than located in universalistic criteria of discovery and evaluation. This transition encompasses a reversal of the quest for valid generalizations and a foundational warrant for knowledge. Lather's proposals, for instance, define a variety of possible grounds for validity, none of them corresponding to the conventional problems of validity and analytic rigor (Lather 1991).

Among other things, the kinds of issues formulated by Lather and other contemporary authors are essentially anticriterial. They are proposed as transgressive categories of methodological thought. They do not invoke criteria of methodological adequacy that are simply better attuned to the interpretative traditions of qualitative research. In that sense, they diverge not only from the most "conventional" criteria of validity or reliability, but also from the revisionist criteria proposed by authors such as Lincoln and Guba. Lincoln and Guba suggested criteria for the adequacy of qualitative research—for instance in the context of qualitative evaluation—that paralleled the conventional categories, but transposed them into the vocabulary of qualitative research.

Lincoln and Guba (1985) outlined a set of criteria for what they termed "naturalistic" inquiry. Rather than the conventional appeal to the "internal validity" of research, they proposed to substitute the criterion of "credibility." This is guaranteed primarily through checking of analyst's accounts by members or informants. Likewise, the external validity, or generalizability, of research is replaced with the test of its "transferability." The latter does not depend on procedural criteria such as establishing the representativeness of a sample, but by providing sufficiently rich and recognizable accounts of social settings that readers can discern their *transferability* to other social contexts. The conventional preoccupation with reliability was also replaced with the notion of *dependability*. This is warranted by the possibility that researchers' activities are available to be audited: the requirement is that the processes of data collection and analysis should be transparently available to the scrutiny of other researchers. Finally, the conventional criterion of objectivity is replaced by one of *confirmability*. This latter is represented, claim Lincoln and Guba, in more open-ended, negotiable terms than conventional notions of objectivity. It is clear that Lincoln and Guba intend to insert interpretative judgments concerning the adequacy of research in place of objectivist accounts that depend on impersonal and decontextualized criteria of objective science. This is an approach to inquiry that stresses the active and engaged role of the researcher, and lays emphasis on the principle of reflexivity.

In contrast, formulations like that of Lather are not founded on the substitution of one set of criteria for another in the attempt to generate a parallel canon. Rather, the stance is oppositional. The proliferation of validities clearly denies the very notion of "validity" itself. One cannot retain even a residual commitment to notions of validity in research while simultaneously advocating a spiraling proliferation of alternative criteria. Clearly the intellectual program of Lather and other contemporary commentators is quite different. The criteria for adequacy become conflated with other kinds of concerns, primarily political and ethical. This diversity of criteria reflects an equally diverse set of assumptions about the proper ends and conduct of qualitative research, and indeed of social inquiry in general.

ESSENTIAL TENSIONS

It would be wrong to conclude from the preceding discussion that "old fashioned" notions of adequacy have been swept away by a landslide of postmodernist alternatives. Rather, we want to suggest that these differences represent a continuation of a recurrent set of tensions and contestations that have marked the history of qualitative research and the disciplines within which it is conducted. Indeed, it is our contention that the creative vitality of ethnographic and other qualitative research lies in the essential tension between the various positions, rather than in one orthodoxy or one or more oppositional tendencies.

It is in keeping with this general stance, therefore, that we fully endorse neither of the extreme positions we have sketched in here. We do not advocate a return to a purely "convergent" view of the adequacy of research. We do not believe that we ought to endorse the earlier position that sought to assimilate qualitative research to the same canons of rigor as those characteristic of other research traditions. Indeed, we want to emphasize that there is an older tradition of qualitative, ethnographic research that predates the canonical methodological texts, and that does not rely upon the vocabularies of validity, reliability, and the like.

Arguably, the standard methodological preoccupations are not congruent with the development of social research in the twentieth century. The main lines of ethnographic, life history, documentary, and other modes of qualitative research were developed in Chicago and other research centers, with little if any reference to the now standard notions of methodological rigor. Likewise, the parallel traditions of social and cultural anthropology developed in the United States and the United Kingdom, respectively, with virtually no preoccupations with methodological or epistemological problems. The community studies that fell somewhere between the two main disciplinary schools (Bell and Newby 1971) also developed with little or no methodological preoccupation. The rhetoric of validity, reliability, and associated concepts were introduced into the language of social research from elsewhere.

We should regard these methodological precepts and standards as vocabularies of justification that became pervasive among the social sciences at a particular juncture in their development and dissemination. Rather than regarding them as gold standard criteria of research adequacy that stand independently from particular perspectives, we should rather think of the rhetoric of validity and reliability as part and parcel of particular kinds of research rhetoric. When research methods were first becoming enshrined in authoritative papers, anthologies, and textbooks, it was perfectly natural to assimilate at least some of the key features of field research to the prevailing canons and rhetorics of social science. The distinctive characteristics of field research were thus adjusted and trimmed to fit the Procrustean bed of prevailing orthodoxy. We have, in many ways, continued in that vein. All social researchers face similar kinds of external scrutiny and pressures. We all compete for resources in the same marketplaces—of recognition, rewards, and research grants. It can, therefore, make perfect pragmatic sense to translate the canons of ethnographic research into the vocabularies of justification that have been invented elsewhere in the intellectual field. We have recognized, however, that this is an act of translation. It is not in itself a process that warrants or legitimates the research we do.

If we recognize some diversity of aims and criteria of adequacy for qualitative research, then, are we free to abandon all notions of validity, reliability, or any of the other kinds of standards that have been applied to all social research in the past decades? Do we have license to say that, in effect, anything goes? We think that is not a warranted conclusion or outcome. The escape from inappropriate criteria and vocabularies leads us to search for appropriate ones, not to abandon the exercise altogether. Difference or divergence in this spatial metaphor does not imply the complete loss of criteria. If we escape from the straitjacket of some notion of "gold standard" methodology, that does not release us from all obligations to be methodical. If we reject oversimplified characterizations of theory building, that does not absolve us from the imperative to have ideas, and to use our fieldwork to generate ideas.

It is important to move away from formulaic criteria for the adequacy of research and the reliance on ritualized prescriptions. It has been abundantly clear that the conventional "textbook" formulations of validity and reliability are of little practical value in guiding and interpreting ethnographic or other qualitative-interpretative research. They have few points of engagement. Indeed, in retrospect it is apparent that they were and remain part of textbook knowledge, rather than being the guiding principles of active researchers. They remain at the level of methodology, almost completely divorced from practical methods and practical research in the field. They are but one instance of the dead hand of methodological teaching that deals in pedagogical simplification. The standard formulations of epistemology and methodology were an odd kind of Procrustean bed: all research had to be adapted to a single set of prescriptions. It is not altogether clear how and why such formulations were so widely endorsed. They rarely came out of the research community of sociologists or anthropologists, and existed entirely in their own discursive domain. They were the stuff of research methods courses and examinations. They were rarely, if ever, part of the craft knowledge of practicing research workers. Since anthropology remained largely innocent of research methods teaching in anything but the most rudimentary sort, the discipline remained mercifully free from gratuitous methodological impositions; it was sociology among the social and cultural disciplines that was especially victim to the dead hand of abstracted methodology. (This latter paralleled what C. Wright Mills called abstracted empiricism; both were also abstracted from general sociological theory, which has for many years trodden paths well removed from any field research in the social world.)

Methodological discourse, therefore, created the criteria for validity and so on, on a purely self-referential basis. It created imperatives for research that bore little resemblance to the practice of social research. Equally, the process of methodological oversimplification affected the attempts of practical researchers to formulate guiding principles that were rooted in practice. Consider, for instance, the very familiar ideas that we have outlined earlier in the chapter—analytic induction, grounded theory, and triangulation. It is clear that they represent collections of ideas that are derived from the everyday conduct of practical research. In many ways they are summary representations of what social researchers actually do in the field, and what they do when interpreting their data. For instance, grounded theory is clearly not—as some misguided commentators would have us believe—a type of theory. It is not a distinctive theoretical tradition, as is, say symbolic interactionism or phenomenology. Rather, it is a description of how ideas can be generated from the practical and systematic engagement of the researcher with the social world at hand. In its original formulation by Glaser and Strauss (1967), the notion of grounded theory is far from being a formulaic set of prescriptions. It is not proposed as a sociological analysis in its own right. It must be recalled that the overall rationale for grounded theorizing was to remedy the prevailing philosophical orthodoxy that stressed the testing of ideas rather than their generation. Grounded theory is intended to put into methodological terms the pragmatist concern for the exploration of the world through practical transactions. Grounded theory, it is apparent from the book itself rather than from secondary treatments of it, can be generated from a diverse range of data types and research strategies. The general idea relates to the dialectic between data, ideas, and research strategies (Charmaz and Mitchell 2001; Melia 1996). While far from being a justification for purely inductive data dredging, the approach stresses the emergent nature of ideas as the researcher engages with the social world. The approach is, therefore, intended to be flexible and based on multiple strategies: ideas can be generated from diverse sources, including numerical and literary information.

Moreover, the "discovery of grounded theory" is prescriptive only in the sense that it enjoins the development of ideas, and it advocates the conduct of research according to strategic development, driven by the ideas, and the data. In contrast, it is descriptive of strategies that researchers can and do follow in order to think and act creatively in the course of unfolding research projects, and in response to the data they collect. In its original spirit, then, grounded theory is not a recipe for the production of an analytic straitjacket. We should rather think in terms of a set of heuristic principles that guide productive research. The problem seems to be that the heuristic has been progressively transformed into the prescriptive. Strauss himself contributed to that process.

We can enter similar pleas concerning ideas like analytic induction (Manning 1982). In its various formulations, it looks like a prescriptive program for research conduct. It certainly has the appearance of a somewhat mechanistic approach. If approached in the same spirit as we advocate interpreting grounded theory, then we can think of it in similarly heuristic terms. Indeed, the two sets of ideas seem to hang together coherently to add up to a sensible package of advice to any social researcher. Taken overall, the two ideas inspire an approach to research design and data analysis that encourage the active interpretation of data, the production and modification of ideas in the light of data collection, and the collection of data in accordance with the emergent ideas of practical research. Analytic induction, seen from this perspective, then, is not a second-class way of guaranteeing procedural validity. It is a characterization of how creative social scientists think— whether or not they are consciously following analytic induction as a methodological precept. What the descriptions of grounded theory and analytic induction really achieve, then, is to make explicit what researchers have done implicitly before and since. They have engaged with the social world about them and have engaged with the data they collect in strategic and creative ways. They have continued to do so since the ideas were published and popularized through secondary formulations.

Indeed, the same sort of argument can be entered on behalf of triangulation. As we have seen, and as has been discussed on previous occasions, the overly rigid view of triangulation implies that the combination of data sources, data types, or observers enhances the validity of research findings in accordance with conventional procedural criteria. The temptation for qualitative methodologists has been to use such ideas to "tidy up" field research in order to produce the appearance of orthodox criteria of adequacy. Triangulation could all too easily look like a handy repair kit that could be used to remedy apparent weaknesses in qualitative field research. If participant observation could be criticized for not generating quantitative measures, then it could apparently be complemented by survey data, through interviewing or the administration of questionnaires. The addition of quantitative measures can be interpreted as a means of shoring up the data and guarding the research against selective weakness. The vulgar version of triangulation, therefore, interprets the principle in terms of rigid categories and prescriptive thought-styles. It is based on the notion that there are "best" matches of research strategies given research problems, and the data types need to be chosen and evaluated against an evaluative matrix of strengths and weaknesses. Some methodological writings have sustained this view of triangulation, incorporating the iconography of matrices that compare the strengths and weaknesses of different data types, implying the aggregation of research methods in order to establish the most robust of data sets and interpretations.

It is clear, however, that this is not the most productive way of thinking about these issues. At best, different kinds of data collection strategies generate different kinds of information. They may not be completely incommensurable, but they certainly cannot simply be combined additively. The significant thing about data of different types—such as the differences between participant observation and interviewing or conducting surveys—is that they bear on different kinds of issues. In the same way, within the normal confines of qualitative research, different kinds of data cannot be combined uncritically. The analysis of situated action through participant observation or participant recording is neither improved nor repaired by the addition of interviews with key actors, nor with focus groups, nor yet with the analysis of narrative and rhetoric. Each approach, each type of data, and each analytic strategy gives us a different array of analytic possibilities. We have argued and exemplified this general point with reference to the classic comparison between participant observation and interviewing (in chapter 3), and it can be extended to cover all varieties of additive research strategies.

If triangulation retains any value, it does so in the same spirit as we have suggested that grounded theory and analytic induction might be interpreted most productively. None of them constitutes a prescriptive protocol for the collection and interpretation of field data. None of them provides a formula to guarantee the adequacy of any given research project.

The analogy we would invoke here is Blumer's distinction between definitive and sensitizing concepts (see Hammersley 1989). The difference does not convey a literal pair of definitions. It should be thought of somewhat more metaphorically. The general connotations of Blumer's approach are clear enough, however. He grounds it in an unnecessary contrast with other kinds of scholarly or scientific research that we shall not pursue. Instead, we focus on the positively productive implications of Blumer's thought. He suggests that social scientists—especially those committed to the kind of field research that we are discussing—deal in sensitizing concepts. They are not susceptible to precise algorithmic specification or absolute categorization. They are essentially heuristic devices, based on fuzzy categories. Their value lies in guiding empirical research rather than satisfying the requirements of epistemological purists. These are ideas for researchers rather than ideas for methodologists or teachers. They escape the simplifying procedures that characterize the work of the latter.

CONCLUSIONS

Throughout the chapters of this book we have traced ways in which qualitative methods have become progressively more fragmented, more complex, and—in many ways—more contested. These trends have meant that the existence of orthodox or canonical modes of analysis and reasoning have become difficult to sustain. Some commentators and practitioners have apparently tried to do so. Some have attempted to derive specific paradigms or quasiparadigms of qualitative research, and to promote them. Some researchers have even tried to assert that the various general strategies of qualitative research, their intellectual traditions, and their epistemological commitments are virtually incommensurable—and that researchers therefore should restrict their activities so as to work unequivocally and exclusively within one such intellectual framework. The attempts to devise and impose such versions of orthodoxy are quite misplaced. There are no grounds for assuming that there are such mutually incompatible systems of method and theory.

Equally, we are skeptical of those attempts to elevate simplified versions of "grounded theory" as the canonical approach to analyzing qualitative data (or any other data for that matter). At the most general of levels, all productive research ideas are "grounded" in the sense that there is a demonstrable and systematic relationship between ideas and data about the social world. The true legacy of Glaser and Strauss is a collective awareness of the heuristic value of developmental research designs and exploratory data-analytic strategies, not a "system" for conducting and analyzing research.

Equally, we are aware of the danger and the limitations of tying analytic strategies to narrow implementations of computer software for the management and analysis of qualitative data. There is nothing inherent in such software that constrains one approach to analysis and excludes others. But—often linked with naïve versions of grounded theory—there are too many examples of the mechanistic application of such software to the "analysis" of field data, interview transcripts, and other data. The most fundamental problem associated with such narrow and ultimately misleading approaches is the implicit equation of qualitative data analysis with the inductive inspection of data and the derivation of categories from such data dredging, whether by manual indexing or by computer software. While we do not believe that there is a single right way of doing things, there are wrong-headed approaches—and these are among them. Qualitative research is not well served by formulations that imply that it is a primarily inductive exercise.

If there are some tendencies towards orthodoxy and formulaic prescriptions for data analysis, there are also tendencies that imply a carnivalesque proliferation of perspectives and criteria for the adequacy of analysis. Such perspectives reject any invocations of "traditional" criteria, such as conventional commitments to reliability and validity. Proponents of postmodernist perspectives on social research tend to reject such conventions as unacceptably modernist, in fact, all but *positivist*. They tend to equate all such conventional criteria with outmoded science-based attempts to impose inappropriate models on qualitative research. They celebrate the proliferation of divergent approaches: postmodernism appeals to difference in many ways, and that is true of analytic perspectives as well.

We do not think that it is helpful to equate all but the most recent approaches to qualitative research as positivist or modern (in the sense that they contrast with postmodern). Such formulations do not do justice to the long traditions of interpretative social research with which qualitative research has been closely associated. It is clearly nonsense within sociology, for instance, to equate strands of research associated with symbolic interactionism or phenomenology with "positivism." It does violence to the history of the subject, and is a betrayal of those scholars who struggled to assert the distinctiveness of interpretative and hermeneutic social research against the claims of approaches that really were based on appeals to positivist science.

What is needed, therefore, is a collective appreciation that there are appropriate methods for the analysis of qualitative data on social life. Those analytic strategies do not need to be constrained by more-or-less arbitrary frameworks that are the province of the methodologist rather than the practical researcher. They do, however, need to respond to the intrinsic forms of social life—being attentive to the systems and conventions of talk and action, performance and rhetoric, that constitute everyday life. They also need to reflect the distinctive theoretical and epistemological ideas of social science disciplines and traditions. Adequate research and productive analyses are not guaranteed simply by appeals to "qualitative" data. Data of any sort need to be used to have and to generate, and to extend *ideas*. We do not need to invoke unduly restrictive canons of rigor in order to recognize the need for systematic and demonstrable relationships between data and ideas. We also need to have and use ideas that have significance within broader systems of ideas. (And it is not necessary to strive toward a "cumulative" science in order to develop relations between ideas within disciplinary frameworks.) Likewise, it is not unduly "positivist" to suggest that research might be methodical, careful, and systematic. Equally, it should be explicitly grounded in and informed by the theoretical commitments of social science. We do not need to go to the extremes of "postmodernist" confusion and disarray in pursuing a distinctively interpretative social science, rooted in ethnographic and other qualitative forms of engagement with the social world. Qualitative research of any sort is not a self-justifying activity. In the absence of disciplinary ideas, qualitative research is as idle as any other. We do not proceed productively, therefore, if we endorse solipsistic criteria for analysis, entirely divorced from wider disciplinary knowledge.

7

FROM STYLES OF REPORTING
TO POETICS AND BEYOND

WRITING ETHNOGRAPHY

Debates over the representation of social life and cultural phenomena have become a familiar aspect of contemporary ethnography. Several of the pivotal issues in this chapter are paralleled by the material on autoethnography rehearsed in chapter 2. The changes in our conventions about how we write about our data have developed in conjunction with changes in our conventions about who, what, and where we collect the data. These debates have been vigorous, occasionally acrimonious, and have focused on the extent to which ethnographic texts construct reality.

One outcome of these contestations has been to encourage a more self-conscious approach to textual production. Another has been a growing awareness, and some utilization of alternative (or experimental) textual forms. Hence one characterization of ethnographic representation has been a shift away from authoritative or monovocal texts toward a diversity of forms and types (Denzin and Lincoln 2000). This perceived shift is our starting point for this chapter, which we have titled From Styles of Reporting to Poetics and Beyond. This title captures something of the intellectual coolness of distance and difference often used to characterize various classic formulations of ethnographic writing, and the textual, narrative turn articulated by recent poststructural approaches. Like the other chapters in this book, we begin by revisiting an earlier paper.

The pivotal paper, by Lofland, is remarkable as an early exploration of how qualitative research, or rather American sociological qualitative research, was being written up for potential publication. It is not a classic in the sense that it has been much reprinted and anthologized, nor is it routinely cited today. It has not had the impact of Lofland's textbook (Lofland

1971; Lofland and Lofland 1984 and 1995) nor of his empirical studies of social movements. However, with the benefit of hindsight, Lofland's choice of topic was prescient. It is also noticeable that Lofland's strictures and expostulations did not prevent hundreds of qualitative researchers from submitting papers to journals that display the same faults. The editors of contemporary journals of ethnography could analyze the evaluations of 200 articles submitted in 2002 and report similar categories. Indeed, it would be wrong for anyone to conclude that even after decades of critical reflection on the textual practices of ethnographic and other qualitative research, the majority of researchers have either transformed how they write, or even improved how they do so.

John Lofland's paper appeared in *The American Sociologist* (1974). The paper—entitled "Styles of Reporting Qualitative Field Research"—addressed the variety of ways in which qualitative research was written for publication. Drawing on editor, referee, and consultant evaluations of 200 unpublished articles and book-length reports of qualitative field research, Lofland identified five dimensions of evaluation and twelve different styles of writing. He suggested that evaluator commentary focused on five dimensions. These signified the degree to which a report: (1) had a generic conceptual framework; (2) was novel or original; (3) was elaborated and developed; (4) was eventful —"abundantly documented with qualitative data" (102); and (5) was "interpenetrated with the empirical materials" (102).

Lofland termed this overall approach to qualitative writing "the generic style" and suggested that these dimensions provided some kind of benchmark alongside which reports were judged. Lofland was able to identify (from the evaluations he analyzed) eleven other styles of qualitative research writing in addition to the generic style, all of which were open to some critical comment from referees. For completeness, we briefly outline these below.

1. *The Moral Style.* The writer has some moral stake in the research, for example in exposing mistreatment, or improving a situation. Genericists may recognize this as good writing, but question whether it is social science, due to the lack of attention to processes or structures.

2. *The Protocol Style.* This style usually has a short introductory statement followed by a set of transcripts in full. Hence the raw data are left to speak for themselves, without a conceptual framework.

3. *The "Then They Do This" Style.* Writer uses direct observation of (repetitive) everyday activities to organize a report. This is not dis-

missed out of hand, and it is recognised that much excellent field-work is reported in this style. However it can be criticized for lacking a frame, and for "working best" with exotic settings (of intrinsic interest). A variation of this style is multi-page quotes from unedited fieldnotes. "This, declare evaluators, is a literary monstrosity, both in the sense of hugeness and in the sense of marked malformation, smacking of giantism and obesity. The field notes are ungrammatical and free-flowing, running on in wandering fashion. . . . Authors are charged with believing their flabby, chaotic scribblings are precious." (Lofland 1974: 104)

4. *The Vacillating Style.* This might be thought of as "over-framing." This is not so much a criticism of multiple frames present in a report, but rather a lack of clarity. The author switches from frame-to-frame or concept-to-concept; the paper "starts" more than once.

5. *The Slightly Late Style.* Lofland describes this as trying "to be new and novel by using other people's new and novel frames" (105). Hence the paper or report is appropriately framed, but cannot claim a novel or original contribution.

6. *The Intro Text Style.* This style overstates the obvious, or rehearses the well known or taken for granted, "textbook" style. Lofland suggests there are limitations to the extent that this style can claim novelty, as it demands that new subtypes or kinds of familiar concepts are specified or developed.

7. *The Unelaborated Style.* This is similar to the intro text style, and often compounded with it. A report does not go beyond a very elementary frame, rendering the empirical illustrations overly abstract. This might suggest a lack of analytical elaboration. "Genericists become virtually enraged when the author is . . . pledging allegiance to symbolic interactionism, ethnomethodology, 'actors' definitions of the situation and/or their 'artful practices.' The reported materials suggest an enormously complex and shifting series of definitions and artful practices, but the author does not strive actually to analyze them." (Lofland 1974: 107)

8. *The Abstracted Conceptualism Style.* In this style, the author becomes overly involved in frameworks and concepts, at the expense of an adequate reporting of the data. Hence the data themselves remain underreported, and the paper is largely divorced from the empirical materials.

9. *The Hyper-Eventful Style.* This is a report that might well be novel, appropriately framed and elaborated, but where there is too much going on. Examples, incidents, episodes, and events are shared in multiple abundance—which can render the paper repetitive or boring.

10. *The Segregated Style.* Here, there is little or no attempt to integrate data with the specified concepts and frameworks. Hence the paper is compartmentalized and segregated in style, with distinct sections virtually unrelated to each other. Lofland (1974: 109) describes this as "a late effort to appear sociological."

11. *The Forced Style.* This is·where frame and data are integrated in the physical sense, but still lack convincing interpenetration. This might be where the author has "borrowed" a conceptual framework and used it uncritically. Hence the paper seems strained or ill fitting.

Lofland concluded from his analysis that there is considerable diversity in the reporting practices of qualitative research. He suggested that qualitative field researchers fall into a number of camps, and that one of these, the genericists, are the most vociferous in the codification of research reports. He offered two possible causes for this textual diversity. Firstly, the conventional wisdom is that qualitative methods are in themselves exploratory and discovery devices, and that this is "transmuted into an ideological celebration of creativity, *verstehen*, and 'do your own thing.'" Hence,

> the notion of discovery, beginning as legitimation for doing forward-edge work, is broadened and softened into a mandate for reporting anything "social" in virtually any verbal or nonverbal manner whatsoever. In this broadened and softened mandate, little distinction is drawn between sociology and other writing about social life. (Lofland 1974: 110)

Secondly, Lofland argued that the diversity in reporting qualitative research was indicative of the low levels of collectivity and technology among qualitative researchers. He made the case that it is collectivization (arising in part from technological sophistication) that fosters uniformity. Without these factors, there is a tendency to individualized and diverse practices.

We have chosen to revisit this paper because it raises a number of issues and questions that continue to vex qualitative research. The paper is not especially classic, or well cited, but does provide a way of setting the scene for the contemporary debates about qualitative research writing and representation.

Lofland's paper stands on the axis between Denzin and Lincoln's second and third "moments" of qualitative research, although it seems to be harking back rather than looking forward. It is suggestive of a modernist phase, seeking to address the issue of codification in research writing.

Although Lofland does not explicitly side with the genericist style, the tone of his paper certainly suggests that this style of writing offers the "preferred" or "best" way of qualitative research writing, alongside which all other styles are to be (critically) judged. The paper does, however, acknowledge diversity in the formats of reporting, and perhaps this could be identified as a "blurring of genres" (cf. Denzin and Lincoln 1994). Certainly Lofland recognizes, although does not necessarily condone, pluralism. He identifies different and diverse styles of reporting, although he does not choose to capture these in terms of a rounded complement of paradigms or strategies. The styles that he identifies rely on editorial or referee judgements about the generic qualities of the paper, rather than the identification of alternative (comparable) genres. There is little time given in this paper (and seemingly by the sociological "refereeing" community) to the view that "the essay as an art form was replacing the scientific article" (Denzin and Lincoln 2000: 15).

His conclusions also suggested that diversity is not necessarily desirable. For Lofland identifies diversity as an indicator of a "softened" mandate, a "lack" of distinction between sociology and other writing, and a "low" level of collectivization (and technology).

We could also view Lofland's paper as ahead of its time. Indeed it is one of the earliest papers to address writing at all in qualitative research. Prior to the late 1970s, there had been little attention paid to ethnographic writing (Spencer 2001). However limited Lofland's grappling with representations may seem in retrospect, at least he was writing about writing. His identification of writing diversity present within qualitative research, and his observation that these "represent real differences of evaluative belief and action" (102) are also important, given the debates about representation and authorship that were to ensue in later years. Lofland also stopped short of laying down a gold standard in qualitative writing. He does not, for example, suggest that the diversity is a recent phenomenon (although he does not provide any historical context in his paper). Nonetheless, one cannot help but be struck by Lofland's lack of engagement with alternative paradigms or genres, and his implicit stance that there is a right or preferred way to write qualitative research. He also appears rather sanguine at the lack of technology and collectivization, and unconvinced by calls to the blurring of genres.

Lofland's paper, then, provides a rich backdrop from which to examine contemporary debates about writing and representation in qualitative research. As a departure point the paper establishes the reality of writing diversity, and the possibility of critically examining the reports of qualitative research. It recognizes the presence of the author (in the moral style for example), and raises questions about the different genres and the use of technology. In essence, then, it provides glimpses of debates that were to come and that are still taking place.

THE CRISIS OF REPRESENTATION

The publication of *Writing Culture* (Clifford and Marcus 1986) is conventionally taken as the start of a greater reflexivity in qualitative research writing. There had been some earlier explorations, such as Anderson (1978) and Brown (1977 and 1983) in the United States, and Edmonson (1984) in the United Kingdom. These are evaluated in Atkinson (1990) and not rehearsed here. *Writing Culture*, an edited collection that was the outcome of a research seminar, building in part on the earlier work of Geertz (1973 and 1983), addressed the issue of representation in ethnography, recognizing the varied textual practices of qualitative researchers. This volume served as a reminder that ethnographic writing incorporated both politics and poetics (both present in the subtitle to the volume). It fueled debates over cultural representation and asserted dialogic, innovative, and reflexive approaches. Not least, it prompted a self-conscious and critical approach to authoritative texts, challenging the qualitative researchers' claims to "textual" authority.

While *Writing Culture* is an important consolidation of critiques about representation, we would question whether it constituted a "profound rupture" (Denzin and Lincoln 2000: 16). The impact of Clifford and Marcus was initially greater on American than British anthropology, or on qualitative sociology or the applied areas in either country. It was still possible to find sociological ethnographers in the United Kingdom in 1999 who had not read the book and did not feel that they could or should have done, as we discovered when editing Atkinson et al. (2001). The British anthropological collection (James, Hockey, and Dawson 1997) came out a decade after the original. Spencer (2001: 443) in an essay on ethnography "after postmodernism" argues that *Writing Culture* was an accident waiting to happen; "many ethnographers in the generation of fieldworkers trained in the late 1970s and early 1980s had simply ceased to believe in the models of scientific and textual authority provided by our disciplinary ancestors."

The so-called "crisis" of representation and consequent rethinking of qualitative research texts has been associated with postmodernist and poststructuralist agendas. Indeed, as Denzin and Lincoln (2000) argue, the crisis of representation can be seen alongside other crises confronting qualitative researchers (the crises of legitimation and praxis), all of which are embedded in the discourses of postmodernism and poststructuralism. However, we would not want to overplay the impact of these discourses. Indeed many of the current tendencies in writing and representation can be seen as developments of earlier perspectives, rather than radical departures from them.

Woods (1996) has sidelined the postmodern turn, perceiving postmodern approaches to ethnography and text as logical extensions of interactionist practices. Hence he argues that these developments are transgressive rather than progressive—as an emergent means of expressing research. Others see such developments as implying much more—reflexive, self-conscious research and texts that draw on new conceptual frameworks of aesthetic understanding and more complex considerations or authorship and audience.

Qualitative writing has always reflected variety—encompassing different disciplinary styles, textual conventions, and subject matter (Atkinson 1982 and 1992). However, it is fair to say that the crisis of representation crystallized this representational diversification and contestation. Despite recognition that the production of the qualitative research text has never been wholly static or monolithic, more recent debates about the textual representation of social reality have provided a platform for a critical reappraisal. Emerging from social anthropology, but now more widespread in sociology and related disciplines, has come a rereading of ethnography and its (textual) products. Influences have come from a number of spheres, including a rediscovery of rhetorical practices.

The "rediscovery of rhetoric" is a wide and diffuse intellectual movement spanning a range of disciplines. It has long been acknowledged that the Enlightenment saw a separation of rhetoric and science. This implied a clear distinction between two contrastive sets of commitments: on the one hand science, logic, reason, method, and evidence; on the other hand art, persuasion, opinion, and rhetoric. A consequence of such a distinction has been the consignment of rhetorical forms to the margins of legitimate scholarship. The aspirations of the *modern* ethnography have been rooted in this stark duality. The dichotomy established the possibility and perceived reality of ethnographic observers armed with a neutral and "scientific" language of observation, untainted by rhetoric and opinion. The rediscovery of rhetoric has had a profound impact on the way disciplinary knowledge is conceptualized. For example, scientific accounts have been recast as having rhetorical qualities and features (Law and Williams 1982; Lutz and Collins 1993; Lynch and Woolgar 1990), and taken-for-granted concerns have been reassessed. Moreover the dichotomy between the "reality" of the natural scientific world and the narrative accounts of the social world have been problematized.

Alongside the move to recognize the textual practices by which social reality is rendered meaningful have come more ideological critiques. Said's (1978) sustained commentary on the orientalizing tendencies of academic representation of the non-Western world strengthens the case that ethnographic texts can be both privileged and privileging. Postcolonial perspectives have revealed the ways in which observation and representation have reduced many cultures to the subjugated and muted objects of dominating discourse (Ardener 1975). The observer is cast as privileged ("with voice")—able to classify and write the (exotic) characteristics of an (oriental) "other." Authority is thus established and maintained through the production of texts of exploitation, description, and classification (Marcus 1992). The critique of postcolonialism is of more general significance than that of race or color. It is not limited simply to the sustained observation and writing of a distant other. The same set of issues is relevant to observation and writing of cultures "at home," where the representation of "otherness" remains salient (see Fordham 1996).

Representational issues have also formed part of a sustained dialogue between feminism and ethnography. The privileged positioning of author has been both acknowledged and challenged by feminist theory and research praxis (Stanley and Wise 1993). The feminist critique of social research goes beyond straightforward appraisals of gender balance. Standpoint research, for example, has taken up the criticism of women marginalized (or indeed absent) from research accounts, and brought to the fore the relationships between women's knowledge and their situated experiences (see Farrell 1992; Harding 1987; Haraway 1997; Langellier and Hall 1989; Olesen 2000). Recent dialogues between feminist standpoint research and poststructural approaches have further clarified the "pluralities of power relations" (Harding 1996: 451) within social research. Others have added to the debates about the relationships between feminism and ethnography (see Skeggs 2001). Clough (1992) has argued that many realist accounts of ethnography incorporate unconscious fantasies and desires concerning gender (and race). Clough also suggests that the ethnographic pursuit of the realist genre (see Atkinson and Coffey 1995) has served to disguise the exploitative processes at work. Mascia-Lees et al. (1989) made a similar point by suggesting that ethnographic texts should be rethought in terms of representation and power. Of course, as M. Wolf (1992) has argued, feminist ethnographers have been exploring the issues of power, authority, and representation for a long time, almost independent of the wider attention they have recently enjoyed. Jennaway (1990), for example, has argued that calls to a postmodern ethnography have (dis)located feminist discourse.

> The move toward egalitarian relations of textual production, dialogic, and polyphonic cultural scripts, collaborative authorship, the de-centering of self and the dis-alienation of the ethnographic other, the move away from systems of representation which objectify and silence the ethnographic other, i.e. the general reflexive stance, are things to which feminist theory (if not specifically feminist anthropology) has long been adverting. (Jennaway 1990: 171)

In keeping with this view, there has been a sustained feminist response to *Writing Culture* (see Babcock 1993; Bell 1993; Gordon 1988; Mascia-Lees et al. 1989; M. Wolf 1992), discussed in chapter 3.

The use of textual conventions to produce written texts has also been identified as a point of discontent within ethnography. We must recognize—as in other contexts of social-scientific discourse—that there is no neutral medium of representation for the ethnographer. We use the conventions of written language in the reading and writing of our texts. In that sense, the formats that academics (including qualitative researchers) use are *conventional*. There is no "natural" way of writing about social and cultural life. Even though we may be used to some ways of writing that we treat uncritically, this should not blind us to the fact that they are conventional resources. The authors of academic texts draw on a repertoire of conventional devices in order to construct authoritative texts. Equally, readers of academic texts draw on the same stock of literary devices. We should recognize that there are socially shared conventions of reading and writing that exert a major influence on the production and reception of all academic texts. Hence we have become accustomed to particular kinds of texts that are conventionally adopted to represent the results of ethnographic work. Or to put it more formally, there are particular genres of ethnographic writing (Atkinson 1992). These genres have close affinities with other academic writing, as well as links with certain kinds of fictional writing.

In general, the conventional genres of ethnographic writing reflect conventional assumptions about realism and authenticity in written accounts. What we might think of as "traditional" ethnographic monographs share textual conventions with other kinds of nonfiction writing—such as history, biography, and travel. They also share some stylistic features with realist fiction—such as conventions for narrating events and conveying character (Atkinson 1990).

The writing of anthropological or sociological monographs has also become a collection of genres in its own right. The traditional anthropological monograph, for instance was a powerful device through which a diverse array of societies and cultures were reconstructed in relatively uniform ways. The styles of writing anthropology, therefore, helped to define the discipline and to define its objects of study (Boon 1982). There are, moreover, recognizable subgenres within anthropology. There are distinctive traditions for reporting different regions, for instance, and there are different national styles. Likewise, if one turns to community studies, the construction of small-scale settings (such as villages) is partly accomplished through the textual conventions of monographs. The urban ethnography associated with the Chicago School of Sociology and its derivatives is yet another distinctive genre. (See Atkinson 1992 for a more detailed review of ethnographic genres.)

The historical and stylistic continuities between ethnography and fiction can also be traced to the early years of ethnographic sociology at the University of Chicago. (See Krieger 1984 and 1991 for discussions of the affinities between fictional and ethnographic writing.) The urban sociologists and novelists of 1920s Chicago had common subject matter, and adopted similar approaches to the production of texts (Cappetti 1993). Sociologists and novelists occupied the same city space, described the same social landscapes, and shared an intellectual and social milieu. These were by and large the "new" intellectuals, sharing the same canvases and inspirations. Both adopted a realist approach.

Van Maanen (1988) has identified literary realism as the dominant mode of ethnographic representation. He characterizes the realist approach as implying an impersonal, all but invisible author. It presents the "story" of one (impartial) author whose point of view is the dominant (and often the only) one. It is a genre of authoritative reportage. Such realist writing represents a style and a set of literary devices that are massively familiar, especially in the construction of "factual," authoritative accounts. There is, therefore, the danger of taking these devices for granted, and treating them as the "natural" and only way of representing the social. However, despite this tendency towards the realist approach, it is by no means clear whether this represents the best way to produce accounts of varied and complex social worlds. Most ethnographers recognize the complexity of social life, and the fundamentally constitutive nature of language. Given this, adopting the realist approach might be seen as somewhat of a paradox. Conventional realism treats language as a taken-for-granted resource, and shows little concern for the language of representation itself. Hence the realist approach may actually result in rather *thin* descriptions (Atkinson 1982) that do not do justice to the complexity of cultural forms and social life.

Van Maanen's own analysis of the conventions of ethnographic writing identified two further styles beyond the realist mode. If the realist style constructs relatively impersonal, cool, and detached texts, the others are distinct from it. What Van Maanen described as "impressionistic" writing—less used in traditional texts but increasingly incorporated into ethnographic texts—more self-consciously uses "literary" language. It generates a less factual style of reportage, aiming instead at the vivid evocation of a setting, mood, or event. Thirdly, the confessional style is in sharp contrast to the realist mode. Here the approach is an overtly personal one: the ethnographer writes explicitly about her or his personal experiences of life "in the field."

If the realist mode places the author outside of the text and constructs her or him as an impersonal observer and reporter, the confessional mode writes the ethnographer into the text as an actor within the research process itself. As Van Maanen points out, the traditional approach to confessional autobiographical accounts was to keep them separate from the realist reportage. They were consigned to appendices or anthologies of first-person accounts of fieldwork. This separation functioned, if anything, to affirm the factual, authoritative status of realist texts by translating the personal to a genre of its own. For a recent example of this type of autobiographical account, on the dilemmas of fieldwork in postsocialist states, see the anthology edited by De Soto and Dudwick (2000).

In relatively recent years, ethnographic writing has become much more variegated, with authors mixing impressionistic and autobiographical writing with the reportage of their data and its analysis. On the other hand, realist writing continues to define the taken-for-granted methods of textual representation. Experimental texts that are impressionistic and deploy a variety of textual styles continue to be placed within a genre of their own rather than replacing the more standard realist mode of representation.

Whether or not one sees the "crisis" of representation as revolution or evolution; as a result of poststructural discourses, or emergent from a wider variety of sources, there are a number of elements that can be highlighted. The variety of critiques about qualitative research writing have exposed the conventionality of texts and laid the path for alternative representations and textual forms. The authorship of qualitative research has also been made "visible," and highlighted as privileged and privileging. Ethnographic texts have been conceptualized within wider discourses of power and exploitation, and the authority of the text has been subjected to critical scrutiny. Moreover conventional ethnographic texts have been exposed as monovocal—and not necessarily the best means by which the complexity of social reality can be represented. The "observed" are represented as "other," and often rendered mute, deprived of a "voice" and culturally legitimized means of expression; visible and audible only through the eyes, voice(s), and texts of the dominant group. In the next section, we consider the extent to which these points have been addressed by calls to more alternative and creative representational forms.

The celebration of alternative and creative representations produces a tension for those whose research has been funded to address policy issues, and/or wish to bring about social change. This has always been a danger: the famous novel about the Chicago stockyards in the 1890s was partly intended to produce action to improve the lives of the workers. The public outcry actually focused on the unhygienic nature of the meat being produced. Policy makers, politicians, the media, and those hostile to all social science can be dismissive of very plain, conventional texts, and can seize upon the "wrong" things. Brettel's *When They Read What We Write* and the hostile reception of Scheper–Hughes (1977 and 2001) and McDonald (1989) by the communities they worked in are salutary. However poetry, dialogues, plays, multivocal texts, and probably the use of visual and technological media are all likely to be at best baffling, and at worst counterproductive, for non-academic readers.

EXPERIMENTS AND ALTERNATIVES

As we have already noted, Denzin and Lincoln's moments model of qualitative research illuminates changes that have occurred to the ways in which ethnography is represented. Denzin and Lincoln's sixth moment, for example, points to experimental representational styles that disrupt and re-center the self. And in Lincoln and Denzin's (2000) vision of the future of qualitative research—the seventh moment—these themes are recurrent and consolidated. The seventh moment "connects the past with the present and the future," and qualitative inquiry is imagined in the twenty-first century as "simultaneously minimal, existential, autoethnographic, vulnerable, performative, and critical" (Lincoln and Denzin 2000: 1048). Selves, autobiographical ethnography, representation, and performance are all part of an envisaged future of qualitative work. There is an emphasis on "making ourselves visible in our texts" (1053); and on not one future but many—to quote from Lincoln and Denzin (2000: 1060):

> . . . not one "moment," but rather many; not one "voice," but polyvocality; not one story, but many tales, dramas, pieces of fiction, fables, memories, histories, autobiographies, poems, and other texts to inform our sense of lifeways, to extend our understandings of the Other, to provide us with the material for "cultural critique."

The critical attention paid to the processes and products of qualitative research writing has certainly led to a more self-conscious approach to authorship and audience. The impersonal all-but-invisible narrator status of the author has been questioned, alongside a critical appreciation of the power relations of textual production and representation of the social world. In placing the observable into recognizable textual formats, the opportunity to make the social world "readable" has now been located alongside vexed issues of authorship, authenticity, and responsibility. Moreover, conventional ethnographic texts, such as the research monograph, have been criticized for failing to do adequate justice to the polyvocality of social life and the complexity of social forms, experiences, and biographies.

These sustained critiques have prompted, and can be framed within, the articulation, practice, and evaluation of other representational forms. Often referred to as alternative or experimental (though they adopt conventional genres found in the worlds of literature, theatre, and biographical practice), these forms of representation could be viewed as part of an avant garde (or postmodern) spirit of experimentation (see the introduction to this book). They are innovative and creative responses, presenting new ways of seeing and representing. They also reflect a more general (postmodernist/ feminist/critical race theory) agenda of addressing how research is translated into representational and knowledge forms. As we have noted, conventional scholarly texts have been held up as embodying an essentially modernist set of assumptions—predicated on a discovery of social reality through selective, unproblematized, and scientific acts of engagement, inspection, and notation (and told through a realist, narrated genre). Postmodern agendas treat the status of texts in different ways, as *representations* or interpretations of social reality. This allows for the transgression of literary boundaries, and calls for an aesthetic that does not necessarily celebrate consistency of form.

There are a number of ways in which the qualitative researcher's position of privilege has been potentially transformed through representation diversification. However, as Lather (1991) has argued, these alternative representational modes do not necessarily remove issues of power from ethnographic production, and are at risk of falling into "static claims" of authenticity (Lather 2001). Nevertheless, the textual formats of ethnographic representation have been challenged, and a more self-conscious approach has been prompted. Significantly these calls to "new" forms of representation have signified a return of the author to the text (Lincoln and Denzin 2000). Drawing on a dialogic approach to text (Allan 1994; Holquist 1990), many of these "alternative" representational forms actually exploit the conventions of naturalistic conversation or theater or literature, in order to draw out the poetical and performative qualities of everyday life.

Ethnodrama, or ethnographic theater, is one articulation of this approach—producing scripts, or even live performances of social events. Mienczakowski (1995 and 1996) has used ethnodrama extensively to "performance" the experiences of people and a variety of settings (for example experiences of alcohol detoxification, experiences of schizophrenia, police interviews with victims of sexual assaults). Mienczakowski (2001) argues that performed ethnography can make qualitative research more accessible than is the case with conventional texts, and can return the "*ownership*, and therefore the power, of the report to its informants, as opposed to *possessing it* on behalf of the academy" (471). Paget (1990) adopted a performative or dramaturgical approach to give ethnographic representation to experiences of cancer (see also Bluebond–Langer 1980, who used a similar approach to explore the social worlds of dying children). Multivoiced (or split screen) texts have also been used to represent the polyvocality, or multivocality, of social life and research endeavors. For example, Lather and Smithies (1997) used split text formats to give layers of voices (their own and their respondents) in their representation of women living with HIV/AIDS. And Fox (1996) experiments with multivoiced texts to (re)present contested voices and give subversive readings of child sexual abuse.

Ethnopoetry (Richardson 1994) is a further example of a literary form utilized to ethnographic ends. The use of poetry in ethnographic representation can offer a means of capturing the pauses, rhymes, and rhythms of everyday life, enabling the social world to be seen, heard, and felt in new dimensions:

> Writing "data" as poetic representations reveals the constraining belief that the purpose of a social science text is to convey information as facts of themes or notions existing independent of the contexts in which they were found or produced—as if the story we have recorded, transcribed,

edited, and written up in prose snippets is the one and only true one: a "science" story." Standard prose writing conceals the handprint of the sociologist who produced the final written text. (Richardson 2000: 933)

Richardson's story of the life of Louisa May (Richardson 1992) is one of the most cited of the ethnographic poems. Richardson represents her informant's life in poetic form, using Louisa May's "voice, diction, hill-southern rhythms and tone" (Richardson 2000: 933). The result is a striking, historically situated, poetic narrative. Like McCoy's (1997) poetry exploring preservice teacher discourses, Richardson's poetry provides a mode of evocative representation that disrupts conventional, and promotes new, understandings.

Other modes of ethnographic representation have included photographic essays, ethnographic "fiction," the use of diary and journal formats, and multimedia texts (some or all of which have also been utilized in the calls to autoethnography, see chapter 1 of this book). These have all been concerned with challenging taken-for-granted or conventional modes of representing the social world, and with the blurring of literary boundaries. The potential of computer software for qualitative data analysis and representation is also worth mentioning here. We do not wish to rehearse all of the debates about qualitative data analysis software in this chapter (see Coffey, Holbrook, and Atkinson 1996, and chapter 6 of this book); suffice it to say that it embodies two contradictory positions. On the one hand, criticisms have been levelled at computer software approaches for encouraging an overly simplified and mechanical application to analysis and grounded theorizing (interestingly this would fit in well with Lofland's contention that a greater reliance on technology might lead to a standardization of form). On the other hand, contemporary technology can offer significant representational potential for the qualitative researcher (see Dicks and Mason 1998; Mason and Dicks 1996).

Hypertext applications can support a more complex, messy, and cyclical approach to textual production. Similarly, hypermedia applications can allow a multidimensional authoring and reading environment to be created. As approaches to ethnographic representation, these forms are relatively new. Yet, like other alternative representational forms they offer new possibilities—perhaps better placed to recognize and (re)present complex social worlds. In the spirit of creativity and a more self-conscious ethnography, we might cautiously welcome such innovations, although most debates have focussed on written texts (interestingly film has long been part of ethnography).

Alternative representational modes make, then, a number of claims, through which some of the "crises" in qualitative research are addressed. By utilizing different representational styles, we are able to produce more self-conscious and reflective texts, grounded in emotionality and lived experience. Modes of "writing" such as dialogic texts, ethnodrama, poetry, and multi-layered texts are better placed to capture the different dimensions, "voices," and polyvocality of complex social worlds. By challenging conventional representational forms we can make authorship visible and transparent, at the same time providing opportunities for shifting the balance of power. These represent, according to Denzin and Lincoln (2000: 17), the present and future of qualitative research, where "fictional ethnographies, ethnographic poetry, and multimedia texts are today taken for granted."

Despite these claims, we remain cautious of the extent to which alternative representations can and should change the ethnographic landscape. Some commentators (for example, see Lal 1996) have questioned the possibilities of the "textual turn" in relocating the balance of power in qualitative research, while others have made the case that issues of power do not simply disappear (Lather 1991). D. L. Wolf (1996) also argues that textual experimentation often fails to challenge conventionally derived power differentials:

> Despite important efforts to experiment with strategies of representation and authorship, the basic power differentials and the distribution of benefits of research remain the same. Few practical changes that have been attempted translate into radically transforming the researcher's privileged position. While more theorizing on these contradictions is needed, perhaps an acknowledgement of their irreconcilability is also necessary. (D. L. Wolf 1996: 34)

Hence, creative approaches to the production of qualitative texts can promote a reflexive and self-conscious approach to writing and authorship. They can create opportunities for more realistic (complex) pictures of events, and may serve to blur power boundaries, but in themselves they do not solve power differentials (see Mienczakowski 2001). Texts, even creative, experimental, or alternative ones, are still authored, edited, and crafted. Indeed the very artfulness of these texts can actually draw attention to the craftwork of authorship. Ethnodrama, scripts, and poetry, for example, emphasize the creative potential and power of the author, by overtly manipulating the appearance and ordering of words, voices, and texts. These place the ethnographer as author in the foreground and demand that the aesthetic qualities of the text are noted. Rather than simply making the author visible, such calls to aesthetics can increase, rather than diminish, distance between author and "other," making the craftwork of authorship more rather than less visible.

Lather's essay for *The Handbook of Ethnography* (Atkinson et al. 2001) warns, "at risk is a romance of the speaking subject and a metaphysics of presence complicated by the identity and experience claims of insider/ outsider tensions" (Lather 2001: 483). Hence sentiments of authenticity and voice should not be used to "appropriate the lives of others into consumption, a too easy, too familiar eating of the other" (Lather 2001: 484).

As we noted in chapter 2, Mykhalovskiy (1997) has defended various calls to autobiographical sociology, arguing that a charge of narcissism or self-indulgence can actually be perceived as ironic, for it inevitably gives support for "a solitary, authorial voice who writes a text disembodied from the individuals involved in its production" (Mykhalovskiy 1997: 246). On the other hand, reflexivity in textual production, and all it might spawn in terms of alternative representations, should not be used as a justification for self-indulgence or navel gazing (Silverman 1997).

A paper about a diverted flight on September 11, 2001, by Ellis (2002) is a case in point. It is "revealing," in a carefully crafted way, about Ellis. It is not analytic, or even informative about any particular aspects of American culture and social life. It does not even refer to Goffman's darkly pessimistic essay on the "insanity of place" (Goffman 1971, appendix). It does not render flying itself strange, nor does it create any other object of study. To a reader in Spain, Israel, Palestine, or Northern Ireland—where terrorist atrocities or scares routinely disrupt mundane familial and other commitments, it is not even original. We should not lose sight of the fact that research is (and should be) judged by "what it tells us about those under study, not just what it reveals about the social scientist" (Fay 1996: 217). Or as Spencer (2001: 450) argues:

> A formalized version of postmodern ethnography, alternating between stock passages of ethnographic self-consciousness and (carefully edited and positioned) "voices" is in danger of becoming the disciplinary norm, while students have to be constantly warned that sometimes the people they are talking to are more interesting than the people asking the questions.

There is also a major issue around the author's skill as a writer. Producing good, well-written poems, plays, dialogues, and messy texts is much,

much harder than producing coherent traditional academic descriptions and discussions. At least one publisher has told us informally that his desk is awash in experimental writing from ethnographers who simply do not write well enough to be playful with their texts.

A number of cautions have been articulated and debated in discussions about the narrative or textual turn in qualitative research (see for example Atkinson 1997b; Bochner 2001; Ellis and Bochner 2000; Reed-Danahay 2001; Tedlock 2000), and are discussed too in chapter 2. While we do not agree with Snow and Morrill (1995: 361) that postmodern approaches to ethnographic representation signal "the death knell of ethnography as an empirically grounded enterprise," we would not wish to see reflexivity becoming synonymous with autobiographic therapy. It is the case that the tools and scripts of ethnography can be fruitful in exploring and making sense of our own lives and experiences (see, for example, Paget 1990 and 1993; Sparkes 1996). However, such applications should not replace the desire to make sense of other (and help others make sense of their own) lives and complex social worlds.

It would be all too easy to assume that qualitative research is now firmly in the post-post period, where experimental representations and interpretive ethnographic practices are the norm. As Denzin and Lincoln (2000: 23) argue, "it is certain that things will never again be the same. We are in a new age where messy, uncertain, multivoiced texts, cultural criticism, and new experimental works will become more common." But will they, or have they become "more common?" Can we now take for granted this new representational diversity—and the potential (as well as the limitations) it offers? We believe that it would be wrong to take anything for granted in this context. Despite inclusion in the contemporary "state of the art" edited volumes such as the *Handbook of Qualitative Research* (Denzin and Lincoln 2000) and the *Handbook of Ethnography* (Atkinson et al. 2001) it is not the case that all of qualitative research is now taking place in a post-experimental, poststructural, performance space.

A lot of the early debates about representation and legitimacy actually took place in anthropology, rather than in sociology and other related disciplines. And while these debates have now broadened in scope, we are not all operating in a realm of representational experimentation and diversity. In practice, the impact of such articulations on the written products of qualitative research has been peripheral (Delamont, Coffey, and Atkinson 2000). In education, for example, the experimental texts are almost completely confined to the journal *Qualitative Studies in Education* (and they are a minority of articles even in that journal); other journals such as *Teaching and Teacher Education, Gender and Education,* and the *British Journal of Education* all publish qualitative research, but in much the same traditional forms that Lofland's paper commented on in the 1970s. *Anthropology and Education Quarterly* has not changed stylistically at all over the period from 1978 to 1998. In sociology, both in the United Kingdom and in the United States, conventional textual forms predominate in the journals and in the monographs across all the empirical and theoretical specialisms. Only one subset of sociologists in Britain embraced polyvocal forms enthusiastically, and that was a small subgroup in the sociology of science, inspired by the work of Michael Mulkay, who produced a brief flurry of experimental works, but seem to have abandoned that style of work again (Ashmore, Myers, and Potter 1995).

Experimental texts have been more common in the United States than in the United Kingdom and Europe, where it is difficult to point to more than a handful of examples (see for example Rath 2001). And even within the United States the "performance" turn has been largely restricted to a handful of (albeit influential) scholars and their students. For many scholars and students of qualitative research, experimental texts remain a world away. Even in American anthropology many scholars continue to produce texts in classic styles: Sutton's (2000) ethnography of the island of Karpathos, Greece, is structured in essentially the same way as Danforth's study of Ayia Eleni, Greece (1982), and Friedl's (1962) study of the village of Vasilika, also in Greece. These ethnographies display a remarkable continuity of style across forty years.

This does not mean that new forms of representation should be ignored, or dismissed as a minority quirk, far from it. Nor does it mean that we should dismiss many of the past and present texts because they do not fully engage with the so-called new ways of "composing" ethnography (Ellis and Bochner 1996). Spencer (2001) writes of the speed at which the 1980s critique of writing was routinized within mainstream anthropology, and of the potentially corrosive effects of postmodern introspection. He argues for strong reflexivity, "which recognizes that the ethnographer and his or her language are inevitably part of the phenomenon that is being investigated" (450), and the recognition that with this reflexivity comes responsibility—"for the consequences of a particular way of representing the words and practices of other people" (450). This then is a call to complexity and difference, rather than homogeneity or generalization. This recognizes the complexity and partiality of all accounts and representations, without dismissing them out of hand as poor ethnography. In this sense, reflexivity is a liberator, but not a prescription for certain kinds of alternative texts, narrowly defined:

It is now possible to write extraordinarily rich, and even sometimes extraordinarily readable, ethnographies which are quite open about their limitations and partiality, and which manage to acknowledge the complexity of the world, and thus the difficulty of rendering it through words on a page, without sacrificing coherence of clarity. (Spencer 2001: 450)

CONCLUSIONS

We began this chapter by addressing an early publication on the writing of ethnography by John Lofland. We did so for three reasons. First, it is one of the few published reflections on textual formats from the period of our methodological classics that we have used as starting points for our discussions throughout this book. Secondly, it shows that even before the intellectual ferment generated by the so-called crisis of representation, it was possible to identify a variety of styles and representations within the literature of sociological ethnography. It would, therefore, be wrong to assume that prior to more recent developments and experiments there was a single representational style in use. Thirdly, and in contrast to the later interventions, it is clear that Lofland is not seeking to engage in or promote "experimental" writing styles. His work—and it would reflect the more general style of thought at the time—was concerned with advocating what he thought of as the most appropriate modes of ethnographic authorship. He explored textual variety in order to understand how readers of ethnographic texts evaluate them in the course of peer review. He was not suggesting that sociological authors should actively seek to disrupt and transgress those expectations as to what constitutes successful ethnographic writing. In the intervening years, by contrast, the writing of ethnographic and other qualitative research has obviously become yet more diverse. In response to critical reflection that drew on a variety of cultural and literary theory, some anthropologists and sociologists have self-consciously engaged in experimental writing methods. The genres of ethnographic writing have expanded, and some have become more overtly aesthetic. Literary models have been adopted with greater self-consciousness.

   It would be misleading, however, to conclude that the entire face of ethnographic research has been transformed. The greater visibility of experimental writing and the proliferation of texts advocating literary styles and experimental ethnographic texts can readily create a false impression. It is certainly not the case that the entire research community has lurched from a uniform adherence to conventionally realist texts to the wholesale adoption of new literary forms. In fact, the vast majority of sociological, anthropological, and other work deriving from qualitative research continues to be reported and published in modes that are not explicitly literary. The majority of experimental texts remain confined to rather small networks of researchers, and are published in a restricted range of places. A small number of journals, for instance, encourage and publish contributions that are in unconventional forms. There are a few research groupings and associated edited collections of papers that promote alternative and experimental texts. Monographs that reflect new forms of representation are few and far between, mostly restricted to the lists of a small number of publishing houses. We have not, in other words, witnessed a major revolution or paradigm shift in the representation of ethnographic research.

It is sometimes claimed that the "crisis of representation" shook the foundations of cultural anthropology more than any previous disputes. Theoretical disputations in anthropology have been quite common, and they have certainly been acrimonious at times. They have not undermined the most cherished of the discipline's bases, however. Anthropology always had the monograph. Anthropologists could wrangle over the most appropriate interpretation of the ethnographic evidence, and there could always be a margin of dispute over the precise details of ethnographic reportage. But the monograph remained the bedrock of anthropological knowledge. When the crisis of representation took place, it was sometimes alleged that the discipline of anthropology was thrown into disarray because the conduct and representation of ethnography were themselves thrown into question. At the level of epistemological dispute, that may be the case. On the other hand, it clearly has not fundamentally disrupted the production of practical ethnographic monographs and papers. Anthropological fieldwork continues to be reported in conventional ways much as it has been—with notable exceptions—for generations of practitioners and authors.

Sociology has never had the same reliance on the ethnographic monograph. It has long been a much more fragmented domain than anthropology, from that point of view. It has been touched even less by textual crisis. A small number of sociological texts have, as we have said, reflected the literary turn. But the great majority of texts—even those based on quite self-conscious and epistemologically radical premises—continue to inscribe conventional literary styles. It would be even more inaccurate to claim that sociological work has been radically transformed by the literary turn in ethnographic representation. This is not especially surprising, of course. By definition, the avant garde is never the accepted style of the majority. It rarely leads to revolutionary changes that affect the entire academic or artistic field. We should therefore not exaggerate the impact of newer and experimental styles on the relevant academic fields. On the other hand, avant garde movements have a function that is not measured simply by the number of practitioners who adopt their approach. They have the function of making everyone more aware of their own practices and the conventions within which they work. The literary turn in ethnographic writing should not be expected to create a complete transformation in how we all write, or in how we write everything. Indeed, there is something especially annoying and precious in the work of a handful of contemporary authors who seem to write everything in "literary" styles.

The literary turn has created new possibilities in the representation of qualitative research. As we have indicated in the course of this chapter, it helps us to see the conventions of textual representation for what they are—conventions like any other, which can be explored, changed, and overturned. However, there are dangers in the sustained use of self-consciously literary genres. There is a paradox, an irony, in the use of literary forms by at least some authors. The crisis of representation and its aftermath was in part a critique of the monologic, authorial voice of the more traditional ethnographer-as-author. It sought to disrupt the surface of the text so as to render more problematic the authority of the observer/narrator. The development of literary forms such as poetry or drama can throw a renewed emphasis onto the individual author. The basis for "authority" may well shift: the warrant for the work, and the evaluative criteria it invites, include aesthetic values. But the literary work of the individual author still pervades the work. If a life history is to be re-presented as a poem, or if a series of social encounters is to be reconstructed into a drama, then the "voices" that might inhabit that work are still pressed into service to serve the author's own interests. There is a potential tyranny of the literary author, who turns the social world inexorably into her or his own literary style. This danger is compounded when the literary merits of the work are limited. There are already too many texts that follow rather tired styles of "creative writing" classes. Moreover, such writing too often stresses the emotional engagement and response of the author herself or himself. Consequently, there is a clear danger that the literary turn in ethnographic writing could transform social worlds into a series of autobiographical encounters with them, in which the emotional and aesthetic response of the author is granted more prominence than the social actions of the members of those social domains.

Conclusion

CONTINUITIES AND CHANGES

In concluding these chapters, we do not do so with a simple set of methodological precepts or formulae, nor do we intend to proclaim yet another new paradigm or moment in the development of qualitative research. In some ways, we have an anti-conclusion to offer—that perhaps we need less methodological ferment, less novelty, and less emphasis on methodology itself. The positive side of that is: we need more research that is methodical, sensible, accessible, and comprehensible. In any event, it is clearly time to take stock.

In the preceding chapters, we have attempted to take stock of the current situation by looking back and by addressing a series of classic themes in the conduct of and reflection on qualitative research. This is not an empty exercise in retro chic, nor is it a gratuitous invocation of older papers and positions. We have certainly not invoked the work of such distinguished role models as Howard Becker, Blanche Geer, or John Lofland in order to treat them and their arguments as if they were museum pieces. As we have said, we think that their concerns were valid when they were first voiced, and they remain pertinent now. The world has changed, undoubtedly, and one could not—and would not wish to—return to earlier approaches. However, it *could* be argued that too many of today's authors seem to have forgotten earlier contributions, and celebrate novelty with undue enthusiasm and with insufficient attention to the older literatures. We are not convinced by all of the most fashionable of contemporary arguments, while recognizing the positive contribution they also bring to bear. In this concluding section, we recapitulate and reflect on these debates, in order to outline some of our misgivings and criticisms. We believe that there are excesses in the contemporary positions, and that there are problems as well as gains in the developments of recent years.

Let us discuss our themes once more (albeit in a different order from the way they appear in the main body of the book). We begin our conclusion by revisiting the seemingly perennial question encapsulated in Becker's question "Whose side are we on?" Becker's question was by no means rhetorical. The taking of "sides" was of considerable moment among the social scientists he was addressing directly in his presidential address, and indirectly through publication and citation. Becker's advocacy was among the many voices raised (against the claims for "value-free" social science). Social research and social theory too often served and endorsed specific social interests and values, while masking those interests behind claims for scientific neutrality. Becker helped to make values and interests explicit. He stressed for his hearers and his readers that it was incumbent on qualitative researchers *not* to take on trust the taken-for-granted hierarchies of credibility when considering the understandings and perspectives of deviants and others. The social researcher should thus be able to shift his or her own analytic stance, in order to comprehend the rationality and morality of the "underdog." Becker's own formulation of the issue was at once political and methodological. Indeed, it was the strength of his original formulation so eloquently to elide the two. In his hands, the methodological is ideological. It is a methodological issue in that the social researcher must be able to suspend everyday assumptions concerning reason and ethics. Interpretative analysis depends on the capacity to "take the role of the other" and to be able to shift perspective from social position to social position.

It must be remembered, however, that Becker was addressing the Society for the Study of Social Problems. He was primarily concerned with the empirical investigation of "social problems," such as crime and deviance. He contributed with distinction to the burgeoning literature on deviance, and he wrote at a time when sociologists and criminologists were doing a great deal to establish an intellectual commitment, a corpus of work, and a style of intellectual engagement. The empirical work proved durable. Although criminology and deviance studies have developed since Becker first wrote—and Becker's own work developed, too—the studies of drug users and other deviant subcultures are among the classic works of modern sociology. The background to Becker's own pronouncements was an engagement with social issues of some moment. The politics were not revolutionary. The interactionist sociologists were not aligned with the most politicized of sociological movements—notably those of European radicals. Nevertheless, in the tradition of Chicago sociology, they provided an empirical basis for a liberal critique of contemporary society. The reversal of perspective, from alignment with officialdom toward alignment with the

deviant, highlighted the work of social control agents in defining and producing the categories of deviance.

There was, therefore, considerable intellectual commitment involved
in Becker's formulation of partisanship. Equally, as we have discussed, in
the 1960s research methods themselves were not always invested with the
same ethical and ideological commitments that have accrued in recent
years. Becker and his contemporaries clearly did not see the conduct of
fieldwork as entirely neutral. The intellectual and personal commitment
to field research implies an attitude towards everyday life that is—in broad
terms—ethical as well as methodological. One does not have to endorse
the forms of life one studies in order to conduct field research, and one
certainly does not have to like the people one works with. But one cannot successfully conduct research and interpret it without taking seriously
the groups and individuals with whom one works. We take people seriously by applying analytic principles of symmetry to them and to others:
by attributing rational intentions and actions; by assuming a degree of coherence and continuity in their lives; by paying attention to the concrete
details of their everyday lives; by listening attentively, and by acknowledging their status as human subjects. So much was clear in the classic formulations of fieldwork methods and ethics. Attention to the moral order
is itself a moral commitment.

As we have suggested, however, Becker's formulation also helps to
show that the categories within which such precepts were formulated were
themselves relatively simple. In the intervening years, the research process
has become increasingly complex, both methodologically and politically.
We, as intellectuals, are an increasingly diverse constituency, and "we" certainly cannot assume a relatively uniform array of shared values and commitments. The academic world of social science has become almost as fractured as the social worlds we study. Even a relatively stable liberal consensus
cannot be assumed to exist, certainly not in the terms of the 1960s or 1970s.
The increasingly sectional interests of feminist, queer, subaltern, and other
standpoints have rendered problematic the idea of partisanship. At any rate
they have made it much more difficult to assume that there is a liberal consensus that provides a relatively stable position from which the sociologist's
perspectival gaze can be directed. In their wake, however, these various
standpoint analyses carry with them a danger. Too often, we believe, the social problems—such as those engaged with by Becker—have been replaced
with personal and private problems. Too often, contemporary commentators and analysts have treated the political commitment in terms of identity
politics. Too many contemporary authors claim a warrant for the legitimacy

of their research and their interpretations in terms of their own biography and their own identity. Gender, sexual orientation, ethnic heritage, family circumstances, health status, and disability—these and other sources of identity are used to define personal commitments and analytic stances.

The translation of social problems into private issues, and the reliance on identity results in a quite different kind of analytic stance from that advocated by Becker and his contemporaries. Becker's view of fieldwork and its analysis were predicated on shifting perspectives. As we have just suggested, the classic sociological view advocated the capacity to take the role of the "other." It was in part a reflection of even more long-standing and classic formulations of interactionist sociology—such as the notion of the reciprocity of perspectives. It also echoed the influential contribution of theorists like Simmel, in their advocacy of a perspectival social science. This was the view that Karl Mannheim famously sought to articulate as well. That is, the capacity of the social analyst to *shift* her or his interpretative stance. Standpoint theories and related ideological commitments are predicated on quite different principles. They assume that one's personal identity or social position provide a relatively *fixed* point of reference. They assume that the researcher is not capable of shifting perspective and taking the role of the other. They tend to be predicated not on a multiplicity of perspectives, but on an identity between the researcher and the researched. If we are to preserve the essence of the anthropological or sociological imagination, therefore, we need to cultivate still the capacity to *bracket* our own identities and commonsense assumptions, not *only* to celebrate them as personal warrants of knowledge.

We have discussed the remarkable changes that have taken place in the representation of qualitative research through writing practices. It is, on the whole, to the benefit of social research that practitioners, methodologists, and theorists have become increasingly sensitive to the consequences of writing strategies. We cannot now treat the writing of social research as innocent. No student or researcher should think that qualitative research can simply be "written up" in accordance with unquestioned conventions. One may choose to write in "traditional" styles and formats, but following the attention paid to the topic over the past quarter century, one should regard that strategy as a conscious decision, and not a self-evident matter. It is clearly not necessary to go on referring to this as the "crisis of representation." If it is a crisis, then it is a very protracted spasm. In any case, social scientists have gone on reconstructing and representing the social world, using a variety of different representational styles, from the most traditional to the most alternative and literary modes available (verse, drama, visual arts). A mature perspective suggests that we do not need to endorse the cult of the new here. We do not all need to embrace alternative literary forms. Writing is undoubtedly a significant aspect of analysis. Again, we can see that writing and representation can never be innocent. There is no absolutely neutral and transparent medium of social representation. The most tried-and-trusted of realist formats carry specific connotations of authorship and authority.

Extremes of self-conscious authorship and textual innovation carry their own dangers, however. They include the risk of aestheticizing social phenomena. We mean that there is a risk of privileging the stylistic qualities of sociological or anthropological accounts as the primary criterion of value. While all representations are dependent on conventions of writing and reading, some are more overtly dependent on aesthetic criteria: the social scientist who constructs a poem is implicitly inviting evaluation on a different set of criteria from the social scientist who presents a more penny-plain approach. Indeed, we believe that there is a paradox at the heart of the aesthetic movement. The critique of conventional monographs and papers included the charge that such texts inscribed an implicit kind of authority. The researcher-as-author was accused of presenting a hegemonic view, based on the omniscience of the realist author, whose authority was implicitly enhanced by her or his virtual *absence* from the text. The "degree zero" style—as Roland Barthes referred to an equivalent literary style—exerted a powerful constraining force on the reader. The authorial viewpoint was fixed, and the voice monologic. Ironically, however, aestheticizing tendencies have introduced new ways of privileging the author. His or her superiority is claimed not on the basis of authorial absence, but on the basis of overt authorial felicity. All texts are crafted. In that sense they are all fictions. But the elaborately wrought, multilayered text draws attention to its fictive nature with heightened urgency. In producing such a textual work, the author simultaneously draws attention to her or himself *as author*. The celebration of textual experimentation thus generates a new form of authorial superiority. It is grounded not in the monologic, single-viewpoint text of the traditional monograph, but in the self-consciously aestheticizing text of the ethnographer-as-author. In some ways, this exercises a hegemonic relation to the reader and to the subjects of the research even stronger than more simple textual forms. It draws attention to the creative capacity of the author. It resists reinterpretation from other theoretical perspectives, because the analysis is so inextricably intertwined with the presentational mode. It translates the shared social phenomena that are its subject matter into an individualized work. It thus mirrors the process of translating public issues into identity politics. Here, public discourse is translated into a personalized idiom.

The crafts of writing and representation are but one way in which the analytic processes of qualitative research have become diversified, and in which older canonical forms of analytic reasoning have been fragmented and made problematic. In practice, there seem to have been two countervailing tendencies in recent years. On the one hand, there has been a clear trend toward what we have called the "convergent" mode of reasoning. There has emerged a persistent kind of orthodoxy that deals with the analysis of qualitative data in somewhat rigid and stereotyped ways. This approach is not to be found on the wilder shores of postmodern social science, but flourishes in the applied areas of qualitative research (where most of the "work" continues to be conducted). It relies on a rather oversimplified notion of "grounded theory" or some other approximation to inductive data analysis. It usually uses the language of data coding, and is also often—by no means always—accompanied by the use of a code-and-retrieve strategy implemented by means of computer-aided qualitative data analysis software. Now we know that such software does not necessarily and inherently constrain its users to follow a particular methodological strategy. But there has been an elective affinity between the rise of code-and-retrieve functions in those software products and the widespread use of so-called "grounded theory" approaches, in what has become a widely implemented version of analytic orthodoxy.

If this represents a continuing centripetal tendency, there are—as we have seen—centrifugal movements that celebrate and commend a profusion of different analytic strategies, and a similar diversity of criteria for the evaluation of research. In many ways, we welcome this diversity. It is important to emphasize repeatedly that any analytic strategies should be thought of primarily as heuristic devices, and not as procedures to be followed slavishly. In any interpretative discipline—such as those that qualitative research informs—analysis necessarily transcends procedural recipes. The insistence on strict evaluative criteria and canons of analytic practice within a paradigmatic framework is not productive. We are not sympathetic to those who translate exploratory strategies like "grounded theory" into canonical forms. Equally, however, the proliferation of "post-paradigmatic" criteria is dangerous. When it is possible to identify as many criteria for "validity" as there are authors contributing to the debate, then the entire notion seems to be rendered vacuous. We do not need to rely on straitjackets of methodological prescription in order to sustain elementary notions of adequacy: research should be methodical, systematic, careful, attentive to detail, densely grounded in data, and theoretically sensitive. What is urgently needed is not a proliferation of mannerist exaggerations, but a series of approaches that rest on transparent and simpler expressions of methodical procedure.

We have considered a number of other strategic and analytic uses that highlight similar themes. We have in two related chapters considered the nature of actions and accounts. We returned to the classic questions concerning the reliability of informants' accounts. The classic formulations of interview data were partly predicated on a well-established and much-quoted distinction between what people do and what people say they do. In the earlier papers, there was a clear tendency to privilege the observation of social action over informants' accounts. The former represented the gold standard, while the latter were sometimes represented as inferior proxy data *about* unobserved action. In recent years, the literature seems almost to have come full circle. Qualitative methods are often equated with the enactment of interviews and the analysis of interview data. Moreover, the accounts derived from research interviews—personal accounts—have achieved a central place in the repertoire of qualitative researchers. There has, we have suggested, been a subtle but profound change in the attitudes of the research community towards interview-derived data. Where once the observation of action was prized, more recently narrative accounts of personal experience have been more highly valued. Interviews and other sources of biographical materials are treated as if they provided access to personal, even private, experience. Experience—so-called "lived experience"—itself is treated as a central research topic. We have suggested that this transformation is in itself unnecessary and unhelpful. The emphasis on personal experience and on the biographical can divert analytic attention from collectively organized social action. The social world is transformed into a series of sites of personal recollection and feeling. This analytic stance thus parallels the personalizing tendency that we have already identified in other methodological contexts. If we apply a thoroughgoing social analysis, then we need to recognize that accounts, narratives, memories, and all that might count as "experience" are themselves forms of *action*. They are, moreover, culturally shaped and socially organized. If we take seriously the kinds of insights concerning the social construction of reality that most interpretative social scientists would endorse—in one form or another—then distinctions between what people say and what people do become almost irrelevant.

The same is broadly true of the vexed question concerning the truthfulness of informants' accounts. We are not advocating a naïve willingness to accept everything that people say at face value, nor indeed a wholesale cynicism that assumes that informants and other social actors are constantly engaged in misleading the researcher through their self-presentations and deceptive fronts. Rather, we believe that informants' accounts should be neither endorsed nor disregarded: they need to be analyzed. We need to pay serious attention to the biographical and social *work* that personal accounts and narratives perform. We should take seriously the analysis of culturally shared rhetorics and vocabularies, the accounting devices and socially shared narrative formats that are used in the construction of personal accounts. Accounts are not to be equated with private experiences. We ought to maintain our social research at the level of socially shared representations.

Contemporary qualitative research, then, seems unlikely to ask if the informant is telling "the truth" in a traditional way, and is equally skeptical about the possibility of the analyst telling "the truth." It is more likely to bracket the idea of truth altogether. At the same time, there is a repeated search for authenticity. Personal narratives are too often granted an unquestioned authenticity, as providing an unchallengeable source of "lived experience." This latter response is just as troublesome as the earlier attempts to check accounts against external criteria for their accuracy. If we take at all seriously the social performance of actions—including spoken actions—then we also need to regard "truth" or "deception," plausibility and credibility, and informant's invocation of evidence as accomplishments themselves. We need to pay close attention to how actors' portray themselves as credible, or how they *use* anecdote and biographical materials to enact rational accounts, moral accounts, stories of heroism or victimhood. In other words, paying serious attention to narratives does not imply "believing" them or the reverse. It means treating them as kinds of social action and analyzing them accordingly.

Our "classic" authors were also occupied with two closely related issues. They were concerned with the proper relationship between the researcher and the social actors with whom she or he was working; they were also working with notions of cultural strangeness and familiarity. They were exploring the implications of social difference and of interpretative distance. Problems of "over-rapport" were but one set of issues where this was manifest. Commentators warned against unduly close identification with one's informants or the actors with whom one conducted participant observation. Over-rapport in a social sense was seen to limit the perspectival and social freedom of the researcher. Over-identification with particular individuals or subsets of actors would lead to a partial and restricted view of the social setting. It could lead to resentment and suspicion on the part of other members, so restricting the researcher's access to them and hence to significant information about the social world under investigation. In an intellectual sense, over-identification with any or all aspects of the social setting would dull the analyst's capacity to treat the everyday world as "strange." The proper analytic stance was portrayed as a shifting one, balanced between familiarity and strangeness. The social position of the field researcher of liminality or marginality was paralleled by an intellectual stance of disengagement. In more recent years, in contrast, qualitative researchers have tended to endorse and explore processes of intimacy rather than distance. An emphasis on reflexive ethnography has inserted the researcher into the setting, just as the rethinking of representational practice has inserted the ethnographer into written and visual texts. We have no desire to imply that qualitative research should ignore its essentially reflexive nature: the research process is inescapably predicated on the social relations that constitute "the field." Equally, it is quite impossible to remove the ethnographer's self from the research process. Social inquiry cannot be rendered in impersonal terms.

There are cautions to be leveled at some of the personalizing tendencies in contemporary qualitative research. There may be dangers inherent in overemphasizing the personal aspects of research. Autoethnography and similar exercises are important additions to the repertoire of research strategies and outcomes. Nevertheless, a primary goal of most social research is to understand "other" social worlds, rather than to explore and transform the identity of the researcher. Understanding "others" does not have to imply the "othering" connoted by orientalism and other examples of distancing and exoticizing. Rather, it means, in the best and longest-established traditions of interactionist and other interpretative social science, a capacity to take the role of the other, and to participate in the reciprocity of perspectives between social actors.

We have, therefore, used a number of themes to explore some contemporary tendencies in social research. We have made reference to the claims of "postmodernism" in these methodological contexts. We have not, however, couched our discussion in terms of a dichotomy between "modern" and "postmodern" strategies or paradigms. This is deliberate. Appeals to postmodern culture and to postmodern research perspectives are frequently employed to justify what we have referred to as the avant-garde approach. Too often, however, postmodernism is used as a catch-all term, too rarely explored in explicit detail, used to warrant a diverse range of attitudes and approaches. It is not clear, however, that there is a coherent postmodern position, nor is it clear that contemporary avant-garde methodology bears a consistent set of relations with postmodernist social theory. (The further confusions of postmodernism in the context of literary and aesthetic theories confound the general position even more.)

In any event, we do not believe that currently fashionable contrasts between today's postmodernism and the modernism of yesteryear are altogether warranted, in a consideration of qualitative research. Such contrasts are at best oversimplified, and at worst, thoroughly misleading representations of the development of qualitative research. Our own rhetorical device in structuring this collection of essays could too readily be interpreted as reinforcing such distinctions. We have contrasted a particular contemporary style of thought with the publications of an earlier generation when methodological issues were being formulated most explicitly. This is not intended to reflect a simple, unidirectional developmental line, however. As well as having reservations about aspects of so-called postmodern methodology, we also have reservations about the reconstructed intellectual histories that are used to justify the postmodern position. Recent accounts of ethnography, and of qualitative research more generally, have tended to suggest a field in turmoil, characterized by an accelerating rate of change, increasingly divorced from its intellectual roots. Such characterizations are themselves narrative constructions, and they contribute to the wider narratives of change at the century's end. We suggest that these narratives gain their force in part from neglect of the ambiguities and nuances of the ethnographic project that have extended over many decades.

The general historical framework developed by authors like Denzin and Lincoln captures the current sense of fragmentation and diversity in ethnography. They picture an intellectual field undergoing ever-accelerated change, growth, and reconfiguration.

The narratives of postmodernism (and poststructuralism, postfeminism, postcolonialism, and so on) are used to describe one specific type of historical "past" for ethnographic research methods. They outline a developmental trend that culminates in contemporary practices. Such narratives can mislead, or distort the intellectual field—of the past, the present, and the future. We do not wish to dissent totally from Lincoln and Denzin in their account of the current state of play in qualitative or ethnographic research. The multiplicity of perspectives and practices are not in doubt, are well rehearsed and documented (Atkinson and Silverman 1997; Coffey and Atkinson 1996). Ethnography can indeed be characterized in terms of its own cultural diversity; we are, however, less convinced by Denzin and Lincoln's attempt to periodize the development of qualitative research, and even less convinced by the particular developmental narrative they seek to impose. Their "story" is but one of several. The contrast between previous positivist, modernist, and self-confident (but narrow) perspectives, and the contemporary carnivalesque diversity of standpoints, methods, and representations is perhaps too sharply drawn. It could be taken to imply that all contemporary qualitative research takes place from a position of an intellectual field teeming with contested ideas and experimental texts, which is manifestly not the case. Equally, we would suggest that such a chronological and linear view of development perhaps does a disservice to earlier generations of ethnographers.

It is far from clear that there ever were such monolithically "positivist" and "modernist" phases, as identified by Denzin and Lincoln. We argue that it is as wrong to assume that all ethnography in past generations was conducted under the auspices of a positivistic and totalizing gaze as it is to imply that we are all "postmodern" now. We would wish to take issue with the narrow view that there was a traditional, hegemonic ethnographic approach that has been completely transcended by contemporary innovations. Over the development of ethnography, there has been a repeated dialectic between what might be thought of as a dominant orthodoxy, and other, centrifugal forces that have promoted difference and diversity. There is, for instance, little need to appeal only to recent developments in ethnographic writing and commentary as evidence of blurred representational genres. Relationships between the aesthetic and the scientific, or between the positivist and interpretivist have been detectable for many years—indeed, throughout the development of ethnographic research this century. (Admittedly, they have not been equally remarked on, nor taken the same form at all times.) It is a well-known aspect of the history of sociology—but it bears repetition in this context—that the early period of urban ethnography in Chicago drew on aesthetic and literary models as much as on models of "scientific" research. The sociological perspective was fuelled by the textual conventions of realist fiction. The sociological celebration of the "life"— through the life history and ethnographic approach—was influenced by the development of the novel. Equally, some of the literary inspirations drew broadly speaking on a sociological perspective. More generally still, the ethnographic tradition and literary genres in the United States have displayed intertextual relationships over many decades. The styles of urban realism, the literary creation of characters and types in the city, and the narrative of modern fiction—these have all contributed to the styles of ethnographic representation. The systematic *analysis* of these intertextual relations may be a fairly recent preoccupation, but the genres are more enduring *and* more blurred than contemporary enthusiasms might suggest.

The nature of those intertextual linkages deserves attention. It is clearly insufficient to deal with a monolithic social science on the one hand and an equally undifferentiated literature on the other. The specific relationships between American fiction and ethnographic reportage are but one aspect of the long history of influence between anthropological and sociological research and literary and other aesthetic influences. Realist modes of ethnographic writing are reflections of aesthetic as well as scientific influences. There is a constant interplay between literary modes of fiction and nonfiction of various sorts. Ethnographic writing has never been entirely devoid of aesthetic influence, while pioneering authors—especially from within anthropology—have looked to various literary genres. In American anthropology, the foundational work of Franz Boas was born out of a complex mix of epistemological and aesthetic commitments, while Ruth Benedict's particular development of one strand of Boasian anthropology was hardly conceived and reported in a narrowly scientistic manner. Zora Neale Hurston's experimental ethnographies (see Hernandez 1995) mingled social reportage with aesthetic commitments long before anybody announced a "crisis of representation" or invoked so-called "alternative" literary forms for ethnographic texts. In other contexts too, aesthetic influences included the impact of surrealism in literature, drama, and graphic art on anthropology and on the British Mass Observation experiment.

Our point here is not to review yet again fairly well known commentaries on ethnography, literature, and aesthetics. Rather, we emphasize the extent to which ethnography in sociology or anthropology—whether conceived in terms of method or its textual products—has never been a stable entity. It has been marked by contrasts and tensions that are not merely departures from an established orthodoxy. The conduct of ethnographic research has rarely, if ever, been established solely under the auspices of positivist orthodoxy. American cultural anthropology, for instance, has displayed a repeated tension between the "nomothetic" search for law-like regularities, and the "idiographic" interpretation of cultures. In the same sense, there have been repeated tensions between the "scientific" and the "aesthetic." The point is that these dividing lines were never starkly drawn in the first place. Furthermore, given the highly personalized nature of anthropological fieldwork and authorship, it is far from clear that any major practitioner ever subscribed to a purely scientistic or positivist perspective. Indeed, although it is virtually impossible to demonstrate, one suspects that the social and academic elite members of the community of anthropologists never subscribed to anything quite as vulgar or artisan as a single "scientific method" or its equivalent.

In other words, for all the tidying up of recent methodologists' accounts, ethnographic research has always contained within it a variety of perspectives. As a whole, it has never been totally subsumed within a framework of orthodoxy and objectivism. There have been varieties of aesthetic and interpretative standpoint throughout nearly a century of development and change. The ethnographic approach to understanding cultural difference has itself incorporated a diversity of intellectual cultures. There have been changing intellectual fashions and emphases, and the pace of change has undoubtedly been especially rapid in recent years, although here again we would take issue with models that have change moving ever more quickly and developmental phases becoming increasingly truncated. These "trends" actually reflect long-standing tensions, rather than constituting a new and unique moment in ethnographic research. They continue the centrifugal and centripetal tendencies that have been perceptible for many years, and represent the diverse and broad concerns of past as well as present qualitative social inquiry. Rather than a developmental model, therefore, we would rather conceptualize the field of ethnography in terms of continuing tensions. Indeed, those tensions themselves give the field much of its vigor and impetus. The repeated, and indeed long-standing, tensions between "scientific" and "interpretative" inquiry; between "realist" and "experimental" texts; between impersonal and experiential analyses—are recurrent motifs in ethnography. Recent innovations do not have to be seen as wholesale rejections of prior positions.

REFERENCES

Abbott, A. 1999. *Department and Discipline: Chicago Sociology at One Hundred.* Chicago: University of Chicago Press.

Abbott, A., and E. Gaziano. 1995. "Transition and Tradition." In *A Second Chicago School?,* ed. G. A. Fine, 221–72. Chicago: University of Chicago Press.

Adler, P. 1985/1993. *Wheeling and Dealing: An Ethnography of an Upper Level Drug Dealing and Smuggling Community.* New York: Columbia University Press.

Adler, P., and P. Adler. 1999. "The Ethnographers' Ball—Revisited." *Journal of Contemporary Ethnography* 28 (5): 442–50.

Agar, M. 1980. *The Professional Stranger: An Informal Introduction to Ethnography.* New York: Academic Press.

Aguilar, J. L. 1981. "Insider Research: An Ethnography of a Debate." In *Anthropologists at Home in North America: Methods and Issues in the Study of One's Own Society,* ed. D. A. Messerschmidt, 15–26. Cambridge: Cambridge University Press.

Allan, S. 1994. "'When Discourse Is Torn from Reality': Bakhtin and the Principle of Chronologoplicity." *Time and Society* 3: 193–218.

Altheide, D. L., and J. M. Johnson. 1994. "Criteria for Assessing Interpretive Validity in Qualitative Research." In *Handbook of Qualitative Research,* ed. N. K. Denzin and Y. S. Lincoln, 485–99. Thousand Oaks, Calif.: Sage.

Amit, V., ed. 2000. *Constructing the Field: Ethnographic Fieldwork in the Contemporary World.* London: Routledge.

Anderson, E. 1978. *A Place on the Corner.* Chicago: University of Chicago Press.

Anderson, N. 1923. *The Hobo: The Sociology of the Homeless Man.* Chicago: University of Chicago Press.

Angrosino, M. 1998. *Opportunity House: Ethnographic Stories of Mental Retardation.* Walnut Creek, Calif.: AltaMira Press.

Ardener, S., ed. 1975. *Perceiving Women.* London: J. M. Dent.

Ashmore, M., G. Myers, and J. Potter. 1995. "Discourse, Rhetoric and Reflexivity." In *Handbook of Science and Technology Studies,* S. Jasanoff, G. Markle, J. Petersen and T. Pinch, 321–341. London: Sage Publications.

201

Atkinson, J. M., and J. Heritage, eds. 1984. *Structures of Social Action*. Cambridge: Cambridge University Press.

Atkinson, P. A. 1981. *The Clinical Experience: The Construction and Reconstruction of Medical Reality*. Aldershot: Gower.

———. 1982. "Writing Ethnography." In *Kultur und Institution,* ed. H. J. Helle, 77–105. Berlin: Duncker und Humblot.

———. 1990. *The Ethnographic Imagination: Textual Constructions of Reality*. London: Routledge.

———. 1992. *Understanding Ethnographic Texts*. Newbury Park, Calif.: Sage.

———. 1995. "Perils of Paradigms." *Qualitative Health Research* 5 (1): 117–24.

———. 1996. *Sociological Readings and Re-readings*. Aldershot: Gower.

———. 1997a. *The Clinical Experience: The Construction and Reconstruction of Medical Reality,* 2nd edition. Aldershot: Ashgate.

———. 1997b. "Narrative Turn Or Blind Alley?" *Qualitative Health Research* 7 (3): 325–44.

Atkinson, P. A., and A. Coffey. 1995. "Realism and Its Discontents: On the Crisis of Cultural Representation in Ethnographic Texts." In *Theorizing Culture: An Interdisciplinary Critique after Post-Modernism,* ed. B. Adam and S. Allan, 41–57. London: UCL Press.

Atkinson, P. A., A. Coffey, and S. Delamont. 1999. "Ethnography: Post, Past and Present." *Journal of Contemporary Ethnography* 28 (5): 460–71.

———. 2001. "A Debate about Our Canon." *Qualitative Research* 1 (1): 5–22.

Atkinson, P. A., A. Coffey, S. Delamont, J. Lofland, and L. Lofland, eds. 2001. *Handbook of Ethnography*. London: Sage.

Atkinson, P. A., and S. Delamont. 1980. "The Two Traditions in Educational Ethnography." *British Journal of Sociology of Education* 1 (2): 139–52.

Atkinson, P. A., S. Delamont, and M. Hammersley. 1988. "Qualitative Research Traditions." *Review of Educational Research* 38 (20): 231–50.

Atkinson, P. A., and W. Housley. 2003. *Interactionism: An Essay in Sociological Amnesia*. London: Sage.

Atkinson, P. A., and D. Silverman. 1997. "Kundera's *Immortality:* The Interview Society and the Invention of the Self." *Qualitative Inquiry* 3 (3): 304–25.

Babcock, B. 1993. "Feminism/pretexts: Fragments, Questions and Reflections." *Anthropological Quarterly* 66 (2): 59–66.

Ball, S. 1990. *Politics and Policy Making in Education*. London: Routledge.

Ball, S., and S. Gewirtz. 1997. "Is Research Possible?" *British Journal of Sociology of Education* 18 (4): 575–86.

Banks, A., and S. P. Banks, eds. 1998. *Fiction and Social Research: By Ice or Fire*. Walnut Creek, Calif.: AltaMira Press.

Batchelor, C., E. Parsons, and P. Atkinson. 1997. "The Rhetoric of Prediction, Skill and Chance in the Research to Clone a Disease Gene." In *The Sociology of Medical Science and Technology,* ed. M. A. Elston, 101–25. Oxford: Blackwell.

Bauman, Z. 2000. *Liquid Modernity*. Cambridge: Polity.

Becker, H. S. 1958. "Problems of Inference and Proof in Participant Observation." *American Sociological Review* 23: 652–60. Reprinted in *Issues in Participant Observation*, ed. G. J. McCall and J. L. Simmons. 1969, 245–54. Reading, Mass.: Addison-Wesley; and in *Sociological Work*, H. S. Becker. 1970, 25–38. Chicago: Aldine.

———. 1963. *Outsiders*. New York: The Free Press.

———. 1967. Whose Side Are We On? *Social Problems* 14: 239–48. Reprinted in *Sociological Work*, H. S. Becker. 1970, 123–36. Chicago: Aldine; and in *Howard Becker on Education*, ed. R.G. Burgess. 1995. Buckingham: Open University Press.

———. 1970. *Sociological Work*. Chicago: Aldine.

———. 1971. Footnote. In *Anthropological Perspectives on Education*, ed. M. Wax, S. Diamond, and F. Gearing, 3–27. New York: Basic Books.

———. 1986. *Writing for Social Scientists*. Chicago: University of Chicago Press.

———. 1989. *Tricks of the Trade*. Chicago: University of Chicago Press.

Becker, H. S., and B. Geer. 1957a. "Participant Observation and Interviewing: A Comparison." *Human Organization* 16: 28–32. Reprinted in *Qualitative Methodology*, ed. W. J. Filstead. 1970, 133–142. Chicago: Markham.

———. 1957b. "Participant Observation and Interviewing: A Rejoinder." *Human Organization* 16: 39–40. Reprinted in *Qualitative Research*, ed. W. J. Filstead. 1970, 150–152. Chicago: Markham.

Becker, H. S., B. Geer, and E. C. Hughes. 1968. *Making the Grade*. New York: Wiley.

Becker, H. S., B. Geer, E. C. Hughes, and A. L. Strauss. 1961. *Boys in White: Student Culture in Medical School*. Chicago: University of Chicago Press.

Behar, R. 1986. *Santa Maria del Monte*. Princeton, N. J: Princeton University Press.

———. 1993. *Translated Woman*. Boston: Beacon Press.

———. 1995. "Introduction: Out of Exile." In *Women Writing Culture*, ed. R. Behar and D. A. Gordon, 1–32. Berkeley, Calif.: University of California Press.

———. 1999. "Cherishing Our Second-fiddle Genre." *Journal of Contemporary Ethnography* 28 (5): 472–84.

Behar, R., and D. A. Gordon, eds. 1995. *Women Writing Culture*. Berkeley, Calif.: University of California Press.

Bell, C., and H. Newby. 1971. *Community Studies*. London: Allen and Unwin.

Bell, D. 1993. "The Context." In *Gendered Fields*, ed. D. Bell, C. Caplan, and W. J. Karim, 1–19. London: Routledge.

Benjamin, W. 1986. *Moscow Diary*. Ed. Gary Smith, trans. Richard Sieburth. Cambridge, Mass.: Harvard University Press.

———. 2000. *The Arcades Project*. Ed. Rolf Tiedemann, trans. Howard Eiland and Kevin McLaughlin. Cambridge, Mass.: Belknap Press, Harvard University Press.

Berger, P., and T. Luckman. 1967. *The Social Construction of Reality*. London: Allen Lane.

Berliner, D., and B. Biddle. 1995. *The Manufactured Crisis?* New York: Longman.

Berreman, G. 1962. *Behind Many Masks*. Ithaca, N.Y.: Cornell University Press.

Beynon, J. 1987. "Zombies in Dressing Gowns." In *Enter the Sociologist*, ed. N. P. McKeganey and S. Cunningham-Burley, 144–73. Aldershot: Avebury.

Blackwood, E. 1995. "Falling in Love with An-other Lesbian: Reflections on Identity in Fieldwork." In *Taboo: Sex, Identity and Erotic Subjectivity in Anthropological Fieldwork*, ed. D. Kulick and M. Willson, 51–75. London: Routledge.

Bluebond-Langer, M. 1980. *The Private Worlds of Dying Children*. Princeton, N.J.: Princeton University Press.

Blumer, H. 1954. "What's Wrong with Social Theory?" *American Sociological Review* 19: 3–10.

Bochner, A. P. 2001. "Narrative's Virtues." *Qualitative Inquiry* 7 (2): 131–57.

Bochner, A. P., and C. Ellis. 1996. "Talking over Ethnography." In *Composing Ethnography: Alternative Forms of Qualitative Writing*, ed. C. Ellis and A. P. Bochner, 13–45. Walnut Creek, Calif.: AltaMira Press.

Boden, D., and D. Zimmerman, eds. 1991. *Talk and Social Structure*. Cambridge: Cambridge University Press.

Bolton, R. 1995. "Tricks, Friends and Lovers: Erotic Encounters in the Field." In *Taboo: Sex, Identity and Erotic Subjectivity in Anthropological Fieldwork*, ed. D. Kulick and M. Willson, 140–67. London: Routledge.

Boon, J. A. 1982. *Other Tribes, Other Scribes: Symbolic Anthropology in the Comparative Study of Authors, Histories, Religions and Texts*. Cambridge: Cambridge University Press.

Bourgeois, P. 1995. *In Search of Respect*. Cambridge: Cambridge University Press.

Bowen, E. S. 1964. *Return to Laughter*. London: Gollancz.

Brettell, C. B., ed. 1993. *When They Read What We Write*. Westport, Conn.: Bergin and Garvey.

Briggs, J. 1986. "Kapluna Daughter." In *Women in the Field*, 2nd ed., ed. P. Golde, 19–44. Berkeley, Calif.: University of California Press.

Brodribb, S. 1992. *Nothing Matters*. Melbourne: Spinifex.

Brown, D. D. 1986. *Umbanda: Religion and Politics in Urban Brazil*. Ann Arbor, Mich.: UMI Research Press.

Brown, R. H. 1977. *A Poetic for Sociology*. Cambridge: Cambridge University Press.

———. 1983. "Dialectical Irony, Literary Form and Sociological Theory." *Poetics Today* 4 (3): 543–64.

Brunt, L. 2001. "Into the Community." In *Handbook of Ethnography*, ed. P. Atkinson, A. Coffey, S. Delamont, J. Lofland and L. Lofland, 80–91. London: Sage.

Bruyn, S. 1966. *The Human Perspective: The Methodology of Participant Observation*. Englewood Cliffs, N. J.: Prentice-Hall.

Bucher, R., and J. G. Stelling. 1971. *Becoming Professional*. Beverley Hills, Calif.: Sage.

Bunton, R. B. 1986. *Reproducing Psychiatry: An Ethnographic Study of Entry to an Occupation*. Ph.D. thesis, University of Wales, Cardiff.

Burawoy, M., ed. 1991. *Ethnography Unbound*. Berkeley, Calif.: University of California Press.

Burgess, R.G., ed. 1989. *Ethics in Educational Research*. London: Falmer.

———. 1995a, ed. *Howard Becker on Education*. Buckingham: Open University Press.

———. 1995b, ed. *Computing and Qualitative Research: Studies in Qualitative Methodology* Vol. 5. Greenwich Conn.: JAI Press.

Burns, T. 1992. *Erving Goffman*. London: Routledge.

Butler, J. 1990. *Gender Trouble*. London: Routledge; 2nd ed., 1999.

Cannon, S. 1992. "Reflections on Fieldwork in Stressful Situations." In *Studies in Qualitative Methodology* Vol. 3: *Learning about Fieldwork*, ed. R. G. Burgess, 147–82. Greenwich, Conn.: JAI Press.

Cappetti, C. 1993. *Writing Chicago: Modernism, Ethnography and the Novel*. New York: Columbia University Press.

Cassell, J. 1998. *The Woman in the Surgeon's Body*. Cambridge, Mass.: Harvard University Press.

Chafe, W., and J. Nichols, eds. 1986. *Evidentiality: The Linguistic Coding of Epistemology*. Norwood, N.J.: Ablex.

Chafetz, J. S. 1997. "Feminist Theory and Sociology." *Annual Review of Sociology* 23: 97–120.

Chagnon, N. 1968. *Yanomamo: The Fierce People*. New York: Holt, Rinehart and Winston.

Charmaz, K., and R. G. Mitchell, Jr. 1997. "The Myth of Silent Authorship: Self, Substance and Style in Ethnographic Writing." In *Reflexivity and Voice,* ed. R. Hertz, 193–215. Thousand Oaks, Calif.: Sage.

———. 2001. "Grounded Theory in Ethnography." In *Handbook of Ethnography,* ed. P. Atkinson, A. Coffey, S. Delamont, J. Lofland and L. Lofland, 160–73. London: Sage.

Clifford, J. 1981. "On Ethnographic Surrealism." *Comparative Studies in Society and History* 23 (4): 539–64.

———. 1983. "On Ethnographic Authority." *Representations* 2: 118–46.

———. 1988. *The Predicament of Culture*. Cambridge, Mass.: Harvard University Press.

Clifford, J., and G. Marcus, eds. 1986. *Writing Culture: The Poetics and Politics of Ethnography*. Berkeley, Calif.: University of California Press.

Clough, P. T. 1992. *The End(s) of Ethnography*. Newbury Park, Calif.: Sage.

Coffey, A. 1999. *The Ethnographic Self*. London: Sage.

Coffey, A., and P. Atkinson. 1996. *Making Sense of Qualitative Data*. Thousand Oaks, Calif.: Sage.

Coffey, A., B. Holbrook, and P. Atkinson. 1996. "Qualitative Data Analysis: Technologies and Representations." *Sociological Research On-Line* 1, <http://www.socresonline.org.uk/socresonline/1/1/4.html> [accessed 11/27/02].

Cohen, I. J., and M. F. Rogers. 1994. "Autonomy and Credibility: Voice as Method." *Sociological Theory* 12 (3): 304–18.

Coles, A., ed. 2000. *Site-Specificity: The Ethnographic Turn*. London: Black Dog Publishing.

Coles, R. L. 2002. "Black Single Fathers." *Journal of Contemporary Ethnography* 31(4): 411–39.

Collier, J., Jr. 1988. "Survival at Rough Rock: An Historical Overview of the Rough Rock Demonstration School." *Anthropology and Education Quarterly* 19 (3): 253–71.

Collins, P. H. 2000. "Comment on Hekman's 'Truth and method: feminist standpoint theory revisited': Where's the power?" In *Provoking Feminisms*, ed. C. Allen and J. Howard, 43–49. Chicago: University of Chicago Press.

Cooley, C. H. 1930. *Sociological Theory and Social Research*. New York: Holt.

Cornwell, J. 1984. *Hard-Earned Lives: Accounts of Health and Illness from East London*. London: Tavistock.

Crick, M. 1992. "Ali and Me: An Essay in Street Corner Anthropology." In *Anthropology and Autobiography*, ed. J. Okely and H. Callaway, 175–92. London: Routledge.

Danforth, L. 1982. *Death Rituals of Rural Greece*. Princeton, N.J.: Princeton University Press.

Davies, C. A. 1999. *Reflexive Ethnography: A Guide to Researching Selves and Others*. London: Routledge.

Dean, J. F., and W. F. Whyte. 1958. "How Do You Know If the Informant Is Telling the Truth?" *Human Organization* 17: 34–38. Reprinted in *Issues in Participant Observation*, ed. G. J. McCall and J. L. Simmons, 105–14. Reading, Mass.: Addison Wesley.

Deegan, M.-J. 1995. "The Second Sex and the Chicago School." In *A Second Chicago School?*, ed. G. A. Fine, 332–64. Chicago: University of Chicago Press.

———. 2001. "The Chicago School of Ethnography." In *Handbook of Sociology*, ed. P. Atkinson, A. Coffey, S. Delamont, J. Lofland and L. Lofland, 11–25. London: Sage.

Delamont, S. 1987. "Clean Baths and Dirty Women." In *Enter the Sociologist*, ed. N. P. McKeganey and S. Cunningham-Burley, 127–43. Aldershot: Avebury.

———. 1995. *Appetites and Identities*. London: Routledge.

———. 1999. "Gender and the Discourse of Derision." *Research Papers in Education* 14 (1): 3–22.

———. 2000. "The Anomalous Beasts: Hooligans and the Sociology of Education." *Sociology* 34 (1): 95–112.

———. 2002. *Fieldwork in Educational Settings*, 2nd ed. Falmer: London.

Delamont, S., and P. Atkinson. 1990. "Writing about Teachers." *Teaching and Teacher Education* 6 (2): 111–25.

———. 1995. *Fighting Familiarity: Essays on Education and Ethnography*. Cresskill, N.J.: Hampton Press.

Delamont, S., P. A. Atkinson, A. Coffey, and R. G. Burgess. 2001. *An Open Exploratory Spirit? Ethnography at Cardiff 1974–2001*. Cardiff: School of Social Sciences Working Paper No. 20, <http://www.cf.ac.uk/socsi/publications/index.html>

Delamont, S., P. Atkinson, and O. Parry. 2000. *The Doctoral Experience*. London: Falmer.

Delamont, S., A. Coffey, and P. Atkinson. 2000. "The Twilight Years? Educational Ethnography and the Five Moments Model." *Qualitative Studies in Education* 13 (3): 223–38.

Delgardo, R. 1984. "The Imperial Scholar." *University of Pennsylvania Law Review* 132 (3): 561–78.

deMarrais, K. B., ed. 1998. *Inside Stories*: Qualitative Research Reflections. Mahwah, N.J.: Erlbaum.

Denuvo, R. 1992. "No Anthro-apologies, or Der(r)id(a) a Discipline." In *Writing the Social Text: Poetics and Politics in Social Science Discourse,* ed. R. H. Brown. New York: de Gruyter.

Denzin, N. K. 1970. *The Research Act*. Chicago: Aldine; 2nd ed., 1978, McGraw-Hill.

———. 1991. *Images of Postmodern Society: Social Theory and Contemporary Cinema*. Thousand Oaks, Calif.: Sage.

———. 1992. *Symbolic Interactionism and Cultural Studies*. Cambridge, Mass.: Blackwell.

———. 1995. *The Cinematic Society: The Voyeur's Gaze*. Thousand Oaks, Calif.: Sage.

———. 1997. *Interpretive Ethnography: Ethnographic Practices for the 21st Century*. Thousand Oaks, Calif.: Sage.

———. 2002. "Confronting Ethnography's Crisis of Representation." *Journal of Contemporary Ethnography* 31 (4): 482–89.

Denzin, N. K., and Y. Lincoln, eds. 1994. *Handbook of Qualitative Research*. Thousand Oaks, Calif.: Sage.

———. 2000. *Handbook of Qualitative Research,* 2nd ed. Thousand Oaks, Calif.: Sage.

De Soto, H. G., and N. Dudwick, eds. 2000. *Fieldwork Dilemmas: Anthropologists in Postsocialist States*. Madison: University of Wisconsin Press.

Deyhle, D., and F. Margonis. 1995. "Navaho Mothers and Daughters." *Anthropology and Education Quarterly* 26 (2): 135–67.

Dicks, B., and B. Mason. 1998. "Hypermedia and Ethnography: Reflections on the Construction of a Research Approach." *Sociological Research Online* 3 (3), <http://www.socresonline.org.uk/socresonline/3/3/3.html> [accessed 11/25/02].

Ditton, J., ed. 1980. *The View from Goffman*. London: Macmillan.

Drew, P., and A. Wootton, eds. 1988. *Erving Goffman: Exploring the Interaction Order*. Cambridge: Polity.

Dubisch, J. 1995. "Lovers in the Field." In *Taboo: Sex, Identity and Erotic Subjectivity in Anthropological Fieldwork,* ed. D. Kulick and M. Willson, 29–50. London: Routledge.

Duneier, M. 1992. *Slim's Table: Race, Responsibility and Masculinity*. Chicago: University of Chicago Press.

Eadie, J. 2001. "Boy Talk: Social Theory and Its Discontents." *Sociology* 35 (2): 575–82.

Edmonson, R. 1984. *Rhetoric in Sociology*. London: Macmillan.

Ellis, C. 1995. *Final Negotiations: A Story of Love, Loss and Chronic Illness*. Philadelphia: Temple University Press.

———. 2002. "Shattered Lives." In *Journal of Contemporary Ethnography* 31 (4): 375–410.

Ellis, C., and A. P. Bochner. 1992. "Telling and Performing Personal Stories: The Constraints of Choice in Abortion." In *Investigating Subjectivity: Research on Lived Experience*, ed. C. Ellis and M. G. Flaherty, 79–101. Newbury Park, Calif.: Sage.

———. 2000. "Autoethnography, Personal Narrative, Reflexivity: Researcher As Subject." In *Handbook of Qualitative Research,* 2nd edition, ed. N. K. Denzin and Y. S. Lincoln, 733–68. Thousand Oaks, Calif.: Sage.

Ellis, C., and A. P. Bochner, eds. 1996. *Composing Ethnography*. Walnut Creek, Calif.: AltaMira Press.

Ellis, C., and M. G. Flaherty, eds. 1992. *Investigating Subjectivity: Research on Lived Experience*. Newbury Park, Calif.: Sage.

Ellis, C., C. E. Kiesinger, and L. M. Tillman-Healy. 1997. "Interactive Interviewing." In *Reflexivity and Voice,* ed. R. Hertz, 119–49. Thousand Oaks, Calif.: Sage.

El-Or, T. 1997. "Do You Really Know How They Make Love? The Limits on Intimacy With Ethnographic Informants." In *Reflexivity and Voice,* ed. R. Hertz, 169–89. Thousand Oaks, Calif.: Sage.

Ely, M., R. Vinz, M. Downing, and M. Anzul. 1997. On *Writing Qualitative Research: Living by Words*. London: Falmer.

Emerson, R. M., R. I. Fretz, and A. L. Strauss. 1995. *Writing Ethnographic Fieldnotes*. Chicago: University of Chicago Press.

Epstein, S. 1996. *Impure Science*. Berkeley, Calif.: University of California Press.

Erikson, D. 1970. "Custer *Did* Die for Our Sins." *School Review* 79 (1): 76–93.

Evans-Pritchard, E. E. 1937. *Witchcraft, Oracles and Magic Among the Azande*. Oxford: Clarendon Press.

———. 1940. *The Nuer*. Oxford: The Clarendon Press.

Eyring, M. 1998. "How Close Is Close Enough?" In *Inside Stories,* ed. K. B. de Marrais, 139–50. Mahwah, N.J.: Erlbaum.

Fabian, J. 1983. *Time and the Other: How Anthropology Makes its Object*. New York: Columbia University Press.

Farrell, S. A. 1992. "Feminism and Sociology." In *Revolutions in Knowledge,* ed. S. Rosenberg Zalk and J. Gordon-Kelter, 57–62. Boulder, Colo.: Westview.

Favret-Saada, Jeanne. 1980. *Deadly Words*. Cambridge: Cambridge University Press.

———. 1989. "Unwitching as Therapy." In *American Ethnologist* 16 (1): 40–56.

Fay, B. 1996. *Contemporary Philosophy of Social Science*. Oxford: Blackwell.

Festinger, L., H. Riecken, and S. Schachter. 1956. *When Prophecy Fails*. St. Paul: University of Minnesota Press.

Fielding, N., and Fielding, J. 1986. *Linking Data*. Newbury Park, Calif.: Sage.

Fielding, N., and R. Lee, 1998. *Computer Assisted Qualitative Research*. London: Sage.

Fielding, N., and R. Lee, eds. 1991. *Using Computers in Qualitative Research*. London: Sage.

Filstead, W. J., ed. 1970. *Qualitative Methodology: Firsthand Involvement with the Social World*. Chicago: Markham.

Fine, G. A. 1985. "Occupational Aesthetics." *Urban Life* 14 (1): 3–32.

———. 1996. *Kitchens*. Berkeley, Calif.: University of California Press.

Fine, G. A., ed. 1995. *A Second Chicago School? The Development of a Postwar American Sociology*. Chicago: University of Chicago Press.

Fine, M., L. Weis, L. C. Powell, and L. M. Wong, eds. 1997. *Off-White: Readings on Race, Power and Society*. New York: Routledge.

Flaherty, M.G. 2002a. "The Crisis in Representation." *Journal of Contemporary Ethnography* 31 (4): 478–81.

———. 2002b. "The 'Crisis' in Representation: Reflections and Assessments." *Journal of Contemporary Ethnography* 31 (4): 508–16.

Fleck, L. 1937/1979. *The Genesis and Development of a Scientific Fact*. Chicago: University of Chicago Press.

Fordham, S. 1996. *Blacked Out: Dilemmas of Race, Identity and Success at Capital High*. Chicago: University of Chicago Press.

Fowler, C. S. 1994. "Beginning to Understand: Twenty Eight Years of Fieldwork in the Great Basin of Western North America." In *Others Knowing Others: Perspectives on Ethnographic Careers*, ed. D. D. Fowler and D. L. Hardesty, 146–66. Washington, D. C.: Smithsonian Institute Press.

Fowler, D. D., and Hardesty, D. L., eds. 1994. *Others Knowing Others: Perspectives on Ethnographic Careers*. Washington, D. C.: Smithsonian Institution Press.

Fox, K. V. 1996. "Silent Voices: A Subversive Reading of Child Sexual Abuse." In *Composing Ethnography: Alternative Forms of Qualitative Writing*, ed. C. Ellis and A. P. Bochner, 330–56. Walnut Creek, Calif.: AltaMira Press.

Frank, A. W. 1995. *The Wounded Storyteller: Body, Illness and Ethics*. Chicago: University of Chicago Press.

Frankenberg R. 1993. *White Women, Race Matters: The Social Construction of Whiteness*. London: Routledge.

Freilich, M., ed. 1970. *Marginal Natives: Anthropologists at Work*. New York: Harper and Row.

Friedl, E. 1962. *Vasilika*. New York: Holt, Rinehart, and Winston.

Frisby, D. 1985. *Fragments of Modernity: Theories of Modernity in the Work of Simmel, Kracauer and Benjamin*. Cambridge: Polity Press.

Galliher, F. F. 1995. "Chicago's Two Worlds of Deviance Research." In *A Second Chicago School?*, ed. G.A. Fine, 164–87. Chicago: University of Chicago Press.

Garfinkel, H. 1967. *Studies in Ethnomethodology*. Englewood Cliffs, N.J.: Prentice-Hall.

Gearing, J. 1995. "Fear and Loving in the West Indies: Research from the Heart (As Well As the Head)." In *Taboo: Sex, Identity and Erotic Subjectivity in Anthropological Fieldwork*, ed. D. Kulick and M. Willson, 186–218. London: Routledge.

Geer, B. 1964. "First Days in the Field." In *Sociologists at Work: Essays on the Craft of Social Research*, ed. P. E. Hammond, 372–98. New York: Basic Books.

Geertz, C. 1973. *The Interpretation of Cultures*. New York: Basic Books.

———. 1983. *Local Knowledge: Further Essays in Interpretive Anthropology*. New York: Basic Books.

Gellner, D. N., and E. Hirsch, eds. 2001. *Inside Organizations*. Oxford: Berg.

Gibson, M. 1982. "Reputation and Respectability." *Anthropology and Education Quarterly* 13 (1): 3–28.

Gilbert, N., and M. Mulkay. 1980. *Opening Pandora's Box: A Sociological Account of Scientists' Discourse*. Cambridge: Cambridge University Press.

Glaser, B. 1978. *Theoretical Sensitivity*. Mill Valley, Calif.: Sociology Press.

———. 1992. *Emergence Versus Forcing*. Mill Valley, Calif.: Sociology Press.

Glaser, B., and A. L. Strauss. 1967. *The Discovery of Grounded Theory*. Chicago: Aldine.

Goffman, E. 1959. *The Presentation of Self in Everyday Life*. Garden City: Anchor.

———. 1961a. *Asylums*. New York: Anchor.

———. 1961b. *Encounters: Two Studies in the Sociology of Interaction*. Indianapolis: Bobbs-Merrill.

———. 1963a. *Behavior in Public Places*. Glencoe: Free Press.

———. 1963b. *Stigma: Notes on the Management of Spoiled Identity*. Englewood Cliffs, N.J.: Prentice-Hall.

———. 1971. *Relations in Public: Microstudies of the Public Order*. London: Allen Lane.

———. 1992. "An Interview with Erving Goffman 1980." *Research on Language and Social Interaction* 26: 317–48.

Goodall, H. L. 2000. *Writing the New Ethnography*. Walnut Creek, Calif.: AltaMira Press.

Gordon, D. A. 1988. "Writing Culture: Writing Feminism—the Poetics and Politics of Experimental Ethnography." *Inscriptions* 3 (4): 7–24.

Gouldner, A. 1973. *For Sociology*. Harmondsworth: Penguin.

Greeley, A. 1990. "The Crooked Lines of God." In *Authors of Their Own Lives*, ed. B. A. Berger, 133–151. Berkeley, Calif.: University of California Press.

Gross, P. R., and N. Levitt. 1998. *Higher Superstition*, 2nd ed. Baltimore: Johns Hopkins University Press.

Gross, P. R., N. Levitt, and M. W. Lewis, eds. 1996. *The Flight from Science and Reason. Annals of the New York Academy of Sciences*, Vol. 775 (June 24).

Gubrium, J., and J. Holstein. 1997. *The New Language of Qualitative Method*. New York: Oxford University Press.

Gubrium, J. F., and J. A. Holstein. 2002. "From the Individual Interview to the Interview Society." In *Handbook of Interview Research: Context and Method*, ed. J. F. Gubrium and J. A. Holstein, 3–32. Thousand Oaks, Calif.: Sage.

Guedon, M. F. 1994. "Dene Ways and the Ethnographer's Culture." In *Being Changed by Cross Cultural Encounters,* ed. D. E. Young and J-G. Goulet, 39–70. Peterborough, Ontario: Broadview Press.

Gusfield, J. 1967. "Moral Passage: The Symbolic Process in the Public Designations of Deviance." *Social Problems* 15: 175–88.

———. 1982. "The Scholarly Tension: Graduate Craft and Undergraduate Imagination." In *General Education in the Social Sciences,* ed. J. MacAloon. Chicago: University of Chicago Press.

Hammersley, M. 1989. *The Dilemma of Qualitative Method: Herbert Blumer and the Chicago Tradition.* London: Routledge.

———. 1991. *Reading Ethnographic Research.* London: Longman.

———. 2000. *Taking Sides in Social Research.* London: Routledge.

———. 2001. Whose Side Was Becker On? *Qualitative Research* 1 (1): 91–110.

Hammersley, M., and P. Atkinson. 1983. *Ethnography: Principles in Practice.* London: Tavistock; 2nd edition, 1995, London: Routledge.

Hanmer, J., and S. Saunders. 1984. *Well Founded Fear: A Community Study of Violence to Women.* London: Hutchinson.

Hannerz, U. 1969. *Soulside.* New York: Columbia University Press.

———. 1980. *Exploring the City.* New York: Columbia University Press.

Haraway, D. 1997. *Modest_Witness@Second_Millennium.FemaleMan (c)_Meets_ OncoMouse (tm): Feminism and Technoscience.* London: Routledge.

Harding, S. 1987. *Feminism and Methodology.* Bloomington: Indiana University Press.

———. 1996. "Gendered Ways of Knowing and the Epistemological Crisis of the West." In *Knowledge, Difference and Power,* ed. N. Goldberger, J. Tarule, B. Clinchy and M. Belenky, *Knowledge, Difference and Power,* ed. 431–34 New York: Basic Books.

———. 2000. Comment on Hekman's "Truth and Method: Feminist Standpoint Theory Revisited." In *Provoking Feminisms,* ed. C. Allen and J. A. Howard, 50–58. Chicago: University of Chicago Press.

Hartsock, N. C. M. 2000. Comment on Hekman's "Truth and Method: Feminist Standpoint Theory Revisited." In *Provoking Feminisms,* ed. C. Allen and J. A. Howard, 35–42. Chicago: University of Chicago Press.

Have, P. 1999. *Doing Conversation Analysis.* London: Sage.

Hekman, S. 2000. "Truth and Method: Feminist Standpoint Theory Revisited." In *Provoking Feminisms,* ed. C. Allen and J. A. Howard, 9–34. Chicago: University of Chicago Press.

Hendry, J. 1992. "The Paradox of Friendship in the Field." In *Anthroplogy and Autobiography,* ed. J. Okely and H. Callaway, 163–74. London: Routledge.

Heritage, J. 1984. *Garfinkel and Ethnomethodology.* Cambridge: Polity.

Hernandez, G. 1995. "Multiple Subjectivities and Strategic Positionality." In *Women Writing Culture,* ed. R. Behar and D. Gordon, 148–66. Los Angeles: University of California Press.

Hertz, R., ed. 1997. *Reflexivity and Voice.* Thousand Oaks, Calif.: Sage.

Hess, D. J. 1994. *Samba in the Night: Spiritism in Brazil.* New York: Columbia University Press.

Heyl, B. 1979. *The Madam as Entrepreneur.* New Brunswick, N.J.: Transaction Books.

Hier, S. P., and C. L. Kemp. 2002. "Anthropological Stranger: The Intellectual Trajectory of Hortense Powdermaker." *Women's History Review* 11 (3): 253–72.

Hobbs, D. 2001. "Ethnography and the Study of Deviance." In *Handbook of Ethnography,* ed. P. Atkinson, A. Coffey, S. Delamont, J. Lofland and L. Lofland, 204–19. London: Sage.

Hobbs, D., and M. May, eds. 1992. *Interpreting the Field.* Oxford: Clarendon Press.

Hochschild, A. 1983. *The Managed Heart.* Berkeley, Calif.: University of California Press.

Holquist, M. 1990. *Dialogism.* London: Routledge.

Holstein, J. A., and J. F. Gubrium. 2000. *Constructing the Life Course.* Dix Hills, N.Y.: General Hall.

hooks, b. 1981. *Ain't I a Woman?* Boston: South End Press.

———. 1989. *Talking Back: Thinking Feminist, Thinking Black.* Boston: South End Press.

———. 1990. *Yearning.* Toronto: Between-the-Lines.

Hough, P., and M. Kalman. 1992. *The Truth About Alien Abductions.* London: Blandford.

Hughes, E. C. 1971. *The Sociological Eye: Selected Papers.* New York: Aldine-Atherton.

Hughes, H. McG. 1961. *The Fantastic Lodge.* Greenwich, Conn.: Fawcett.

Jackson, A., ed. 1987. *Anthropology at Home.* London: Tavistock.

Jackson, J. E. 1990. "Déjà Entendu: The Liminal Qualities of Anthropological Fieldnotes." *Journal of Contemporary Ethnography* 19 (1): 8–43.

James, A., J. Hockey, and A. Dawson, eds. 1997. *After Writing Culture.* London: Routledge.

Jennaway, M. 1990. "Paradigms, Postmodern Epistemologies and Paradox: The Place of Feminism in Anthropology." *Anthropological Forum* 6: 167–89.

Jessor, R., A. Colby, and R. A. Schweder, eds. 1996. *Ethnography and Human Development.* Chicago: University of Chicago Press.

Jones, S. H. 1998. *Kaleidoscope Notes.* Walnut Creek, Calif.: AltaMira Press.

Kaminsky, M. 1992. Introduction to B. Myerhoff, *Remembered Lives: The Work of Ritual, Storytelling and Growing Older,* 1–97. Ann Arbor: University of Michigan Press.

Katz, Jack. 1982. *Poor People's Lawyers in Transitions.* New Brunswick, N.J.: Rutgers University Press.

Kelle, U., ed. 1995. *Computer-Aided Qualitative Data Analysis.* London: Sage.

Knorr-Cetina, K. 1995. "Laboratory Studies." In *Handbook of Science and Technology Studies,* ed. S. Jasanoff, G. E. Markle, J. C. Petersen and T. Pinch, 140–66. Thousand Oaks, Calif.: Sage.

Koertge, N., ed. 1998. *A House Built on Sand.* Oxford: Oxford University Press.

Kolker, A. 1996. "Thrown Overboard: The Human Costs of Health Care Rationing." In *Composing Ethnography: Alternative Forms of Qualitative Writing,* ed. C. Ellis and A. P. Bochner, 132–59. Walnut Creek, Calif.: AltaMira Press.

Kondo, D. K. 1990. *Crafting Selves: Power, Gender and Discourses of Identity in a Japanese Workplace*. Chicago: University of Chicago Press.

Krieger, S. 1983. *The Mirror Dance: Identity in a Women's Community*. Philadelphia: Temple University Press.

———. 1984. "Fiction and Social Science." In *Studies in Symbolic Interactionism,* ed. N. Denzin, 269–86, Vol. V. Greenwich, Conn.: JAI Press.

———. 1991. *Social Science and the Self: Personal Essays On An Art Form*. New Brunswick, N. J.: Rutgers University Press.

Kuhn, T. 1962. *The Structure of Scientific Revolutions*. Chicago: University of Chicago Press.

Kwon, M. 2000. "Experience vs. Interpretation: Traces of Ethnography in the Works of Lan Tanzon and Nikki S. Lee." In *Site-Specificity: The Ethnographic Turn,* ed. A. Coles, 74–91. London: Black Dog Publishing.

LaFontaine, J. S. 1998. *Speak of the Devil: Tales of Satanic Abuse in Contemporary England*. Cambridge: Cambridge University Press.

Lal, J. 1996. "Situated Locations: The Politics of Self, Identity, and Other in Living and Writing the Text." In *Feminist Dilemmas in Fieldwork,* ed. D. L. Wolf, 185–214. Boulder, Colo.: Westview.

Langellier, K., and D. Hall. 1989. "Interviewing Women: A Phenomenological Approach to Feminist Communication Research." In *Doing Research on Women's Communication: Perspectives on Theory and Method,* ed. K. Caiter and C. Spitzack, 193–200. Norwood, N. J.: Ablex.

Lareau, A., and J. Shultz, eds. 1996. *Journeys Through Fieldwork*. Boulder, Colo.: Westview.

Lather, P. 1991. *Getting Smart: Feminist Research and Pedagogy With/in the Postmodern*. London: Routledge.

———. 2001. "Postmodernism, Post-structuralism and Post(critical) Ethnography: Of Ruins, Aporias and Angels." In *Handbook of Ethnography,* ed. P. Atkinson, A. Coffey, S. Delamont, J. Lofland and L. Lofland, 477–92. London: Sage.

Lather, P., and C. Smithies. 1997. *Troubling the Angels: Women Living with HIV/AIDS*. Boulder, Colo.: Westview.

Law, J., and R. J. Williams. 1982. "Putting the Facts Together: A Case Study of Scientific Persuasion." *Social Studies of Science* 12 (4): 535–58.

Leacock, S., and R. Leacock. 1972. *Spirits of the Deep*. New York: Doubleday.

LeCompte, M. 2002. "The Value of Authenticity." *Qualitative Research* 2 (3): 283–99.

Lederman, R. 1990. "Pretexts for Ethnography: On Reading Fieldnotes." In *Fieldnotes,* ed. R. Sanjek, 71–91. Ithaca, N.Y.: Cornell University Press.

Lee, R., and N. G. Fielding. 1991. "Computing for Qualitative Research." In *Using Computers in Qualitative Research,* ed. N. G. Fielding and R. Lee, 1–13. London: Sage.

Levinson, B. A. 1998. "Student Culture and the Contradictions of Equality at a Mexican Secondary School." *Anthropology and Education Quarterly* 29 (3): 267–96.

Lieblich, A., and R. Josselson, eds. 1994. *The Narrative Study of Lives, Vol. 2: Exploring Identity and Gender*. Thousand Oaks, Calif.: Sage.

Liebow, E. 1967. *Tally's Corner: A Study of Negro Streetcorner Men*. London: Routledge and Kegan Paul.

Lincoln, Y. S., and N. K. Denzin. 1994. "The Fifth Moment." In *Handbook of Qualitative Research*, ed. N. K. Denzin and Y. S. Lincoln, 575–86. Thousand Oaks, Calif.: Sage. Reprint in 1998.

———. 2000. The Seventh Moment: Out of the Past." In *Handbook of Qualitative Research*, ed. N. K. Denzin and Y. S. Lincoln, second edition, 1047–65. Thousand Oaks, Calif.: Sage.

Lincoln, Y. S., and E. Guba. 1985. *Naturalistic Inquiry*. Thousand Oaks, Calif.: Sage.

Lofland, J. 1971. *Analyzing Social Settings*. Belmont, Calif.: Wadsworth.

———. 1974. "Styles of Reporting Qualitative Field Research." *The American Sociologist* 9 (2): 101–11.

Lofland, J., and L. H. Lofland. 1984. *Analyzing Social Settings*, 2nd ed. Belmont, Calif.: Wadsworth; 3rd ed., 1995.

Lofland, L. H. 1985. *A World of Strangers: Order and Action in Urban Public Space*. Prospect Heights, Ill.: Waveland Press (orig. pub. 1973).

———. 1997. "From 'Our Gang' to 'Society For': Reminiscences of an Organization in Transition." *Symbolic Interaction* 20 (2): 135–40.

———. 1998. *The Public Realm: Exploring the City's Quintessential Social Territory*. Hawthorne, N.Y.: Aldine de Gruyter.

Lonkila, M. 1995. "Grounded Theory As an Emerging Paradigm for Computer-assisted Qualitative Data Analysis." In *Computer-Aided Qualitative Data Analysis*, ed. U. Kelle, 41–51. London: Sage.

Lorber, J. 1984. *Women Physicians: Career, Status and Power*. London: Tavistock.

Lutz, C. 1990. "The Erasure of Women's Writing in Sociocultural Anthropology." *American Ethnologist* 17 (4): 611–27.

Lutz, C. A., and J. L. Collins. 1993. *Reading National Geographic*. Chicago: University of Chicago Press.

Lyman, S., and M. Scott. 1970. *A Sociology of the Absurd*. New York: Appleton-Century-Crofts.

Lynch, M., and S. Woolgar, eds. 1990. *Representation in Scientific Practice*. Cambridge, Mass.: MIT Press.

Mac an Ghaill, M. 1994. *The Making of Men*. Buckingham: Open University Press.

Macintyre, M. 1993. "Fictive Kinship or Mistaken Identity?" In *Gendered Fields: Women, Men and Ethnography*, ed. D. Bell, P. Caplan and W. J. Karim, 44–62. London: Routledge.

Maines, D. R. 2001. *The Faultlines of Consciousness: A View of Interactionism in Sociology*. New York: Aldine de Gruyter.

Malinowski, B. 1922. *Argonauts of the Western Pacific*. New York: E. P. Dutton

———. 1967. *A Diary in the Strict Sense of the Term*. London: Routledge and Kegan Paul.

Manning, P. [Philip] 1992. *Erving Goffman and Modern Sociology*. Cambridge: Polity.

Manning, P. K. [Peter] 1977. *Police Work: The Social Organization of Policing*. Cambridge, Mass.: MIT Press.

———. 1982. "Analytic Induction." In *Handbook of Social Science Methods Vol. II–Qualitative Method,* ed. R. B. Smith and P. K. Manning. Cambridge, Mass.: Ballinger.

———. 2002. "The Sky Is Not Falling." *Journal of Contemporary Ethnography* 31 (4): 490–97.

Marcus, G. E. 1998. *Ethnography Through Thick and Thin.* Princeton, N.J.: Princeton University Press.

———. 2001. "From Rapport under Erasure to Theaters of Complicit Collaboration." *Qualitative Inquiry* 7 (4): 519–28.

Marcus, G. E., and M. M. J. Fischer. 1986. *Anthropology as Cultural Critique.* Chicago: University of Chicago Press.

Marcus, J. 1992. *A World of Difference.* London: Zed.

———. 2001. "Orientalism." In *Handbook of Ethnography,* ed. P. Atkinson, A. Coffey, S. Delamont, J. Lofland and L. Lofland, 109–17. London: Sage.

Mascia-Lees, F. E., P. Sharpe, and C. B. Cohen. 1989. The Postmodernist Turn in Anthropology: Cautions from a Feminist Perspective." *Signs* 15 (1): 7–33.

Mason, B., and B. Dicks. 1996. "The Digital Ethnographer." *Cybersociology* 6. <http://www.socio.demon.co.uk/magazine/6/dicksmason.html> [accessed 11/25/02].

McCall, J., and J. L. Simmons, eds. 1969. *Issues in Participant Observation: A Text and Reader.* Reading, Mass.: Addison-Wesley.

McCarty, T. L., S. Wallace, R. H. Lynch, and A. Benally. 1991. "Classroom Inquiry and Navaho Learning Styles." *Anthropology and Education Quarterly* 22 (1): 42–59.

McCoy, K. 1997. "White Noise—the Sound of Epidemic: Reading/writing a Climate of Intelligibility Around the 'Crisis' of Difference." *Qualitative Studies in Education* 10 (3): 333–48.

McDonald, M. 1989. *We Are Not French!* London: Routledge.

McDonogh, G. 1986. *Good Families of Barcelona.* Princeton, N.J.: Princeton University Press.

Mead, M. 1928. *Coming of Age in Samoa.* Reprint 1949, New York: Mentor Books.

Melia, K. 1996. "Rediscovering Glaser." *Qualitative Health Research* 6 (3) 368–78.

Messerschmidt, D. A. 1981. "On Anthropology 'At Home.'" In *Anthropologists at Home in North America: Methods and Issues in the Study of One's Own Society,* ed. D. A. Messerschmidt, 3–14. Cambridge: Cambridge University Press.

Messerschmidt, D. A., ed. 1981. *Anthropologists at Home in North America: Methods and Issues in the Study of One's Own Society.* Cambridge: Cambridge University Press.

Mienczakowski, J. 1995. "The Theatre of Ethnography: The Reconstruction of Ethnography in Theatre with Emancipatory Potential." *Qualitative Inquiry* 1 (4): 360–75.

———. 1996. "The Ethnographic Act: The Construction of Consensual Theatre." In *Composing Ethnography,* ed. C. Ellis and A. P. Bochner, 244–64. Walnut Creek, Calif.: AltaMira Press.

————. 2001. "Ethnodrama: Performed Research—Limitations and Potential." In *Handbook of Ethnography,* ed. P. Atkinson, A. Coffey, S. Delamont, J. Lofland and L. Lofland, 468–76. London: Sage.

Miller, S. M. 1952. "The Participant Observer and 'Over-rapport.'" *American Sociological Review* 17 (2): 97–99. Reprinted in *Issues in Participant Observation,* ed. G. J. McCall and J. L. Simmons, 87–89. Reading, Mass.: Addison-Wesley.

Millman, M., and R. M. Kanter, eds. 1975. *Another Voice.* New York: Anchor.

Mills, C. W. 1940. "Situated Actions and Vocabularies of Motive." *American Sociological Review* 5: 439–52.

Minh-ha, T. 1989. *Woman, Native, Other.* Bloomington: Indiana University Press.

Mishler, E. 1984. *The Discourse of Medicine: Dialetics of Medical Interviews.* Norwood, N.J.: Ablex.

Monaghan, L. 2001. *Bodybuilding, Drugs and Risk.* London: Routledge.

Moreno, E. 1995. "Rape in the Field." In *Taboo: Sex, Identity and Erotic Subjectivity in Anthroplogical Fieldwork,* ed. D. Kulick and M. Willson, 219–50. London: Routledge.

Motzafi-Haller, P. 1997. "Writing Birthright: On Native Anthropologists and the Politics of Representation." In *Auto/Ethnography,* ed. D. Reed-Danahay, 195–222. Oxford: Berg.

Murphy, E., and R. Dingwall. 2001. "The Ethics of Ethnography." In *Handbook of Ethnography,* ed. P. Atkinson, A. Coffey, S. Delamont, J. Lofland and L. Lofland, 339–51. London: Sage.

Myerhoff, B. 1978. *Number Our Days.* New York: E. P. Dutton.

————. 1992. *Remembered Lives: The Work of Ritual, Storytelling and Growing Older.* Ann Arbor: University of Michigan Press.

Mykhalovskiy, E. 1997. "Reconsidering 'Table Talk': Critical Thoughts on the Relationship between Sociology, Autobiography and Self-indulgence." In *Reflexivity and Voice,* ed. R. Hertz, 229–51. Thousand Oaks, Calif.: Sage.

Nader, L. 1972. "Up the Anthropologist—Perspectives Gained from Studying Up." In *Reinventing Anthropology,* ed. D. Hymes, 284–311. New York: Vintage Books.

Oakley, A. 1981. "Interviewing Women: A Contradiction in Terms." In *Doing Feminist Research,* ed. H. Roberts., 30–61 London: Routledge and Kegan Paul.

————. 1998. "Gender, Methodology and Peoples' Way of Knowing." *Sociology* 32 (4): 707–31.

Olesen, V. 1993. "Unfinished Business: The Problematics of Women, Health and Healing." *The Science of Caring* 5: 3–6.

————. 1994. "Feminisms and Models of Qualitative Research." In *Handbook of Qualitative Research,* ed. N. K. Denzin and Y. Lincoln, 158–74. Thousand Oaks, Calif.: Sage.

————. 2000. "Feminisms and Qualitative Research at and into the Millennium." In *Handbook of Qualitative Research,* ed. N. K. Denzin and Y. S. Lincoln, 2nd ed., 215–55. Thousand Oaks, Calif.: Sage.

Olesen, V. and Whittaker, E. 1968. *The Silent Dialogue: A Study in the Social Psychology of Professional Socialization*. San Francisco: Jossey-Bass.

Ortiz, S. M. 2001. "How Interviewing became Therapy for Wives of Professional Athletes." *Qualitative Inquiry* 7 (2): 192–220.

Ortner, S. 2002. "Burned like a Tattoo: High School Social Categories and American Culture." *Ethnography* 3 (2): 115–48.

Paget, M. A. 1990. "Performing the Text." *Journal of Contemporary Ethnography* 19: 136–55.

———. 1993. *A Complex Sorrow: Reflections on Cancer and an Abbreviated Life*. Philadelphia: Temple University Press.

Park, Robert and E. Burgess. 1925. *The City*. Chicago: University of Chicago Press.

Platt, J. 1995. "Research Methods and the Second Chicago School." In *A Second Chicago School?*, ed. G. A. Fine, 82–107. Chicago: University of Chicago Press.

Plummer, K. 1995. *Telling Sexual Stories: Power, Change and Social Worlds*. London: Routledge.

———. 2001. *Documents of Life 2: An Invitation to Critical Humanism*. London: Sage.

Powdermaker, H. 1966. *Stranger and Friend*. New York: W. W. Norton.

Preissle, J. 1999. "An Educational Ethnographer Comes of Age." *Journal of Contemporary Ethnography* 28 (6) 650–65.

Quinney, R. 1996. "Once My Father Travelled West to California." In *Composing Ethnography: Alternative Forms of Qualitative Writing*, ed. C. Ellis and A. P. Bochner, 357–82. Walnut Creek, Calif.: AltaMira Press.

Rath, J. 2001. "Representing Feminist Educational Research With/in the Postmodern." *Gender and Education* 13 (2): 117–36.

Reed-Danahay, D. 2001. "Autobiography, Intimacy and Ethnography." In *Handbook of Ethnography*, ed. P. Atkinson, A. Coffey, S. Delamont, J. Lofland, and L. Lofland, 407–25. London: Sage.

Reed-Danahay, D., ed. 1997. *Auto/Ethnography: Rewriting the Self and the Social*. Oxford: Berg.

Richardson, L. 1990. *Writing Strategies: Reaching Diverse Audiences*. Newbury Park, Calif.: Sage.

———. 1992. "The Consequences of Poetic Representation: Writing the Other, Writing the Self." In *Investigating Subjectivity: Research on Lived Experience*, ed. C. Ellis and M. G. Flaherty, 125–37. Newbury Park, Calif.: Sage.

———. 1994. "Writing: A Method of Inquiry." In *Handbook of Qualitative Research*, ed. N. K. Denzin and Y. S. Lincoln, 516–29. Thousand Oaks, Calif.: Sage. 2nd ed., 2000, 923–48.

Richardson, L. and E. Lockeridge. 1991. "The Sea Monster: An 'Ethnographic Drama.'" *Symbolic Interaction* 13(1): 77–83.

Riessman, C. K. 1990. *Divorce Talk: Women and Men Make Sense of Personal Relationships*. New Brunswick, N.J.: Rutgers University Press.

———. 1993. *Narrative Analysis*. Newbury Park, Calif.: Sage.

Ronai, C. R. 1996. "My Mother Is Mentally Retarded." In *Composing Ethnography: Alternative Forms of Qualitative Writing*, ed. C. Ellis and A. P. Bochner, 109–31. Walnut Creek, Calif.: AltaMira Press.

Rose, N. 1990. *Governing the Soul: The Shaping of the Private Self*. London: Routledge.

———. 1997. *Inventing Ourselves: Psychology, Power, and Personhood*. Cambridge: Cambridge University Press.

Rosenberg, H. 1988. *A Negotiated World*. Toronto: Toronto University Press.

Sacks, H. 1992. *Lectures on Conversation*, ed. Gail Jefferson. Oxford: Blackwell.

Said, E. 1978. *Orientalism*. London: Routledge and Kegan Paul.

Sanjek, R. ed. 1990. *Fieldnotes: The Making of Anthropology*. Ithaca, New York: Cornell University Press.

Schatzman, L., and A. Strauss. 1973. *Field Research: Strategies for a Natural Sociology*. Englewood Cliffs, N.J.: Prentice-Hall.

Scheper-Hughes, N. 1977. *Saints, Scholars and Schizophrenics: Mental Illness in Rural Ireland*. Berkeley: University of California Press; 2nd ed., 2001.

Schmalenbach, H. 1977. *On Society and Experience*, ed. and trans. G. Lüscher and G. P. Stone. Chicago: University of Chicago Press.

Schutz, A. 1964. "The Stranger: An Essay in Social Psychology." In *Collected Papers Vol. 2*. The Hague: Martinus Nijhoff.

———. 1967. *The Phenomenology of the Social World*. Chicago: Northwestern University Press.

Seale, C., G. Gobo, J. F. Gubrium, and D. Silverman, eds. 2003. *Qualitative Research Practice*. London: Sage.

Shaw, R. 1930. *The Jack-Roller: A Delinquent Boy's Own Story*. Chicago: University of Chicago Press.

Silverman, D. 1985. *Qualitative Methodology and Sociology*. Aldershot: Gower.

———. 1993. *Interpreting Qualitative Data: Methods for Analyzing Talk, Text and Interaction*. London: Sage.

———. 1997. "Towards an Aesthetics of Research." In *Qualitative Research*, ed. D. Silverman, 239–53. London: Sage.

———. 2000. *Doing Qualitative Research: A Practical Handbook*. London: Sage.

Simmel, G. 1971. *On Individuality and Social Forms*, ed. D. N. Levine. Chicago: University of Chicago Press.

Simpson, B. 2001. "Swords into Ploughshares: Manipulating Metaphor in the Divorce Process." In *Inside Organizations*, ed. D. Gellner and E. Hirsch, 97–116. Oxford: Berg.

Sinclair S. 1996. *Becoming Doctors*. Oxford: Berg.

Skeggs, B. 2001. "Feminist Ethnography." In *Handbook of Ethnography*, ed. P. Atkinson, A. Coffey, S. Delamont, J. Lofland, and L. Lofland, 426–42. London: Sage.

Smith, A. T. 2001. *Diary of an Abduction*. Charlotteville, Va.: Hampton Roads Publishing Co.

Smith, D., 2000. Comment on Hekman's "Truth and Method: Feminist Standpoint Theory Revisited." In *Provoking Feminisms,* ed. C. Allen and J. A. Howard, 59–65. Chicago: University of Chicago Press.

Smith, G., ed. 1999. *Goffman and Social Organization: Studies in a Sociological Legacy.* London: Routledge.

Snow, D. A. 2002. "On the Presumed Crisis in Ethnographic Representation." *Journal of Contemporary Ethnography* 3 (4): 498–509.

Snow, D., and C. Morrill. 1995. "Ironies, Puzzles and Contradictions in Denzin and Lincoln's Vision of Qualitative Research." *Journal of Contemporary Ethnography* 22 (4): 358–62.

Sokal, A., and J. Bricmont. 1997. *Impostures Intellectuelles*. Paris: Odile Jacob.

Sparkes, A. 1995. "Writing People: Reflections on the Dual Crises of Representation and Legitimation in Qualitative Inquiry." *Quest* 47 (2): 158–95.

———. A. 1996. "The Fatal Flaw: A Narrative of the Fragile Body-self." *Qualitative Inquiry* 2: 463–94.

Spencer, J. 2001. "Ethnography after Postmodernism." In *Handbook of Ethnography,* ed. P. Atkinson, A. Coffey, S. Delamont, J. Lofland, and L. Lofland, 443–52. London: Sage.

Spindler, G., and L. Spindler. 2000. *Fifty Years of Anthropology and Education.* Mahwah, N.J.: Lawrence Erlbaum.

Spivak, G. 1988. "Can the Subaltern Speak?" In *Marxism and the Interpretation of Culture,* ed. C. Nelson and L. Grossberg, 271–313. Urbana, Ill.: University of Illinois Press.

———. 1990. *The Post-Colonial Critic*. London: Routledge.

Spradley, J. P. 1979. *The Ethnographic Interview*. New York: Holt, Rinehart and Winston.

———. 1980. *Participant Observation*. New York: Holt, Rinehart and Winston.

Springwood, C. F., and C. R. King. 2001. "Unsettling Engagements: On the Ends of Rapport in Critical Ethnography." *Qualitative Inquiry* 7 (4): 403–17.

Stanfield, J. H. 1994. "Ethnic Modeling in Qualitative Research." In *Handbook of Qualitative Research,* ed. N. K. Denzin and Y. S. Lincoln, 175–88. Thousand Oaks, Calif.: Sage.

Stanley, L. 1993. "On Auto/biography in Sociology." *Sociology* 27: 41–52.

———. 2001. "Mass-observation's Fieldwork Methods." In *Handbook of Ethnography,* ed. P. Atkinson, A. Coffey, S. Delamont, J. Lofland, and L. Lofland, 92–108. London: Sage.

Stanley, L., ed. 1992. *The Auto/biographical I.* Manchester: Manchester University Press.

Stanley, L., and S. Wise. 1983. *Breaking Out*. London: Routledge.

———. 1993. *Breaking Out Again*. London: Routledge.

Strathern, M. 1981. *Kinship at the Core.* Cambridge: Cambridge University Press.

———. 1987. "The Limits of Auto-anthropology." In *Anthropology at Home,* ed. A. Jackson, 16–37. London: Tavistock.

Strauss, A. L. 1987. *Qualitative Analysis for Social Scientists.* Cambridge: Cambridge University Press.

Strauss, A. L., and J. Corbin. 1998. *Basics of Qualitative Research: Grounded Theory Procedures and Techniques,* 2nd ed. Thousand Oaks, Calif.: Sage.

Strauss, A. L., L. Schatzman, R. Bucher, D. Ehrlich, and M. Sabshin. 1964. *Psychiatric Ideologies and Institutions.* New York: Free Press.

Strong, P. 1979. *The Ceremonial Order of the Clinic.* London: Routledge and Kegan Paul; 2nd edition, 2001, Burlington, Vt.:Ashgate.

Sutherland, C. 2001. *In the Company of Angels:Welcoming Angels into Your Life.* Dublin: Gateway.

Suttles, G. 1968. *The Social Order of the Slum: Ethnicity and Territory in the Inner City.* Chicago: University of Chicago Press.

Sutton, D. E. 2000. *Memories Cast in Stone.* Oxford: Berg.

Swartz, L. 1994. "Being Changed by Cross-cultural Encounters." In *Being Changed by Cross Cultural Encounters,* ed. D. E. Young and J.-G. Goulet, 209–36. Peterborough, Ontario: Broadview Press.

Tedlock, B. 2000. "Ethnography and Ethnographic Representation." In *Handbook of Qualitative Research,* 2nd ed., ed. N. K. Denzin and Y. S. Lincoln, 455–86, Thousand Oaks, Calif.: Sage.

Tesch, R. 1990. *Qualitative Research: Analysis Types and Software Tools.* London: Falmer.

Texeira, Thierry M. 2002. "'Who Protects and Serves Me?': A Case Study of Sexual Harassment of African American Women in One U.S. Law Enforcement Agency." *Gender and Society* 16 (4): 524–45.

Tierney, W. G. 1993. "Self and Identity in a Postmodern World: A Life Story." In *Naming Silenced Lives: Personal Narratives and the Process of Educational Change,* ed. D. McLaughlin and W. G. Tierney, 119–34. New York: Routledge.

———. 1999. "Introduction: Praxis at the Millennium." *Qualitative Studies in Education* (Special issue on Queer Theory) 12 (5): 451–56.

———. 2002. "Interviewing in Education." In *Handbook of Interview Research,* ed. J. F. Gubrium and J. A. Holstein, 453–72. London: Sage.

Tillman-Healy, L. M. 1996. "A Secret Life in a Culture of Thinness: Reflections on Body, Food and Bulimia." In *Composing Ethnography: Alternative Forms of Qualitative Writing,* ed. C. Ellis and A. P. Bochner, 76–108. Walnut Creek, Calif.: AltaMira Press.

Tooley, J., and D. Darby. 1998. *Educational Research: An OFSTED Critique.* London: OFSTED.

Trice, H. M. 1970. "Outsider's Role in Field Study." In *Qualitative Methodology: Firsthand Involvement with the Social World,* ed. W. J. Filstead, 77–82. Chicago: Markham.

Trosset, C. 1993. *Welshness Perfomed: Welsh Concepts of Person and Society*. Tucson: University of Arizona Press.

Trow, M. 1957. Comment on "Participant Observation and Interviewing: A Comparison." *Human Organization* 16: 33–35. Reprinted 1970 in *Qualitative Methodology*, ed. William J. Filstead, 143–49. Chicago: Markham.

Troyna, B., and B. Carrington. 1989. "Whose Side Are We On?: Ethical Dilemmas in Research on Race and Education." In *The Ethics of Educational Research*, ed. R. G. Burgess, 205–26. London: Falmer.

Turnell, K. D. 1998. "Interviewing the Incarcerated." In *Inside Stories*, ed. K. B. deMarrais, 127–38. Mahwah, N.J.: Erlbaum.

Turner, V. 1978. Foreword to B. Myerhoff *Number Our Days*, ix–xiii. New York: E. P. Dutton.

Van Maanen, J. 1988. *Tales of the Field: On Writing Ethnography*. Chicago: University of Chicago Press.

Verhoeven, J. 1992. "Backstage with Erving Goffman." *Research on Language and Social Interaction* 26 (3): 307–16.

Vidich, A. J., and S. Lyman. 1994. "Qualitative Methods: Their History in Sociology and Anthropology." In *Handbook of Qualitative Research*, ed. N. K. Denzin and Y. Lincoln, 23–59. Thousand Oaks, Calif.: Sage.

Voysey, M. 1975. *A Constant Burden*. London: Routledge and Kegan Paul.

Walford, G., ed. 1994. *Researching the Powerful in Education*. London: UCL Press.

Warren, K. B. 1997. "Narrating Cultural Insurgency: Genre and Self-representation for Pan-Mayan Writers." In *Auto/Ethnography: Rewriting the Self and the Social*, ed. D. Reed-Danahay, 21–45. Oxford: Berg.

Wax, M. 1970. "Gophers or Gadflies: Indian School Boards." *School Review* 79 (1): 62–7.

Weaver, A., and P. A. Atkinson. 1994. *Microcomputing Strategies for Qualitative Data Analysis*. Aldershot: Avebury.

Weitzman, E., and M. Miles. 1995. *Computer Programs for Qualitative Data Analysis*. Thousand Oaks, Calif.: Sage.

Whyte, W. F. 1981. *Street Corner Society*, 3rd edition. Chicago: University of Chicago Press.

Wolcott, H. F. 1990a. "On Seeking—and Rejecting—Validity in Qualitative Research." In *Qualitative Inquiry in Education*, ed. E. W. Eisner and A. Peshkin, 121–52. New York: Teachers College Press.

———. 1990b. *Writing Up Qualitative Research*. Newbury Park, Calif.: Sage Publications.

———. 1994. *Transforming Qualitative Data: Description, Analysis and Interpretation*. Thousand Oaks, Calif.: Sage.

Wolf, D. L. 1996. "Situating Feminist Dilemmas in Fieldwork." In *Feminist Dilemmas in Fieldwork*, ed. D. L. Wolf, 1–55. Boulder, Colo.: Westview.

Wolf, M. 1992. *A Thrice Told Tale: Feminism, Postmodernism and Ethnographic Responsibility*. Stanford, Calif.: Stanford University Press.

Woodhead, C. 1998. "Academia Gone to Seed." *New Statesman,* 20 March 1951–1952.

Woods, P. 1996. *Researching the Art of Teaching: Ethnography for Educational Use.* London: Routledge.

Young, D. E., and J.-G. Goulet, eds. 1994. *Being Changed by Cross-Cultural Encounters.* Peterborough, Ontario: Broadview Press.

Zelditch, M. 1962. Some Methodological Problems with Field Studies." *American Journal of Sociology* 67 (2): 566–76.

INDEX

Abbott, A., 85
abduction, 129
accounts: actions and, 97–98, 106–10,
  117; analysis of, 120–22, 130–40,
  193–94; events and, 100–104;
  veracity and, 120–22, 193–94. *See
  also* interviews
actions: interviews and observation
  and, 97–98, 104–10, 113–15,
  116–17, 119, 193; motive and, 125
actors, 105–6, 113–15
Agar, Michael, 16
Aguilar, J. L., 38–39
Altheide, D. L., 155
American Anthropology Association,
  34
American Educational Research
  Association, 88–89
American Sociological Association, 89
amnesia, sociological, xi
analysis: of accounts, 120–22, 130–40,
  193–94; analytic induction, 143–44,
  146, 160, 161–62; change in,
  130–40, 155–64, 192–93; coding,
  150–51, 152–54, 163, 179, 192;
  continuity in, 157–64, 192–93;
  convergence in, 146–47, 148,
  151–54, 157–64, 192; divergence in,
  155–64; grounded theory and,

148–54, 159–60, 161–62, 162–63,
  179, 192–93; inference and proof,
  generally, 20, 141–43; interviews
  and observation and, 98–104,
  115–16, 144–46, 161; naturalistic
  inquiry, 156; positivism and,
  144–46, 163–64; postmodernism
  and, 163–64; reflexivity and,
  147–48; in sociology, 157;
  triangulation, 144–48, 160–62; truth
  and, 122–23, 132–33, 139–40, 194;
  validity of, 155–64; of veracity,
  130–40, 193–94
analytic induction, 143–44, 146, 160,
  161–62
anthropology: analysis in, 157; applied,
  34–35; basics of, 4–5, 7, 9; change
  in, 198; ethnography rooted in, 2;
  familiarity and strangeness in,
  25–26, 28, 32–47; fieldwork in, 7; at
  home, 33–41; indigenous, 39–41;
  insider research in, 35–41;
  relationships in, 12–13, 49–50;
  representation in, 4, 5, 13, 92–93,
  185; social, 32–33; sociology and,
  37–41; veracity and, 128; writing in,
  170, 174, 182–83. *See also*
  ethnography
antiracist theory, 77–79

ABOUT THE AUTHORS

Paul Atkinson is Research Professor in Sociology at Cardiff University, United Kingdom. He is co-director of the ESRC Research Centre on Social and Economic Aspects of Genomics. His main research interests are the sociology of medical knowledge and the development of qualitative research methods. His publications include: *Ethnography: Principles in Practice* (with Martyn Hammersley, 1983; 2nd ed., 1995), *The Clinical Experience* (1981; 2nd ed., 1996), *The Ethnographic Imagination* (1990), *Understanding Ethnographic Texts* (1992), *Medical Talk and Medical Work* (1995), *Fighting Familiarity* (with Sara Delamont, 1995), *Making Sense of Qualitative Data* (with Amanda Coffey, 1996), *Sociological Readings and Re-readings* (1996), and *Interactionism* (with William Housley, 2003). Together with Sara Delamont he edits the journal *Qualitative Research*. His most recent ethnographic study is of an international opera company.

Amanda Coffey is Senior Lecturer in the School of Social Sciences, Cardiff University, United Kingdom. Her research interests include the sociology of education, gender, youth transitions, and contemporary ethnography. She is currently co-directing an ESRC funded project on ethnography for the digital age. Her publications include: *The Ethnographic Self* (1999), *Making Sense of Qualitative Data* (with Paul Atkinson, 1996), and *Education and Social Change* (2000). She was one of five editors of the *Handbook of Ethnography* (2001).

Sara Delamont is Reader in Sociology at Cardiff University, United Kingdom. She was the first woman to be president of the British Education Research Association, and the first woman to be dean of Social Sciences at

Cardiff. Her research interests are educational ethnography, Mediterranean anthropology, and gender. Of her nine published books, the best known is *Interaction in the Classroom* (1976; 2nd ed.; 1983), her favorites are *Knowledgeable Women* (1989) and *Appetites and Identities* (1995). Her most recent books are *Fieldwork in Educational Settings* (2002) and *Feminist Sociology* (2003). She is coeditor of the journal *Qualitative Research*.